Routledge Revivals

The British Economy

Originally published in 1967, this book provides a detailed survey of economic events from the early 1950s to the late 1960s. It provides an excellent source of reference on economic policy issues and will also be invaluable as a textbook of mid-20th century economic history. Part 1 discusses demand management, the balance of payments and regional development before 1961. The authors stress the social and administrative aspects of Britain's mal du siècle. A turning point came in 1961 when the Conservatives set up the National Economic Development Council. This experiment in 'indicative planning' and the changes introduced by Labour after 1964 are described in Part 2. Despite short-term demand mismanagement by successive governments, 'indicative planning' has made it possible to introduce a number of constructive new measures, in particular prices and incomes policy, regional development and the modernization of economic structures to each of which the book devotes a chapter.

The British Economy

Problems and Prospects

John Hackett and Anne-Marie Hackett

Routledge
Taylor & Francis Group

First published in 1967 by George Allen & Unwin Ltd

This edition first published in 2026 by Routledge
4 Park Square, Milton Park, Abingdon, Oxon, OX14 4RN

and by Routledge
605 Third Avenue, New York, NY 10158

Routledge is an imprint of the Taylor & Francis Group, an informa business

For Product Safety Concerns and Information please contact our EU representative GPSR@taylorandfrancis.com. Taylor & Francis Verlag GmbH, Kaufingerstraße 24, 80331 München, Germany

ISBN: 978-1-041-32633-5 (hbk)
ISBN: 978-1-003-78371-8 (ebk)
ISBN: 978-1-041-32634-2 (pbk)

Book DOI 10.4324/9781003783718

THE BRITISH ECONOMY

PROBLEMS AND PROSPECTS

by

JOHN AND ANNE-MARIE HACKETT

with a Foreword by

BRIAN TEW

Professor of Economics, University of Nottingham

London

GEORGE ALLEN & UNWIN LTD

RUSKIN HOUSE · MUSEUM STREET

FIRST PUBLISHED IN 1967

PRINTED IN GREAT BRITAIN
in 10 *point Times Roman type*
BY SIMSON SHAND LTD
LONDON, HERTFORD AND HARLOW

For Eddie and Edith

FOREWORD

by Professor Brian Tew

John and Anne-Marie Hackett will already be known to many English readers for their authoritative book on *Economic Planning in France*, a work which is generally recognized as successfully meeting the need for an Englishman's guide to certain important aspects of the contemporary French economy.

Their present work grew out of a book published in French that was intended to meet the reciprocal need for a Frenchman's guide to substantially the same aspects of the British economy. Only after the French text was ready for publication did the authors (under pressure from English friends) give thought to the case for preparing a revised and up-dated English edition.

I for one am delighted that in the end they were persuaded that the case was a valid one, even thought I admit it did at first blush seem implausible that a book on the British economy written for the benefit of a reader with little initial background knowledge of the UK should also serve the needs of British residents. But the more I reflected the more I was driven to the conclusion that it is precisely their ignorance of the events and the issues treated in *The British Economy: Problems and Prospects* which frustrates my undergraduate students in their initial attempts to grapple with the subject of Economics.

Moreover, it is not just the university freshman whose requirements are met by this book, for many of us who are old enough to have followed day by day the course of post-war events have by now lost our capacity to see the wood for the trees. How many of us recognize the year 1961 as the watershed of post-war economic policy? How many could at all clearly explain the interrelations between the National Plan, regional policy, modernization policy (industrial training, research and development, etc.), policy on restrictive practices, and the prices and incomes policy? I feel sure that many of my contemporaries will, like me, find the book refreshing and helpful even where the factual information marshalled and analysed by the authors relates to events which we have lived through and can still, with some effort, recall to mind.

The dramatic adjustment of British economic policy in 1966, with an unprecedented application of deflationary brakes, has imposed an additional burden on the unfortunate authors by calling for an assessment of the policy implications of recent events in Britain. Yet their burden is our gain, in that they have provided us with a book whose publication could not be more timely. For now is the moment when events force us to take stock of all the policies adopted since 1961. The overall targets of our two National Plans, which both overestimated the productive potential of the economy, have not only been scrapped, but can now be seen to have done harm. For they led the Government to over-stimulate demand, in a desperate effort to get a quart out of a pint pot, and thus (a) brought about an unprecedented balance-of-payments crisis and (b) undermined the Prices and Incomes policy. Moreover they have produced a mis-direction of investment, and in particular excessive investment in industries (e.g. steel, electricity) which took the Plans seriously.

Where then do we go from here? Do we give up the idea of having a National Plan, or do we try to formulate a more realistic one—and if so how should we go about it? Is a National Plan essential to the other economic policies adopted since 1961, or can they stand on their own? Why has the productive potential of the British economy expanded so slowly, despite all the Government's efforts to improve it? These are questions which all of us ought to be urgently considering, and it is vital that we should not succumb to the temptation to throw everything uncritically overboard, but take instead a long cool look at what has actually happened both before and since 1961, and thence identify our successes and our failures, and assess what lessons they hold for the future. We are fortunate indeed that, in this national stock-taking, we shall have at hand this lucid, authoritative and dispassionate guide to the *Problems and Prospects of the British Economy*.

University of Nottingham,
September 1966.

CONTENTS

PART TWO: NEW TRENDS

TABLES

GRAPHS AND MAPS

AUTHORS' NOTE

In 1966, we published in France *L'Economie Britannique: problèmes et perspectives* (Cahiers de la Fondation Nationale des Sciences Politiques, Librairie Armand Colin). The present book is based on the French edition but has been re-written in part to suit the needs of the English-speaking reader. The year 1966 saw a number of policy measures in the economic field and these have been incorporated into the text. We wish to acknowledge the valuable assistance given to us by Mr E. S. Snelling, CBE, in establishing the present text from the French. Thanks are also due to Mrs Maria Jude for help in typing the manuscript.

INTRODUCTION

A study of the present position and prospects of the British economy reveals that there are still serious obstacles preventing the realization of the double aim which the country has been pursuing for some years: faster and more stable economic growth and a satisfactory equilibrium of the balance of payments. The true nature of these obstacles can best be seen in the light of history, for Britain is still in the throes of that 'crisis of the twentieth century' that André Siegfried diagnosed as early as 1931.[1]

This crisis was far from being resolved when war broke out in 1939, and the war left behind it a fresh weakening of the balance of payments structure which has still not been overcome. But the post-war period has brought into being other problems, arising from such varied causes as: political emancipation overseas and a loosening of links with the Commonwealth; new currents of world trade and finance disadvantageous to Britain: the longing for full employment, leisure and well-being in a population which suffered so bitterly from mass unemployment in the 1930s and was exhausted by the war effort; the task, long overdue, of modernizing an economic and social fabric which had for too long been stubbornly resistant to change.

The first post-war years were full of promise, and Britain was brilliantly successful in dealing with many difficulties of reconstruction that had been viewed with foreboding as the war drew to a close. This was a period of intense innovation in economic and social policy. The first Labour Government put through a broad programme of nationalization in the basic industries. Social insurance and health services were placed upon an entirely new footing. The reconversion of the war economy to peacetime activities was carried through in an atmosphere of consistently low unemployment—an immense boon for the British working class. Strict controls over private industry were used to direct scarce resources to priority uses. Thanks to severe rationing of vital commodities and to the discipline accepted by consumers, the social justice of the war years was continued into peacetime. Both sides of industry submitted to voluntary controls over profits and incomes so that the price record of those years was good. And, despite the fiasco of the 1949 experiment with convertibility for the pound and the latter's subsequent devaluation, the export record was excellent whilst import needs were sharply curtailed.

[1] Siegfried, A. *La Crise britannique au XXème siècle*. A. Colin, Paris, 1931.

By 1950, before the end of the second Labour Government's period of office, the innovating ardour of the immediate post-war years was beginning to wane. And, with the knowledge of hindsight, it is clear today that the disappearance, after that date, of wartime controls that had been carried over as expedients into peacetime was bound to reveal unexpected gaps in economic policy where inadequate provision for dealing with future problems had been made. This was particularly the case with medium-term development issues that, despite the wartime conversion of the British Treasury to Keynesian 'full employment' economics, were too long ignored. The negative and unnecessarily irksome character of war controls maintained by Labour after 1945 gave rise understandably to a desire for a return to 'normalcy' that quickly became a major difference between the political parties. Unfortunately, this basically healthy reaction was accompanied by a yearning for an impossible return to the supremacy of traditional economic policy instruments touching notably the pound and credit conditions.

This yearning in the 1950s' liberalizing atmosphere won the day in England. Administrative control over the activities of the private sector were abolished, including price control. Rationing of consumers gave place to changes in the system of budgetary subsidies, accompanied by a rise in the cost of living. Even before the end of the second Labour Government in 1951, ideas of economic planning (nearer indeed in spirit to wartime controls than to new economic thinking) were forced into the background by urgent problems arising from the Korean world inflation and the requirements of rearmament. And already, before then, the trade unions' policy of voluntary wage restraint had practically ceased to exist.

In the field of international economic relations, the two main aims, after 1951, were a return to convertibility of the pound sterling and trade liberalization. From 1955 onwards, the deficit in the balance of payments became the chief preoccupation of economic policy. To correct this, internal growth was severely restricted and expansion was not resumed until 1958. It lasted only two years. But the rate of exchange of sterling remained stable, and the country was able largely to liberalize its trade with the dollar area and at the same time to reduce progressively the area of non-convertibility of the pound. In sum, Britain in the 1950s chose financial stability—achieved only relatively as the rise in prices was appreciable—but did not act to avoid slow and irregular economic growth. British experience was thus different from that of the Continent where growth was rapid—two or three times pre-war rates whereas Britian had exceeded by much less the pre-war trend. These opposite developments help to explain many misconceptions which hampered Britain's understanding, over the 1950s, of the problems and economic policies of Continental Europe. Too many British observers, even as they became increasingly aware of the comparative slowness of the growth of the British economy and of British living standards, tended to attribute the performance of the Continental economies to exceptional and short-lived causes; and this held back a systematic review and reassessment of the aims and instruments of British economic policy.

At present these divergencies in action and thinking are becoming every day less pronounced. This statement may seem surprising, for Britain is still beset by acute economic difficulties on the home and foreign fronts, whereas the Continent is a bastion of strong currency countries, sustained by flourishing balance of payments positions, so much so that gold and currency reserves there are already among the largest in the world and can be increased further whilst growth prospects remain favourable. Nevertheless, as it will be argued later, underlying tendencies in Britain justify the claim that aims and means are today more parallel between Britain and the Continent than for many years.

There has come into being, since 1961, a system of flexible planning which is in many ways reminiscent of Continental planning, particularly the French. This experiment indicates a desire to avoid in future the sequence of unfavourable balance of payments results and the consequent restraints on an expansion of demand. Such a modification of British policy seems to us of vital importance and several chapters of this work will be devoted to it. The move to economic planning forms part of a general climate of opinion in Britain that, at last, recognizes the need for changes, and often for quite drastic changes, in the conduct of the nation's economic affairs. This augurs well for the future. But, meanwhile, it will be apparent that, even though British economic policy has in the last few years taken a turn which is likely to prove decisive, a great deal remains to be done before intentions become realities and before lost ground has all been made up.

Today, as it happens, people on both sides of the Channel are studying economic policy afresh. The immediate task is to reconcile a rapid and sustained rate of growth with a satisfactory balance of payments, and to increase national productivity while improving the adaptability of the economy to new conditions. But beyond these two immediate preoccupations, one may perhaps hopefully discern a common will to define a policy of human ecology to correct those geographic, demographic and social imbalances which are an inevitable accompaniment to the development of a modern economy, and from which no Western countries are exempt. It would be pleasing to think that Britain will be able to make her original contribution to this renewal of ideas on economic and social policy.

The present seems, then, a propitious moment for an examination of British economic problems and prospects. This examination will be in two parts. The first will be devoted to those key problems of British economic policy which dominated the decade 1950–60. Then we shall proceed to an analysis of the new trends which have appeared, since about 1961 largely in response to, and with the object of, solving these problems. It is of course rather artificial to try to give a precise date to economic and social changes which must, by their nature, be subject to a slow evolution. But there are two good reasons for the date which has been chosen; these are, the profound shock to public opinion caused by the balance of payments crisis in July 1961, and the British Government's decision at that time to set up a National Economic Development Council to work out a medium-term plan. It is perhaps worth underlining, especially for those who might be tempted to attribute the 'new trends' dealt with in the second part of this book to the recent change of government in Britain, that the NEDC was the creation of a Conservative Government.

PART ONE

KEY PROBLEMS

INTRODUCTION

For an understanding of current trends in British economic policy, it is necessary to make constant reference to the past. Indeed it is largely due to the inadequacy of the policy followed since the war that attempts are now being made to launch out in new directions.

The economic problems whose origins we are to study in the following chapters are still with us today, and whilst it would be premature to assume that they will be solved satisfactorily, at least they do now seem to have been perceived and the first steps taken towards finding solutions for them. In the first part of the book this 'new look' is still in the future, but an attempt will be made to discover how and why the need for it came to be felt and what lessons the 1950s offer for this rethinking of economic policy.

In this connection the crucial importance of attitudes should be underlined. An observer of the British scene today cannot fail to notice how prevalent is the conviction that traditional attitudes need to be altered, a conviction that cuts right across existing political party lines. This wish for change arises from many causes, the chief of which are reviewed in the first chapter entitled 'A Mal du Siècle', a term which seems to express most adequately the all-pervading sentiment of unease which gathered impetus in the country after about 1955 and which should be seen as the perhaps indispensable precursor of the renewal of thinking on economic and social problems that characterizes the 1960s in Britain.

One of the causes of this *mal du siècle* was that, faced by the problem of stabilizing demand in the short term, British economic policy seemed to have got into a blind alley. This use—or rather misuse—of anti-cyclical policy—nicknamed with critical intent 'stop-go' policy—is of such importance for our subject that a separate chapter is given over to it (Chapter II).

Everything in Britain's economic history led the authorities after the war to focus particular attention on the health of the balance of payments and on the position of the pound sterling, for so long one of the key currencies in international dealings. But changes in the world economy after 1945 were on the whole unfavourable to the pound. To the extent that adaptation to these changes was only partially successful, the weakness of the British balance of payments position acted, and still acts, as a brake on internal economic growth (Chapter III).

The lack of connection between demand management policy and long-term economic policy considerations was general in Britain in the 1950s. But, in relation to regional problems, such considerations had perforce to be allowed for. It is hardly surprising, however, that in the prevailing intellectual climate of the 1950s, regional policy should have been conceived essentially as a series of emergency operations with little by way of unifying principles for action. Experience showed that, both in conception and fulfilment, these efforts were insufficient to counterbalance the powerful attraction of prosperous development in the south. And so, just as British demand management policy took on a new dimension in the 1960s when it was placed in the broader perspective of medium-term economic growth, so regional policy today is becoming part of a policy for more balanced growth in all regions (Chapter IV).

CHAPTER I

A 'MAL DU SIECLE'?

When people in any country become more and more aware that their economy is lagging behind that of other countries, their reactions may be of different kinds.

One very usual group of defensive reactions is to deny the fact or to suggest that its importance has been exaggerated, or to stress non-economic values. These, it is claimed, are superior to the vulgar struggle to increase the production of goods and services and they are even said to be protected by an absence of dynamic quality in the economy. Another reaction, this time more positive, though of limited scope, not only recognizes the relative loss of momentum in the economy but accepts it as part of an out-and-out rejection of traditional values and practices. Maybe these reactions necessarily precede a more methodical attempt to study causes and, even more, remedies. At all events, they bear a close similarity to what happened in Britain between, say 1955 and 1961.

It was after 1955 that people began to be acutely aware of the unsatisfactory growth of the British economy compared with that of many Continental countries, and even compared with the aspirations of many in this country. The initial attempts to defend the *status quo* were soon overwhelmed by a mounting wave of self-criticism that grew in volume in the course of the following years. From 1961, there began a new phase—to be examined only in the second part of this book—in which there is less concern to criticize our failures than to decide on various means to improve matters.

It is in this sense that the years 1955–61 can be seen to have revealed a kind of *mal du siècle* in Britain. The passage of time now makes it clear how much exaggeration and even at times naïvety there was in this movement of opinion, which found expression in a large number of writings.[1] But these discussions have left their mark

[1] This list, selected from among the more serious works, is very incomplete, but it gives an idea of the abundance of writings in this subject: Crosland, C. A. R., *The Conservative Enemy*, Cape, 1962. Hartley, A., *State of England*, Hutchinson, 1962. Koestler, A., ed., 'Suicide of a Nation', special number of *Encounter*, July 1963. Malik, R., *What's wrong with British Industry?* Penguin, 1964. Morris, J., *The Outsiders*, London, 1963. Sampson, A., *Anatomy of Britain*, 1962. Schonfield, A., *British Economic Policy since the War*, Penguin, 1958. Shanks, M. *The Stagnant Society*, Penguin, 1961. Titmuss, R., 'The Irresponsible Society' in *Essays on The Welfare State*, Allen and Unwin, 2nd edn. 1963.

on events today; public opinion was influenced by the particular targets chosen by the critics of English society and as a result a fresh impulse was given to the study of certain key problems. We must not stray from the point, however, since the purpose of this chapter is not to examine the development of public opinion in Britain in recent years, but only to note the main currents in a movement of opinion of capital importance for an understanding of present British economic policy.

In this respect we are faced with a difficult problem of selection since, in the literature dealing with this complex and ill-defined period to which the title '*mal du siècle*' has been given, there is a very great diversity of topics, and many authors have been led to attribute decisive importance to non-economic aspects of national life, in particular the psychological, social and institutional.

According to some authors, for example, the reasons for the *mal du siècle* are essentially psychological. For Arthur Koestler,[1] the malady is more 'functional' than 'structural'. 'Structural diseases,' he says, 'have objective, material causes,' while 'functional diseases have subjective, psychological causes'. Others, like C. A. R. Crosland,[2] present Secretary of State for Education and Science, one of the most far-sighted members of the Labour Party, wonder whether fundamental causes of a social nature are not responsible for the lag in economic growth in Britain. The specialist in political science turns his attention to the part played by institutions and the men who serve them. Professor B. Chapman[3] writes: 'It is my contention that the source of many of our present ills is institutional, and lies in a mistaken veneration for old ideas, and a refusal to examine them coolly and objectively.'

The professional economist,[4] for his part is led, in the last analysis, to blame the politico-social complex, its social structure and habits of thought, its rigid distinction between employer and employee. The TUC itself—a body not given to radical innovation—describes Britain as an old industrial economy tending towards stability, if not stagnation, and in need of radical industrial and economic reforms.[5]

These themes are so closely interlocked that it becomes by no means easy to pick out what is really important. Also movements of self-criticism, once they get under way, tend to generate a momentum of their own that carries them beyond their initial object. But in the

[1] *Encounter*, July 1963.

[2] Crosland, C. A. R., 'On Economic Growth', *Encounter*, April 1961.

[3] Chapman, B., *British Government Observed*, Allen and Unwin, 1963, p. 7.

[4] Cf. Prof. C. F. Carter, Vice-Chancellor of the University of Lancaster, Speech to the British Association, August 1963.

[5] Cf. 'Report on Economic Development and Planning', Appendix A, Annual Congress of the TUC, September 1962, p. 480.

last analysis it seems that opinion was moving towards the view that fundamental changes had become necessary, firstly to bring about a substantial improvement in the growth performance of the economy; secondly, and related to the first, to modernize habits of thought and action among the *élites* of the public and private sectors; and thirdly, to adjust British society to the, as yet ill-digested, phase of affluence brought into being by full employment and the spectacular expansion of the consumer goods industries.

1. THE GROWTH OF THE ECONOMY

It is difficult to date exactly the first manifestation of anxiety about the rate of economic growth in Britain, but early in 1955 criticism began to be sharper and more frequent. It will be helpful first of all to review the sequence of events from the beginning which started in a most promising fashion after the war.

In the first post-war years, say between 1945 and 1950, the reconstruction of the economy and its conversion to a peacetime footing took place, as elsewhere in Europe, faster and more easily than had been foreseen, and the rate of growth of the gross national product, at 4 per cent per annum, was decidedly in advance of the pre-war figure.

Despite the inflationary boom caused by the Korean war and the period of readjustment lasting until 1952 which affected all the countries of Western Europe, Britain continued to enjoy years of sustained expansion up to 1955.[1] The first years of government by the Conservative Party during which controls were relaxed and the economy given its head thus saw substantial progress in output. It was possible to claim that economic development over the ten post-war years had been satisfactory, even very satisfactory compared with pre-war figures.

Living conditions also encouraged optimism. Full employment, of prime importance for a population still remembering the long and bitter experience of mass unemployment between the two wars, had almost been attained since unemployment figures remained negligible—around 1·5 per cent. The austerity of wartime controls was beginning to be lifted between 1952 and 1955 (food rationing went in 1954), accompanied by rapid expansion in the demand for durable consumer goods. Private cars, household appliances, TV sets brought new amenities into many homes. It was not surprising therefore that

[1] Nevertheless the balance of payments crisis following the Korean war revealed the weakness of the British balance of payments which the export drive after 1945 and devaluation in 1949 had not corrected. Cf. for this period Joan Mitchell, *Crisis in Britain*, 1951, Secker and Warburg, 1963.

public opinion felt that all was well with the economy. The rise in prices—fairly considerable, about 4 per cent per annum—which accompanied the new well-being did nothing to weaken this optimism, for, apart from a few small inarticulate groups such as pensioners, incomes were rising too, and more rapidly than prices. When in 1954 Mr Butler[1] coined the slogan 'Invest in success', with the idea of doubling the standard of living in twenty-five years, this seemed in no way an unattainable aim.

The situation became less satisfactory during 1955, for in that year the expansion of demand (consumer and investment) exceeded the supply of goods and services, the rise in prices gathered speed, and the balance of payments became critical as the result of greatly increased imports. Restrictive measures were therefore introduced in the summer of 1955 and remained in force until 1958, and it is important to note that during these three years production remained almost stationary.

The year 1955 was a turning point in the history of the British post-war economy. Nevertheless, optimists still saw no reason for alarm when they considered the recent past. Some, for example, noted that the long-term *per capita* growth of the national product was much the same as between the two wars. But those who examined what was going on abroad felt unable to share this optimism. The economies of many Western European countries were in a state of rapid expansion, in comparison with which British economic growth was lagging seriously behind (cf. Table I). A judgment based upon the British economy viewed in isolation therefore seemed meaningless. Since other economies showed more rapid growth, the reasons for the difference called for examination. This fact remains indeed 'one of the few points on which there is widespread agreement' among British economists.[2]

The explanations offered were various and of unequal validity. Those that did not go beyond accidental causes, such as the extent of war damage and consequent reconstruction on the Continent, or the fact that Continental countries were mostly behind Britain economically to start with, failed to account for the persistent lag in British expansion. It is, of course, true that the vast demands of reconstruction had stimulated production in certain European countries, particularly Germany, where reconstruction had moreover been delayed (growth rate 6·5 per cent between 1950 and 1960); and equally true that, immediately after the Second World War, output per head was lower in Western Europe than in Great Britain. The view that

[1] At that time Conservative Chancellor of the Exchequer. Now Lord Butler.

[2] W. Beckerman in *The British Economy in 1975* by W. Beckerman and associates, Cambridge University Press, 1965, p. 11.

TABLE 1

PER CAPITA GROWTH OF THE GROSS NATIONAL PRODUCT IN THE PRINCIPAL INDUSTRIAL COUNTRIES (ANNUAL AVERAGES)

	1870–1913	1913–50	1950–60
Europe			
Belgium	1·7	0·7	2·3
Denmark	2·1	1·1	2·6
Federal Germany	1·8	0·4	6·5
France	1·4	0·7	3·5
Italy	0·7	0·6	5·3
Netherlands	0·8(*a*)	0·7	3·6
Norway	1·4	1·9	2·6
Sweden	2·3	1·6	2·6
Switzerland	1·3(*b*)	1·5	3·7
North America			
Canada	2·0	1·3	1·2
USA	2·2	1·7	1·6
United Kingdom	1·2	0·8	2·2

(*a*) 1900–13
(*b*) 1890–1913
From Maddison, A., *Economic Growth in the West*, Allen and Unwin, 1964. (We are grateful to the author for allowing us to quote these figures.)

Continental countries were merely catching up by taking advantage of recent technical advances was frequently put forward as an answer to critics. According to this thesis, Britain was paying the price of being a pioneer in industry.

However, the passing of time revealed that such explanations were only marginally adequate, and it became necessary to seek elsewhere the causes of this relative stagnation, notably in the rate of increase in the supply of the factors of production, manpower and capital.

The rate of increase in the population in Britain after the war gathered momentum, as in most developed countries, though remaining fairly moderate (2·1 per cent 1952–6; 2·8 per cent 1957–61). The rise in the labour force was rather more rapid; but, on the whole, the total supply of labour was not very elastic in the period. On the Continent, often with the help of immigration, there were generally faster increases in the labour force, though not in France where there was practically no change during the 1950s. Moreover, Britain was faced with the difficulty that there could be little transfer of labour from the land into industry, for at the end of the war British agriculture employed only a very small proportion (4 per cent) of the total labour force. On the Continent, things were often very different. In France where agriculture accounts for a fifth of the working population still today, the reduction in the number of these workers by about one-quarter (2½ million) between 1954 and 1962 benefited the economy as a whole. Some of the workers who transferred to other industries were in a sense disguised unemployed, and their productivity in agriculture was almost negligible, and all were workers whose productivity in their original jobs was much below what it was to become in their new employment. This sort of flexibility in the labour supply, with the additional windfall of extra production due to differences in productivity levels, was lacking in Britain.

In this country also the large and persistent differences in the level of employment from one region to another (cf. Chapter IV) exacerbated labour shortages which must have affected total production. But it is true that other countries which showed more rapid expansion, like France and Italy, had similar, or even greater, regional differences than Britain.

Attempts have been made to quantify the effect on the British growth record of these manpower trends[1] that were different from those pertaining on the Continent. The results obtained, whilst they show that some 'explanations' of the poor performance of the British economy during the 1950s tended to overstate the importance of demographic factors do not, it seems, entirely dispel the view that such factors have been, and continue to be, important.

With regard to investment and, more particularly, to the percentage of the gross national product devoted to capital formation, Britain found herself, between 1950 and 1960, in a position better indeed than before the war, but below a number of Continental countries. In the comparison which follows, investment in housing is omitted as this has no immediate effect on the level of productivity; productive investment is therefore defined as the total of non-residential building plus purchases of plant and equipment. The figure was only 10 per cent in Britain at the beginning of the 1950s as against 14 per cent in the six countries of the Common Market; this rose to 13 per cent between 1958 and 1960, but to 16 per cent in the Common Market.

There is, of course, no automatic correlation between the investment rate and the *per capita* rate of growth of the gross national product. Indeed experience abroad suggests that the countries with the fastest rate of growth are not necessarily those that devote the largest share of their resources to investment. Nevertheless, if the investment rate remains weak, the stock of capital grows slowly and tends, as a result, to feel the effects of an out-dated structure when compared with the capital structure in countries having a higher

[1] Notably by W. Beckerman, op. cit.

investment rate. And the disparity between experience in Britain and on the Continent—as the figures quoted in the previous paragraph show —was too great to be without influence.

The kind of investment undertaken by British industry during the 1950s can also supply some interesting pointers. Enquiries among British industrialists frequently revealed the simultaneous existence of difficulties in recruiting enough labour and of unused capacity. Certain economists[1] drew the conclusion that investment was too often devoted to extending productive capacity ('capital widening') and not enough to replacing men by machines ('capital deepening'), hence the cases noted of lack of balance between available manpower and productive capacity.

On the whole, then, the growth and distribution of productive investment in Britain during the 1950s were such that they did not provide an adequate basis for more rapid expansion.

The part played in the post-war world by the Welfare State and the substantial increase entailed in public revenues derived from taxation was a favourite theme with some critics who considered that initiative was thus being dampened. Others, too, pointed to the volume of military expenditure, which was unproductive yet consumed valuable resources in manpower and capital, as an impediment to growth. Nevertheless, the proportion of the gross national product in Britain devoted to public expenditure in the civil sector (less than 10 per cent) is much the same as in Continental countries, and the same is true for military expenditure, except for Germany where the figure remains very low. This is not to deny of course that, in all countries with high military expenditures, civilian needs have to be cut back; but this argument does not suffice to explain the British case. The situation is the same as regards taxation. Direct and indirect taxes in Britain represent about 25 per cent of the gross national product, as in most industrial countries in Europe; and although the preponderance of direct taxation in Britain is sometimes thought to discourage individual initiative, it is doubtful whether this has been a valid argument, since the differences in the fiscal structure in England, France and Germany are not very significant.[2]

We shall reserve examination of two further types of explanation of Britain's poor growth performance for the following chapters. They concern respectively the debilitating effect on growth prospects of 'stop-go' demand management policy and the handicap, for

[1] For example Barna, T., 'Investment in Industry: has Britain lagged?', *The Banker*, April 1957.

[2] Cf. the report of the Richardson Committee on the reform of indirect taxation (*Report of the Committee on Turnover Taxation*, Cmd. 2300, 1964).

British industry, of the absence of buoyant demand conditions on external markets. Let it suffice, for the moment, to note that both explanations merit considerable weight in any assessment of the causal factors at work.

Meanwhile, we must return to a consideration of the heavy criticism that has been levelled at British *élites*.

2. BRITISH ELITES

The search for a scapegoat for the unsatisfactory working of the economy was bound to lead observers to challenge the efficiency and dynamism of British *élites*.

English post-war literature remained faithful to its tradition of critical analysis of social structures. But, with the appearance in the 1950s of the 'Angry Young Men', though they proved to be but a passing phenomenon, criticism became more aggressive.[1] At the same time it became customary to group together under the title 'the Establishment' the ruling circles in politics and business, the name being meant to be frankly critical and signifying conservatism, fixed ideas and social exclusiveness. As used by Henry Fairlie,[2] the journalist who gave the term 'the Establishment' its current vogue, the expression attacks the narrow network of personal, and often family, relationships maintained by certain exclusive circles, who are thus able to monopolize key positions in administration, banks, the chief industrial concerns and the Press. Another author, Anthony Sampson, for whom the Establishment is also very much a reality drew from this fact a rather different conclusion when he suggested that the danger lies less in a near monopoly by the Establishment of English political and economic life, than in a lack of contact with the new worlds of science and technology, so that the ruling circles are still trying to cope with contemporary problems by amateur methods which are no longer relevant.[3]

This criticism of the 'pundits' extends equally to those of the Left. Thus Anthony Crosland maintains that the British Labour Movement 'from being the most flexible and empirical has become the most conservative and fundamentalist' in its attitude.[4] Similarly an acute observer of British trade unionism did not hesitate to write, in a generally favourable study of the aims of the Trade Union Movement, that 'the leadership is not keeping pace with the march of

[1] Cf. the joint work of a group of young intellectuals published under the title *Declaration* (MacGibbon and Kee, 1957).

[2] Cf. for example his article 'The BBC' in *Encounter*, August 1959.

[3] Cf., op. cit., p. 632.

[4] Crosland, A. R., *The Conservative Enemy*, Cape, 1962, p. 120.

events' and has been unable to make good 'the deficiencies that have appeared' in the working of the unions.[1]

Let us then examine in turn the criticisms directed against the three main groups which play a predominant part in British economic affairs: the higher circles of the Civil Service, the leaders of industry and of the trade unions.

The Civil Service

In Britain, as elsewhere, in the course of post-war development, the powers of public administrators have become infinitely greater and more varied than they were before the war. Public opinion today holds the Government answerable for all aspects of economic affairs, for rising prices and distressed areas, for the state of foreign trade, for the level of investment. In brief there are few things for which the State is not held responsible and for which the latter refuses to accept such responsibility. In addition, as a result of post-war nationalization, the public sector includes several basic industries, such as electricity, coal and rail transport, the efficiency of whose operation affects the performance of the economy as a whole. And the annual investment bill of the public sector represents nearly half the total investment in the economy.

To fulfil all these new functions, the higher Civil Service—and especially the Treasury which in practice controls all the spending departments—must deal both with policy issues and with highly technical problems which, before the war, were no part of an official's responsibility. Such is the extent today to which the efficient working of the highly complex economies of the Western world is dependent on the quality of the top civil servants and on the decisions which are based on their advice.

Although the Civil Service in Britain remains faithful to the great Victorian reforms in its methods of recruitment, for example, in selection by examination, the willingness to envisage new ideas which inspired the reformers of the last century was lacking after 1945 when the temporary war-time recruits from private industry and the universities returned to their civilian occupations. Until quite recently the 'specialist', if he was a scientist or even an economist, was to be found only in certain technical Ministries, and was seldom seen in the higher ranks of the Service. These posts were in fact, if not in theory, the preserve of men trained in the classics, philosophy or letters. Moreover, in spite of the post-war reforms, and particularly those introduced by Ernest Bevin in the Foreign Office, recruitment still tended to favour the products of Oxford and Cambridge, that is to say, a small minority of university graduates. Such a situation did

[1] Wigham, E., *What's wrong with the Unions?*, Penguin, 1961, p. 21.

not favour the rise to the top posts of men from a varied social background.[1]

The higher Civil Service in Britain was also stigmatized as 'amateurish', and this is not unconnected with the nature of the men recruited. It is significant that the term 'technocrat' is more readily used on the Continent to describe the qualities expected in the top civil servant, whereas in England the word that comes to mind is 'mandarin'. Until 1964 'the junior administrative course (for new recruits) has consisted of three weeks of isolated talks', writes Professor Robson.[2] The worst defect of the administration 'is—or has been—a profound disbelief in training at the centre, by which I mean the Treasury'. What Continental critics of the role of the technocrats in the public service fear is too much expertise and too little political control. It is noteworthy that the British counterparts of such critics apprehended rather a lack of professional competence in technical matters allied with the same insufficiency of political responsibility.

If the Treasury thus became the target of criticism of British officialdom—which, in fairness must be said to have shown a capacity for self-criticism[3]—it is because of the pre-eminence it enjoys over all other departments and because, wielding until recently ultimate authority in economic matters, it undertakes heavy and wide-ranging responsibilities in all spheres of public life. The Treasury approves the expenditure estimates of other Ministries and the investment programmes of public corporations; it prepares the budget, controls public finance, and exercises a decisive role in the field of Civil Service personnel and remuneration; its functions also include contacts with other countries and with international economic organizations.

Until recently, the only 'apprenticeship' which new entrants to the Civil Service received was given 'on the job' and did too little to make up for a university training which had, in general, too little relevance to responsibilities requiring extensive knowledge of economic, social or scientific problems. The very nature of the administrative life of a high official in Britain does nothing to make good the gaps in his educational background. He must maintain a reserve in his dealings with the public much greater than on the Continent; the rule of ministerial responsibility is observed to the letter although, as many observers have pointed out,[4] the complexity and sheer volume of

[1] Cf. Kelsall, R. K., *Higher Civil Servants in Britain*, Routledge & Kegan Paul, 1955.

[2] Robson, W. A., 'The Reform of Government', *Political Quarterly*, April–June 1964, p. 208.

[3] Cf. the remarkable selection of replies by high officials to a question put by the administration, authorized for publication by the Treasury and appearing in the *Economist* for August 8, 1964.

[4] Cf. Chapman, B., *British Government Observed*, Allen and Unwin, 1964.

questions with which a Minister must deal today cause this rule, first brought in to protect the public against bureaucracy, to have the opposite effect.

He tends to have little acquaintance with the problems of the private sector and his contacts with industry are minimal. In addition, until recent years, the strict separation between questions falling to the administration and those concerning the private sector was much more scrupulously maintained than on the Continent. Inside the administration also his professional mobility seems restricted compared with that of a similar official on the Continent.

Nevertheless, the beginnings of change were discernible as the 1950s drew to a close, though the main changes belong to the period dealt with in the second part of this book. For example, a former high official in the Treasury, Sir Leslie Rowan,[1] who went into private industry a few years ago, noted that the current experiment in a planned economy in Britain introduced a new dimension into the relations between administration and the private sector and insisted that the excessive divergence between their ways of thought must be reduced. 'A much better understanding than ever before [by the Treasury] with the world of business, industry and commerce; more effective methods of communication, in both directions' will be required in future, says Lord Bridges who was Permanent Secretary to the Treasury for eleven years after the war. He adds that the introduction of economic planning will involve, for his old department, 'big changes in the way in which the Treasury does this part of its work'.[2] It is noteworthy that, for both these high officials, it is the advent of planning that epitomizes the need for the adoption of new methods.

Industry

British industry, like that of the rest of Europe, has since the war been going through a difficult period calling for rapid adjustments to changes in technology and to the revolution in methods of business administration. Though it is impossible to assess satisfactorily the effect of a certain tardiness shown by British industrialists in adapting themselves to fresh conditions, it is very generally claimed that this factor is not negligible in considering the decline of some branches of industry relative to those on the Continent. The nationalized industries have not escaped their share of such criticisms. Moreover, it has not been difficult to detect many signs of a lack of concern among employers with regard to problems of industrial relations, a gap that

[1] *Barclays Bank Review*, May 1964.
[2] Lord Bridges, *The Treasury*, Allen and Unwin, 1964, p. 203.

has unfavourable repercussions on productivity and collective bargaining arrangements.

The 'cult of the amateur' is not the monopoly of high officials. 'It is well known,' writes M. Shanks, 'that if one wants to reach the top in British industry it is usually fatal to admit any specialist expertise. Otherwise one is apt to find oneself put in charge of a specialist advisory department . . . and there one is liable to stay.'[1] The fact that a degree in engineering is still often considered, even in industry, as inferior to a training in classics or letters must surely deflect many brilliant scientists away from careers in industry.

The same lack of systematic training on the job which is held against the Civil Service in Britain is to be found in the private sector. Although scientific management is taught at all levels in modern branches of industry like electronics, chemistry and oil technology, this is by no means true in many of the traditional branches such as shipbuilding, machine tools and building construction. These are the very industries which employ only a small proportion of qualified engineers and spend limited amounts on scientific research. It was not until 1963 that a business school was planned for higher ranks of industry (cf. Chapter IX).

The problems in the nationalized industries are similar to those in the private sector. Whereas one of the logical consequences of postwar nationalization might have been great technical improvements in those industries which would have had a beneficial effect on the economy as a whole, the facts were very different and such exceptions as there were depended on the personality of individuals. All too often the nationalized industries lacked dynamism because they tended to fall between the two stools of commercial enterprise and public service. The most striking example was that of the railways. When, in 1961, a high executive from private industry—now Lord Beeching—took over, he found that no systematic attempt had ever been made to determine which lines ran at a profit and which at a loss. The methods of control of investment programmes in these industries by the Treasury came in for heavy criticism before moves were made to reform them.

The long period of unemployment between the two wars poisoned the atmosphere of industrial relations in Britain. The years of nearly full employment following the Second World War did little to improve matters, and we shall consider the unions' responsibility for this situation a little later. But it may be noted here that, if employers have a major part to play in creating conditions conducive to good relations with their workpeople, such a part was not fully played in Britain. We will quote, among many such comments, that of a

[1] Op. cit., p. 212.

Swedish businessman who, after noting that industrial relations between employers and employees in England most certainly interfered with productivity, maintained that, to a Swedish employer, the frequency of strikes in England seemed 'a sort of nightmare', and that employers and unions were equally responsible.[1]

One solution would be to have the general guidelines for policy worked out by employers' representatives at the national level on such matters as collective agreements, paid holidays, pensions and compensation for loss of employment. The details could then be left to individual firms, possibly within the framework of each industry. Whatever changes are made, however, and in whatsoever manner they come about, the practice of collective bargaining had come, by the 1950s, to incorporate too many defects. Few agreements dealt with anything but basic rates of pay and the length of the working week. Trade union representatives thus found themselves forced continually to put forward fresh pay claims since, in the eyes of their members, wage increases became the chief evidence of the union's effectiveness. Equally, few employers bothered to follow up matters discussed in agreements which, until recently, were never made binding over a predetermined number of years, but could be abrogated at any time by either signatory.

It is unlikely that there will be any marked change in the attitude of employers in many branches of industry without strong guidance from the employers' organizations. But, until 1964, the employers had no single organization, and none of the existing ones had any real power with their members in the formulation of general policy, or any great concern with industrial relations. The four bodies which represented the employers were differentiated somewhat arbitrarily according to their function: The British Employers' Confederation (BEC), the National Association of British Manufacturers (NABM), the Federation of British Industries (FBI), and the National Association of Chambers of Commerce (NACC). The study of problems of a general nature fell to the FBI; this body, however, did not embrace most of the smaller enterprises which were members of the NABM. Moreover, the FBI had no power to deal with questions of collective bargaining, the concern of the BEC, which, for its part, carefully avoided involvement in general problems. Both the BEC and the FBI were very weak bodies, with no power either to represent their members' corporate views or to put pressure on their members to

[1] Browaldh, T., 'A Swedish view of Britain's economy', *Three Banks Review*, June 1963. An example of what can be done to get agreement among staff to a reorganization of work in a business is given in Flanders, A., *The Fawley Productivity Agreement*, Faber, 1964. This refers to the new refinery built by Esso in the south of England.

make them respect national agreements. This situation aroused growing concern on the setting up of the National Economic Development Council.[1]

Today all these problems are under review and useful progress seems likely. But for a real improvement changes are needed on the union's side too.

The Trade Unions

The British Trade Union Movement is one of the oldest in Europe. It is also, on the surface at least, one of the most powerful. It has close links with the Labour Party, for which it provides the main income, and many trade unionists sit in Parliament. Several hold key posts in nationalized industries; for example, until recently Lord Citrine at the Central Electricity Generating Board, and today Lord Robens at the National Coal Board, a former trade unionist and Labour Minister after the war. After 1945, the members of the Council of the TUC[2] were regularly consulted by the Chancellor of the Exchequer, and the unions were represented on all royal commissions and consultative committees. The membership of the unions is impressive. About half of all wage-earners—9 million workers—subscribe to them, and almost all of these to unions affiliated to the TUC. The British trade unions are not divided on political or religious issues; recognized by the employers, their representatives are the intermediaries between their members and management—the banks being among the few institutions where trade unionism has not yet found a foothold.

Yet, despite its strong position, British trade unionism is going through a period of self-questioning.

One of the causes for concern is the falling off in membership. Economic development has reduced the percentage of workmen in the total of wage-earners, in England as elsewhere. On the borders of the working class there has arisen a class of white-collar workers, draughtsmen, foremen, specialists of various kinds; the so-called 'service sector' has grown. Now these workpeople are slow to join the trade unions and so do not offset the fall in membership among factory workers in general. Moreover, this new class often tends to join unions which are not affiliated to the TUC.[3] There have been blunders and tactical mistakes which have also aroused concern. In 1959, Mr George Woodcock, General Secretary of the TUC, pin-

[1] About which more later (Chapter V and following).

[2] Elected each year by the TUC, the Council represents it to the outside world. Its members are often presidents or general secretaries of unions.

[3] Cf. M. Shanks, op. cit., p. 73.

pointed four of them: unofficial stoppages, demarcation disputes, rowdyism among strikers, the closed shop; all these have damaged the good name of the unions at the present time.

The unions' suspicion of technical progress tends to be very largely due to the fear of loss of jobs. Here Britain is still suffering from the mass unemployment of the inter-war period. This grim experience, lived through by all union leaders over forty-five, has stamped its mark on a whole generation of workers. The spectre of unemployment explains, at least in part, the fundamental conservatism of trade unionists and their representatives in face of changes in working conditions.

The laying off of labour, for whatever reason, is therefore regarded as the worst of all evils—we need refer only to the unions' opposition to any broadening of recruitment, for example, by a simplification and speeding up of training which would entail changes in the traditional shape of apprenticeship. Hence, it is extremely difficult for a firm to derive full benefit in increased productivity from shop-floor reorganization or new investment.

But for this state of affairs responsibility must be shared. The attitude of the employers has not helped to change traditional trade-union reactions to technological advance; it was not until 1963 that the Government took upon itself to override the employers' resistance to its intervention in questions of apprenticeship, and not until 1964 that it brought in compulsory indemnification for loss of employment.

Even the organization of the trade unions is full of time-honoured survivals and reveals a rather negative attitude to the needs of modernization, and it was only through the efforts of Mr George Woodcock, and a few trade union leaders, that in 1962 the annual congress of the TUC passed a motion calling for an examination of these problems.

Although British trade unions are not divided politically, there are nevertheless many differences between them. The 190 odd British unions fall into three groups which have remained distinct despite some blurring of their frontiers since the war. The *craft unions* date back to the nineteenth century and the first associations of highly skilled men from the new industrial working class, and preserve the traditions of apprenticeship and trained workmanship. The *industrial unions* recruit, in theory at least, all the workers in any one branch of industry; here the best example is the National Union of Mineworkers. The *general unions* date from the beginning of this century when the second wave of trade unionism in Britain brought into the movement workmen with no special qualification. Subsequently the craft unions threw open their membership, to some extent, to specialized workmen in industry, particularly in motor manufacture, but were unable to achieve any sort of monopoly among them. The fierceness of industrial competition, the hard fights against employers, especially in the south which became industrialized between the wars, labour difficulties during the long period of unemployment, combined to bring into being a multiplicity of unions in industry and even in individual works. The Ford Motor Company, for example, has to deal with some twenty unions in any negotiations.[1]

Some union leaders have realized the harm done by this fragmentation of the unions. In the view of the president of the Building Trades Union,[2] the struggles with the employers appear tame by comparison 'with the petty jealousies and demarcation disputes' within the union movement. The need for every one of these unions to be represented in negotiations weakens union authority and inhibits discussion on any important question. Mr Weaver also remarked that it was becoming 'well-nigh impossible to develop and co-ordinate long-term policy for improved wage standards', or to work out a policy 'for dealing with the problems of new techniques'.

It might be expected that the TUC would have a unifying influence, and it is indeed now regrouping most of the unions, except certain 'white collar' unions. But none of these unions is prepared to surrender any of its autonomy to the TUC, and each member of the General Council can speak only for those workers whom he controls as leader of a union. Thus, although strong personalities succeed from time to time in giving the TUC a unified leadership,[3] its influence remains considerably weakened. In particular it finds difficulty in formulating any long-term policy, and still more in carrying such a policy through. This organic weakness of British trade unionism affects the movement in other ways.

The British unions lack funds, with calamitous results. The expense of propaganda and staffing is heavy and union subscriptions are very small. They are sometimes less than 1 per cent of wages and have risen little with wage increases.[4] As a result, the poorly paid

[1] But Vauxhall, who was less opposed to union influence, only has to deal with two.

[2] Cf. M. Weaver, speech to the annual congress of building workers in 1961 (quoted by P. E. P., *Structure and Organization of British Trade Unionism*, 1962, p. 437.)

[3] As Ernest Bevin did before the war, and Arthur Deakin, his successor at the head of the powerful Transport and General Workers' Union, immediately after the war.

[4] In 1912 members of The Amalgamated Society of Engineers paid 1s 9d a week. Today (Amalgamated Engineering Union) 2s 6d on wages eight times as large.

union officials frequently earn less than many of the members[1] and they are too few to maintain proper contact with them.[2] This explains why shop stewards have gained considerably in importance, although they cannot really do the work of a responsible permanent official satisfactorily. Originally entrusted by the unions with particular tasks such as the collection of subscriptions, union propaganda and the settlement on the spot of minor grievances, the shop stewards have now become much more important than union representatives as intermediaries between management and workers; especially in the engineering and electrical industries. They deal with such questions as bonuses, piece rates, reclassification of jobs. For many workers it is the shop steward, not the permanent official, who represents the union. In these circumstances, absenteeism at union meetings can be as high as 90 per cent.

It may be that the chronic shortage of permanent union officials makes shop stewards indispensable today, for they take on thankless tasks, unpaid and in their spare time. But one of the disadvantages of this arrangement is a frequent failure of communication between the shop floor and the leaders and vice versa. At the present time Britain has 200,000 shop stewards—70 for every permanent official—with an organization parallel with that of the unions. In every factory there is a shop stewards' committee, and a national association of shop stewards has been formed with a strongly Left-wing bias, which is not true of the leadership of most unions in Britain.

3. THE AFFLUENT SOCIETY[3]

It may seem strange to devote attention to problems arising in England from the higher standard of living, in view of the relatively slow growth of the British economy during the last decade, but the paradox is only apparent.

Like other countries in Western Europe, Britain has witnessed a remarkable change in the habits of consumers consequent on the growth in their purchasing power, but due even more to the vastly increased range of goods offered, especially among durable consumer goods.[4] For reasons which will be made clear, the slow rate of expansion of the British economy has not prevented consumers from moving, like those on the Continent, towards a mass-consumption

[1] The salaries of presidents of the most powerful unions are around £2,000.

[2] 3,000 permanent staff for nearly 9 million trade union members, or 1:3,000.

[3] We owe the phrase to Professor Galbraith's book, *The Affluent Society*, H. Hamilton, 1958.

[4] Cars, household appliances, radio and TV, record players.

society. This explains why economic stagnation has not affected the sense of well-being of most people in England and why they were so slow to realize its dangers.

A study of the most characteristic changes in the attitude of the British consumer will reveal how a new policy of social equilibrium has been slowly evolving.

Transformations in Private Consumption

The average standard of living in the United Kingdom, judged by the growth in volume of domestic consumption per head of the population, has risen faster since the war than during any other period of comparable length; it has increased at the rate of about 2 per cent per annum since 1950, and its growth since that date has been greater than between 1913 and 1950 although this period was more than twice as long. Such a rate may seem modest compared with that in some other countries. But the impact of this moderate growth upon the attitude of householders has been spectacular, as a few examples will suffice to show.

If the motor car is not the only visible sign of the new society, it is certainly the most typical. In 1951 England had less than 2½ million private cars; ten years later she had 6 million and a figure of 15 million has been forecast for 1970. The speed of this tremendous increase surprised even the most far-sighted. For example, the original plans for the new town of Harwell provided one garage for every ten households; before it was completed this had become one for every two.

Changes are numberless within the home: three out of four householders possess a vacuum cleaner, two out of five a washing machine, one in three a refrigerator, and nine out of ten a TV which, according to a recent estimate, working-class families watch on the average four hours a day. Moreover, TV has transformed the use of leisure. People go out much less, especially to the cinema, and workers hurry home in the evening instead of going to the 'pubs'. At home men have got used to helping in the house, while their wives enjoy an undreamed of freedom thanks to this help and the new machines they can buy. And so they have time to think of worth-while leisure occupations, to care for their clothes and personal appearance like women of the traditional middle class. The latter often have to work harder owing to the quasi-disappearance of domestic servants just when working-class women are finding life easier, an upset in the established order which has caused many heartburnings.

Parents may stay at home nowadays watching TV, but the young people go out. They provide a valuable market for a whole group of industries—chiefly in record players, records and scooters—which have expanded rapidly. Their interest in travel, especially in foreign travel, has done much to kill British insularity.

Parallel with this enthusiasm for the goods and services of the new society, traditional tastes have been maintained and even extended. The success of paperback books has been as great in England as abroad, and in the early 1960s British public libraries lent nearly twice as many books as ten years before. Theatres and concerts have never attracted so many people.

Towards a New Social Balance

Changes in social attitudes have blurred many of the class distinctions which were so noticeable before the war. Such was the speed of these changes that the first reactions to them were defensive. Subsequently, however, attempts have been made to get this social revolution into perspective.

Round about 1955, the initial post-war enthusiasm for social progress waned somewhat, both in Left-wing circles and in the traditionally Conservative classes. Many intellectuals were disappointed to find that working-class families were adopting *bourgeois* attitudes—the name itself is significant—as soon as they were able to live in middle-class style.

This phenomenon is not difficult to explain. As Anthony Hartley has noted, 'the means which had to be used to increase the material welfare of the working classes were inevitably destructive . . . of the kind of residual folk culture on which their hopes were based. . . . Such agreeable phenomena as Welsh choirs and self-instructed working men were based on cultural isolation and the lack of educational facilities'.[1]

It was almost inevitable that middle-class people who had known life pre-war should react unfavourably. Though they too had enjoyed the greatly increased range of durable consumer goods, these things had not the same novelty for them as for working-class families, and as, at the same time, other changes were making life less easy for them, they tended to have reservations about the advantages of rapid economic expansion, and indeed about the need for it at all.

These questionings reappear in the political field, and especially among members of the Labour Party, who could not help noting that, for the electorate, much of the gilt had come off their traditional gingerbread, such as the redistribution of wealth by fiscal measures, social innovations and especially further nationalization. On the other hand, since Conservative Governments after 1951 made little

[1] Hartley, A., *A State of England*, Hutchinson, 1963, p. 33.

effort to dismantle the earlier Labour reforms, it became very difficult for the Opposition to differentiate their policy from that of the party in power.[1] The process of readapting the Labour programme to meet the new circumstances began under Hugh Gaitskell in 1950, but the task was long and difficult, and the fierce controversy which accompanied it deflected the party for a time from constructive thought about general economic problems.

For some years, on both the Conservative and the Labour side—to mention only the two main parties—there have been misgivings about the future of the consumer society which came into being in England in the 1950s. It is even more significant that public opinion also seems to be aware of the importance of decisions which must be taken in the near future. We shall not discuss these questions here in detail as they will be the subject of further study in the second part of this book. We may note, however, the direction such study will take.

First, it is very probable that the revolution in durable consumer goods has already reached its climax and that its impact on economic and social attitudes will in future be much less. In some directions, though, the problems arising from the new type of demand are likely to grow much worse, particularly problems of traffic and space. It is agreed today that the motor car is going to make conditions in great urban agglomerations intolerable unless there is a vigorous policy of re-planning in our towns. Internal displacements of population, and especially the drift to the south-east, together with a foreseeable demand for more spacious housing, are bound to lead to a systematic policy for the rational use of space.

The craze for a narrow range of durable goods which was the hallmark of the last decade, gives a very limited idea of the standard of living to which families aspire more and more. For the individual purchaser more variety is being asked for, and this tendency will increase. There will be a demand for more services as well as for more material goods, e.g. travel, amusements and leisure-time occupations generally. This demand, by its very nature, will be more difficult to meet than was the case in the last decade when, by a happy chance, the increased household spending power turned to a few highly mechanized industries which were in a position to expand their production and productivity greatly and thus to reduce their prices relative to other goods and services.

But an important part of this new demand can only be met collectively, for it is directed towards services which the community

[1] In this connection it is very revealing to note the term 'butskellism', concocted from the names of Butler and Gaitskell, the two party leaders, to describe Conservative social and economic policy.

alone is in a position to provide; the use of space, profitable use of leisure, improvement in the health service, greater scope in education. In all these sectors the State will have to play a much more active part than in the past, in conjunction with the local authorities. This theme is developed in the second part of this book.

CHAPTER II

DEMAND MANAGEMENT[1] OR THE POLICY OF 'STOP-GO'

For about 1955 a growing number of observers began to challenge the effectiveness of British anti-cyclical policy and to saddle it with a good measure of the blame for the slow expansion of the economy as compared with most Continental countries.

For a long time, unfortunately, discussion about the value of this policy was rather like a conversation among deaf people. The advocates of rapid economic expansion often put forward too rigid ideas which could not but fail to convince those responsible for policy; and the latter tended to seek refuge in the traditional recipes without asking whether, after all, changed circumstances did not call for changed methods. Further, the right questions were not always asked so that discussion became unprofitable as, for example, in the quarrel during the 1950s about the part that should be played in anti-cyclical policy by the classical instrument of monetary policy as compared with budgetary policy.

Between 1950 and 1961 British anti-cyclical policy was put to the test. The disappointing results obtained led, as will be seen, to a calling into question of the policy and to attempts to evolve new procedures more adapted to present-day circumstances. By way of preface to the study of these issues, let us rehearse briefly the history of 'stop-go'. It will be seen that, since about 1961, fairly general agreement seems to have been arrived at about the need for a different approach. Unfortunately, this did not prevent the re-introduction of restrictive measures after 1964 for reasons which will become apparent in Part Two.

1. WHAT IS 'STOP-GO'?

The development of the British economy between 1950 and 1961 followed a very characteristic zig-zag path unlike anything on the Continent (see graph). This path is not the result of spontaneous

[1] We mean by 'demand management' policy measures designed to preserve, or to restore, overall balance of the economy in the short term, as opposed to a policy for growth over the medium or long term.

—endogenous—trends, but is due, for the most part, to deliberate Government action, in rapid succession, alternately to restrain and to stimulate economic activity.

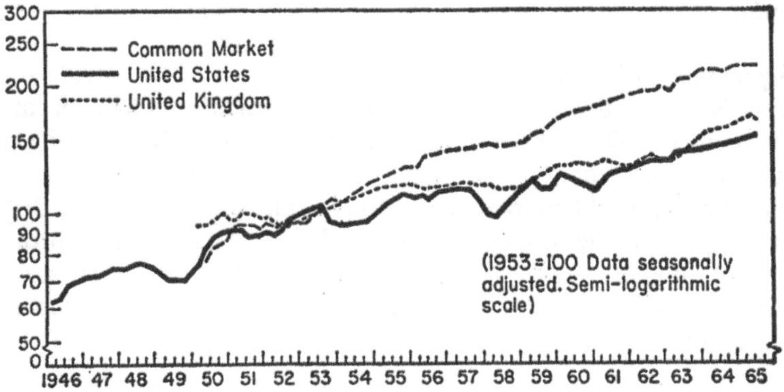

Comparative industrial productions

General Bulletin of Statistics, OECD

The graph shows the development since 1950 of production in Britain, the six countries of the Common Market and the USA. In contrast to what happened on the Continent, where production grew regularly apart from a few periods of slowing down or acceleration, in the United Kingdom as in the United States the progress of production flattens out every few years, and even in the USA shows recession. Each pause, or recession, is followed by a phase of rapid expansion, to be followed after a while by another pause. But the resemblance between the curves for Britain and the USA is only apparent. In the case of the USA we are dealing with a trade cycle very much of the same kind as pre-war, which started again in 1945 and in the period studied had produced four phases of alternate recession and expansion in the old rhythm if not with the old magnitude.[1] But, whereas the recurrent periods of stagnation in the USA were connected with spontaneous economic trends against which the Government refrained from taking remedial action, the repeated recessions in Britain were very largely the result of deliberate actions by the State. In other words the 'stop' was intentional and when the brake was no longer necessary, policy switched over to a stimulant to de-

[1] Hence the use of the term 'recession' instead of 'crisis' or 'depression'. Since 1961 the American authorities have managed to ward off a further recession, unlike Britain, and growth has been both sustained and vigorous. The explanation for this change is the renewal of methods of demand management in the USA in the 1960s under a Democrat administration.

mand, to 'go'. Therefore post-war fluctuations in Britain's economy bear little resemblance to the periodic fluctuations which the country knew in the nineteenth century.

The chronology of British anti-cyclical policy will illustrate the point.

September 1949—June 1951

This is a period of rapid expansion in production which began in September 1949, with the devaluation of the pound. In 1950, the very substantial rise in price of basic products which the Korean war set going in world markets sent up considerably the cost of British imports. But the other countries of the sterling area profited by the higher prices for their exports, and so their sterling balances in London rose, with beneficial effects on the balance of payments.

June 1951—December 1952

In June 1951, the disappearance of the artificial conditions brought about by the Korean war caused a fall in gold and currency reserves in London, while the internal economy began to show signs of inflation. So the Conservative Party, which came into power in September 1951, decided to restrict imports and raise Bank rate. In the spring of 1952, a deflationary budget and a new credit squeeze were adopted. Production slowed down and then, towards the end of 1952, declined, while unemployment figures rose.

Early 1953—October 1955

Between these dates falls the period of most sustained expansion that the United Kingdom has known since the war. In 1953 and 1954 British policy was decidedly expansionist. Already by the end of 1952 the balance of payments had sufficiently improved for the Government's attention to turn anxiously to the slackness in production and its corrollary, unemployment (though unemployment figures were not large). So in February 1953, there was a relaxation of controls over investment, while the April budget in that year was frankly expansionist and included a reduction in direct taxation. Soon afterwards, credit restrictions were removed. These measures conducive to growth were maintained in 1953 and 1954 both in the budget and in monetary policy. But early in 1955 there appeared the harbingers of imbalance in supply and demand (a rapid rise in imports and tension in the labour market). Credit was again made dearer, and although the budget of April 1955, still appeared expansionist, an extraordinary budget in October of that year withdrew the tax reductions conceded in April.

October 1955—October 1958

In spite of an occasional expansionist tendency, these are three years of slack, or even falling, production. At the end of 1958, the production index fell below the 1955 level, and unemployment, which had been below 1·5 per cent up to 1958, rose to 2·4 per cent by the end of that year.

Early in 1956 hire-purchase restrictions were increased and programmes of public investment were severely cut. The position of the balance of payments having improved at the beginning of 1957, and gold and currency reserves having begun to rise again, the budget of that year was slightly expansionist and Bank rate was lowered. But following a sudden speculative run on the pound and an unexpected lowering of the gold and currency reserves, Bank rate was raised again in September; at 7 per cent it was the highest rate since the war. At the same time, credit restrictions and a severe cut in public investment were decided on. There followed a new fall in industrial production and a marked rise in unemployment. However, an improvement in the balance of payments, thanks in part to the attractiveness of high British interest rates to foreign capital, allowed the reserves lost in September 1957, to be quickly made good. The Government could therefore once more think of stimulating the economy by the end of 1958.

October 1958—April 1960

Hire-purchase restrictions were now removed and the 1959 budget afforded substantial tax relief, whence followed rapid expansion of production and the re-employment of the workless. But the balance of payments again became unfavourable at the end of 1959, though the deficit was obscured by the influx of foreign capital attracted by the raising of Bank rate from 4 to 5 per cent in January 1960.

The 1960 budget was neutral, so expansion could continue in spite of certain quantitative credit controls in the spring. But following the Conservative victory at the election of October 1959, investment in private industry grew rapidly and substantially, in the comfortable knowledge that Labour would be in the wilderness for five years.

April 1960—December 1961

Nevertheless, by the spring of 1960, production was again marking time. In March 1961, the weakness of the balance of payments position was thrown into relief by the wave of speculation which followed the revaluation of the deutschmark and the Dutch florin. An agreement with the European central banks bolstered up British gold and currency reserves, but the balance of payments showed no improvement and Britain was compelled to borrow $714m. from the International Monetary Fund in August 1961. In July new restrictive measures included Bank rate raised to 7 per cent again, credit made more difficult to come by, indirect taxation raised, and a 'pause' in wage increases in both the public and the private sector.

Looked at in the perspective of time these decisions in July 1961, seem like the end of an epoch. In spite of efforts to slow down the growth of internal demand, whether in order to avoid excessive pressure on costs and prices, or to redress the balance of payments, or both at once, Britain had been unable to regain economic stability. The rise in prices between 1950 and 1960 was somewhat greater than in the six countries of the Common Market, and whereas those countries' reserves of gold and foreign currency rose by $11,000m. during the decade, the reserves of the United Kingdom rose by only about $400m. It could well be asked whether the policy followed had been worth while for such mediocre results.

This conclusion was indeed being reached by more and more people who felt that Britain had lost on all counts: economic growth, price stability, the strengthening of the balance of payments, and that it was henceforth essential to do something different from 'stop-go'. It was surely not by chance that, on the same day in July 1961, as new restrictive measures were brought in, the Conservative Government invited representatives of employers and labour to join with them in working out a medium-term economic plan.

2. THE INSTRUMENTS OF DEMAND MANAGEMENT POLICY

At the end of the last war all political parties agreed that one of the principal aims of economic policy must be the maintenance of full employment.[1] For several years after 1945, most of those in charge of national economic policy, supported by public opinion, were convinced that, with the end of the period of change-over to a peacetime economy, this would once more become the number one problem economic policy would have to cope with. In the event, British anticyclical policy had mostly to contend with an inflationary trend, with demand in excess of available goods and services and bringing in its wake, if it could not be controlled, an inevitable deficit in the balance of payments. As regards the level of unemployment, despite all the short-term fluctuations just described, it remained mostly under 1·5 per cent, and exceeded 2 per cent only rarely and for a few months at a time.[2] The complete reversal of the economic situation compared

[1] Cf. White paper on Employment Policy, Cmd. 6527, 1944.

[2] The Beveridge Report in 1944 did not foresee that any efforts of the authorities could bring the unemployment figures below 5 per cent. Cf. Beveridge, W., *Full Employment in a Free Society*, Allen and Unwin, 1944.

with pre-war called forth problems with which traditional policy was ill-equipped to deal, and this explains why, after the war, policy decisions were rather a protracted groping after a new conception of demand management policy.

A mass of wartime controls, inherited by the Labour Government, were kept in being until the beginning of the 1950s.[1] But already before 1951, when the Conservatives regained office, the process of dismantling this apparatus of administrative controls had begun. It was to continue with increasing momentum during the following years, to the extent that controls of this type can be neglected as an instrument of anti-cyclical policy during the period under review, i.e. between 1950 and 1961. Rather we must devote our attention to the two principal instruments of policy, the manipulation of public finance in the widest sense,[2] and monetary policy. The use of such measures reveals that, although efforts were made as time went on to achieve more diversity and flexibility in the economic arsenal, those efforts were not fully successful.

Public Finance

Expenditure of the public sector represents nowadays some 30 per cent of the gross national product; it would therefore be unprofitable to discuss what has been described as the economic 'neutrality' of public finance. For better or worse, the public sector does exercise considerable influence on the economy both by its expenditure and by the way it is financed. The real problem is to see that that influence is in the right direction. Neglecting for the moment possible long-term repercussions, let us examine how anti-cyclical policy uses budgetary measures from the point of view of balancing budget receipts and expenditure, manipulating taxation and adjusting expenditure.

(a) Every British Government since the war has accepted and applied the principle that whether the *budget was balanced*, or showed a deficit or a surplus was important, not because the State needed funds, nor because of a doctrinaire dislike of unbalanced budgets, but because it is the chief purpose of the budget to bring about the necessary overall balance between total supply and demand that, according to the analysis of the circular flow of income and the factors that influence it, is needed to ensure full employment equilibrium. Between 1951 and 1961 there was hardly a single budget which did not set out to influence the general balance of the economy in this manner. Thus demand was stimulated in 1953, in the spring of 1954, then in 1961, by an intentional reflation. On the other hand, the need

[1] Consumer rationing, priority allocations of raw materials and basic products to industry, strict import quotas.

[2] That is, including nationalized industries and local authorities.

to restrain expansion of demand in 1952, autumn 1955, 1957, 1960 and July 1961 inspired the deflationary budgets of those years.

(b) In the realm of *taxation*, anti-cyclical policy since 1951 used mainly indirect taxes. The use of direct taxes in order to influence the economy in the short term was limited and usually confined to company taxation.

At the end of the last war income tax was so heavy that it could not be maintained at that level for long, and if reductions of income tax were decided in 1953 and 1955 it was not only in order to underpin an expansionist policy. After 1950, and until the measures taken since 1964 which will be discussed in the second part of this book, there was no increase in income tax, and when it was thought necessary to damp down expansion, it was indirect taxes which were raised. So, over the years, the weight of taxation was moved from direct to indirect taxes.

On the other hand company taxation was changed several times. This applied particularly to allowances on capital investment. Giving firms more or less substantial allowances to set against tax liabilities permits the Government—in theory, at least—to stimulate or hold back re-equipment and thus to affect the total amount of productive investment.[1] Over the ten years 1950–60, this form of taxation varied six times, up or down, according to the state of the business cycle.

Experience showed, however, that such frequent changes in investment allowances had serious disadvantages. It takes a firm a little time to get used to changes in tax relief, and to change its investment plans accordingly, so that rapidity of effect—essential to any instrument of demand management—was bound to be sacrificed. Also too frequent changes introduce an undesirable element of uncertainty into the calculations of firms and may well hold up their efforts to modernize and adapt themselves to the progress of technology. For this reason, in 1961, the Government announced that they would no longer use this tax measure for purely anti-cyclical reasons.

Instead of using direct taxation to influence the behaviour of the private sector, the State can use indirect taxes. This instrument was already available at the end of the war owing to the imposition of purchase tax, between 1939 and 1945, on a whole range of consumer goods. These new indirect taxes were in addition to the traditional excise duty on tobacco, alcohol and petrol. Between 1951 and 1961

[1] Two kinds of tax relief were used: the initial allowance enabled equipment to be paid for more quickly, while the investment allowance was a bonus on investment. It could thus be said that the initial allowance was an interest-free loan from the State to a firm, while an investment allowance was really a tax exemption.

successive budgets altered indirect taxes nine times, either to stimulate consumer demand, as in 1958 and 1959, or to slow it down, especially in 1955, 1960 and 1961.

However, this instrument of anti-cyclical policy lacked flexibility. Since it could only be used with the approval of Parliament, it could really only be introduced in the annual budget, for otherwise the inevitable delays accompanying parliamentary approval might encourage speculation by provoking uncertainty among consumers. Between two annual budgets, then, apart from the very few extraordinary autumn budgets, changes in indirect taxation were hardly ever used by the Chancellor of the Exchequer. The Government were thus led, in 1961, to seek powers, valid for one year and renewable, to modify the whole range of indirect taxes by regulation, the approval of Parliament being required only after the event. This regulatory clause was made even more flexible in 1962 and 1964. At the present time the Government can alter the tax on five groups of consumer goods subject to indirect taxation.[1] The absence of such a handy tool until 1961 was detrimental to British economic policy.

Taken as a whole, the results obtained from 1951 to 1961 by the use of direct and indirect taxation are rather disappointing. The scope of action by the State was limited by administrative and legislative requirements, in particular by the extreme difficulty of using these means outside the annual budget period. Thus the needs of anti-cyclical policy had to be estimated too long in advance, and too exactly, and these estimates were too liable to underrate their impact on the economy. They frequently exceeded calculations of what was required to temper or to stimulate expansion. So that 'the major variations of fiscal policy were in fact not stabilizing, but rather themselves one of the main causes of instability'.[2]

A similar comment could be made on the variations brought about in the total of public expenditure.

(c) Such *expenditure* can be on current account or for investment. The first lends itself little to short-term manipulation, for this expenditure can by its very nature be reduced hardly at all (wages, salaries, expenses in the running of public departments), nor can it be suddenly increased. So it has practically not been used as an economic instrument since the war. The same is true of transfer payments of a social character.

[1] A reduction in rates must be approved by Parliament within twenty-one sitting days, so there is no difficulty if such a decision is taken during the parliamentary vacation. If rates are to be raised, Parliament must approve within twenty-one calendar days.

[2] Dow, J. C. R., *The Management of the British Economy*, 1945–60, Cambridge University Press, 1964, p. 211.

The case is different for investment expenditure which has been used several times for anti-cyclical purposes. For the public sector, in the widest sense, that is, including nationalized industries and local authorities, is responsible for more than 40 per cent of total investment expenditure in the country, so that it provides a powerful lever if the Government decides to use it. But action of this kind during the 1950s came up against certain difficulties.

One of these was due to delays in the carrying out of any decision to alter the level of expenditure. Such delays, arising from Government departmental administration and the devolution of powers to local authorities and nationalized industries, could last a whole year or even more. If delays of this kind cannot be reduced there is a risk that any decisions taken may no longer be appropriate by the time they begin to take effect. In that case, instead of helping to stabilize the economy, they may tend to upset it. Hence the rather disillusioned tone of the White Paper of 1960 on the use of changes in the level of public investment for the purpose of stabilizing demand.[1] According to this document, certain minor modifications can be obtained within a reasonable time, but it is impossible to consider public investment as one of the key instruments of stabilization policy—a conclusion recent events suggest was too timid.

Monetary Policy

This received renewed interest after 1951 as an instrument of anti-cyclical policy, and this was natural enough in a Conservative Government, who preferred it as being more impersonal and more in accord with the idea of a free market, compared with direct controls or even fiscal measures. But the pendulum always tends to swing from one extreme to the other and, for some years, far too much power was attributed to monetary policy, especially as the proponents of its vigorous use were inclined to rely more on intuition than on hard facts or economic reasoning in support of their arguments. Indeed, Sir Robert Hall,[2] former economic adviser to the British Government, remarked that expressions were used more appropriate to magic than to scientific discussion. As a result, there was a certain ambiguity in British economic policy till, in 1959, the report of the Radcliffe Committee put discussions about monetary policy on to a proper footing.

A rise in Bank rate in 1951 marked the beginning of the monetary 'new look'. From 2 per cent, the very low level at which it had remained throughout the post-war period, it rose to $2\frac{1}{2}$ per cent in 1951,

[1] Cf. Public Investment in Great Britain, Cmd. 1203, HMSO, November 1960.

[2] Sir Robert Hall 'Reflections on the practical application of economics', *Economic Journal*, December 1959, p. 648.

then to 4 per cent in 1952, and that was the end of the cheap money policy of the war years. Subsequently the Bank of England made use of variations in Bank rate, and sometimes very large ones, much more frequently than did central banks on the Continent. The rate reached 7 per cent twice, whereas the highest rate introduced on the Continent was 6 per cent in Germany.

For several years, however, the expected results following a rise in Bank rate were never made explicit by the advocates of monetary policy. Although higher interest rates in Britain were likely—other things being equal, and notably confidence in the stability of the exchange rate—to attract imports of short-term capital, their effect on the internal economy was less evident. No doubt a rise in Bank rate indicated that the authorities were making known that, in their view, a certain moderation in demand was needed. But what about the impact of dearer and scarcer credit on decisions to spend and to invest?

The report of the Radcliffe Committee left no doubts that the effects on the actual level of demand in the field either of investment or of consumption of restrictive credit conditions had been oversold. The restriction of bank credit, it noted, falls 'not on projects already in train but on capital projects in their earliest planning stages, implying an effect on spending not immediate but many months later'.[1]

Although it was clearly necessary after the war for the Bank of England to regain control of the banking system whose plethoric liquidity position put it largely beyond the range of action of the Bank, the technical means for manipulating credit conditions, once this initial obstacle had been overcome, proved to be ill adapted to the task, so that considerable changes had to be introduced, after 1960, in the traditional methods of controlling the volume of bank credit.

In 1951 the proportion of liquid assets (essentially Treasury bonds) was very high, nearly 40 per cent of the total. As soon as they came into power, the Conservatives consolidated part of this, bringing down the percentage to its traditional level of 30 per cent. Before 1960 the Bank of England made no attempt to give this Treasury coefficient mandatory force. Nor was there any question of following the American Federal Reserve System or some Continental countries by introducing compulsory variable reserves, although these would, it seems, have allowed quick and flexible action on the total of liquid bank assets, and thereby on the amount of credits the banks could extend to their clients. Instead, the rather roundabout mechanism of

[1] Committee on the Working of the Monetary System. Cmd. 827, HMSO, 1959, paragraph 460.

the discount market was used to influence the lending policy of the commercial banks. The Bank of England also had recourse to the issue of 'requests' to the commercial banks to moderate their lending and to apply priorities, for exporting and productive investment, for example. It hardly seems that the results of these 'requests' were more than marginal.

But in 1960 there were changes in British monetary policy. The Bank of England created the system of 'special deposits' which made the liquidity ratio variable and respect for it more effective. Thanks to these special deposits, which were withdrawn from the clearing banks by the Central Bank, and which were thus excluded from the calculation of the liquidity ratio, thenceforth fixed at 30 per cent of bank assets, a reduction in the banks' liquid assets could be brought about directly.[1] Thus British monetary policy today enjoys a flexibility which it lacked until 1960.

Before that date an instrument of credit control, which was found to be very effective, but which gave rise to mounting criticism, was discovered almost by accident. This was to restrict conditions of hire-purchase so as to control the volume of household expenditure.

The mechanism is simple. Used for the first time in 1952, it consists in changing by regulation either the percentage of the initial deposit at the time of purchase, or the maximum period of repayment, or both together. Such variations will clearly have a marked effect in stimulating or restricting the purchase of those goods most frequently sold with deferred payment, i.e. durable consumer goods. This method of controlling the economy, compared with changes in bank liquidity or budget expenditure and receipts, had the great advantage that it could be used at any moment, by a simple administrative decision, and had a quick effect on spending. That is why it rapidly became a favourite instrument in the armoury of successive Chancellors of the Exchequer.

Between 1952 and 1960 hire-purchase regulations were changed eleven times. Unfortunately, the amount of goods affected was fairly small compared with consumer buying, so that, to have any appreciable effect on the total, the fluctuations in the demand for hire-purchase goods had to be rather large which, in turn, caused frequent serious dislocations in the industries producing durable consumer goods. This is no doubt why the Government made clear in 1960 that they would, in future, try to keep these conditions stable. They were not affected by the austerity programme of July 1961, though, as will be seen, they were modified later on.

[1] In the spring of 1964 the Bank of England authorized the clearing banks to lower the ratio provisionally to 28 per cent. So the principle of a variable ratio is now admitted.

In sum, the years 1951–61 were a difficult period of adjustment to changed conditions for anti-cyclical policy. The experience so painfully gained was not lost, for about 1961 it led to a more exact understanding of the problems to be faced and of the methods capable of solving them. Unfortunately the lessons of this period were rather forgotten after 1962 in the effort to achieve the aims of the two medium-term plans.

3. LESSONS OF THE 1950s

As has been noted by the author of the most thoughtful book on short-economic policy in Britain after the war,[1] 'the major fluctuations in the rate of growth of demand in the years after 1952 were thus chiefly due to Government policy'. The author adds that 'budgetary and monetary policy failed to be stabilizing, and must on the contrary be regarded as having been positively destabilizing'.

This for a number of reasons. First of all, the conditions under which anti-cyclical policy had to operate were markedly different from those of the pre-war period. The acceptance by the authorities, and by public opinion generally, of the prime importance of full employment, and still more the extremely narrow statistical interpretation which came to be given to it, meant that policymakers were faced with an unprecedented task. It called for a degree of precision in forecasting future trends and in dosing appropriately corrective measures that would probably have been too difficult even if an ideal set of demand management instruments had been at hand, which was not in fact the case, as we have just seen. So, in rapid succession, the Government introduced restrictive measures to hold back consumption which showed signs of getting out of hand, but reversed the process and turned to expansion as soon as these measures caused a small increase in unemployment. Hence, anti-cyclical policy found itself operating in a vicious circle of alternate acceleration and braking without ever succeeding in getting the economy squarely into orbit where sustained growth could proceed uninterrupted.

Secondly, the policy was seriously hampered by inflexible handling of the instruments that were available, and by their slowness in coming into effect; a good short-term tool ought to be adaptable to different sets of circumstances and its use should be felt quickly. Clearly the policy measures before 1960 fell far short of these requirements. British fiscal and budgetary policy was often rather crude and it took years even to secure some flexibility in the use of changes in indirect taxation. Attempts to secure reliable quantitative information about the reaction of different sectors of the economy towards

[1] Dow, J. C. R., op. cit., p. 384.

this or that stabilizing measure and about the time interval before it begins to bite are a fairly recent innovation.

A third cause of the disappointing results of British anti-cyclical policy stems from a long-continued misunderstanding about monetary policy. Excessive reliance on this is one reason for slowness in seeking a better use of fiscal measures. Today the reconciliation of outlook between supporters and opponents of monetary measures as a prime instrument of policy has permitted a juster appraisal of the situation. The authors of the Radcliffe Report wrote, 'Monetary measures . . . are not so much a policy in themselves as part of one general economic policy which includes among its instruments fiscal and monetary measures and direct physical controls. There is no prescription which determines the proportion in which at any one period these measures should be combined.'[1]

The severest criticisms of British policy since the war and especially since 1955 have been that it could not fail to cause stagnation, and hamper the growth of investment and productivity, and therefore to block rapid expansion. The echoes of this debate between expansionists and restrictionists have rolled on continually since 1951.

According to Sir Roy Harrod, 'the attempt to bring a halt to cost inflation by demand deflation during the period 1955–62 was a total failure.[2] Professor Phillips has tried to work out the degree of deflation necessary if nominal wages were to remain stable and estimates that an unemployment rate of 5·5 per cent would result.[3] Of course, this author does not suggest that such a figure should be adopted since it would conflict with the promise of both political parties to maintain full employment. But his conclusions about the link between unemployment and pressure on prices join those set forth by Professor Paish, for whom the necessary conditions for long-term price stability would demand the maintenance of a margin of 5 per cent in unemployed productive capacity, of which 2 per cent would be labour.[4] Many authors have drawn attention to the debilitating effects on longer-term growth prospects of 'stop-go'. By depriving businessmen of a reasonably buoyant, and stable, demand prospect, 'stop-go' retarded investment and technological change.[1] In this way, we meet again the search for explanations of slow growth in Britain in the 1950s that was described in Chapter I.[5]

[1] Op. cit., paragraph 980.

[2] Sir Roy Harrod, *The British Economy*, McGraw Hill, 1963, p. 169.

[3] Cf. Phillips, A. W., 'The relation between unemployment and the rate of change of money wage rates in the United Kingdom from 1861 to 1957', *Economica*, November 1958.

[4] Cf. Paish, E. W., *Studies in an Inflationary Economy*, 1961, p. 332.

[5] Cf. for example A. Maddison, *Economic Growth in the West*, Allen and Unwin, 1964, p. 50.

CHAPTER III

THE BALANCE OF PAYMENTS AND ITS PROBLEMS

Post-war British economic policy has been—and continues to be—dominated by questions connected with the balance of payments, and the last chapter showed how often a restriction of internal demand was the result of a worsening of the position relative to external payments.

The problems which arise from the balance of payments in Britain are generally of two kinds: one concerns the state of the current balance which depends essentially on the internal economic situation; the other, not necessarily linked, or at least frequently without any close link with that situation, stems from the part played by sterling as a leading international currency.

The events of the last war and the evolution of the world economy since 1945 have hardly been favourable to the British balance of payments. To the losses of capital invested abroad in financing the war effort must be added the depressing effect on British exports of the centrifugal trading tendencies in the sterling area. The efforts of the British economy to adapt itself to the new conditions were remarkable in the early post-war years, but the difficulties from which the balance of payments still suffers show that readaptation has been incomplete.

This chapter will deal with: the problem of British external payments in the light of long-term development (i.e. since the war), how the short-term fluctuations of the balance of payments have hampered economic expansion, the relationship between the international position of sterling and the difficulty of maintaining a satisfactory balance of payments.

1. EVOLUTION OF THE BALANCE OF PAYMENTS SINCE THE WAR

In the main we shall limit our study to the period between the end of the Korean inflation (1952) and the balance of payments crisis in July 1961. It is, however, necessary to refer back to the years before the Second World War in order to realize the extent of the structural modifications in the balance of payments which became necessary after 1945. A survey of the whole development of the balance in the 1950s will reveal that this readaptation was insufficient.

The Last War and its Consequences

Long before the war the trade balance of the United Kingdom was seriously in deficit, and some writers maintain that this situation goes back to the eighteenth century. But thanks to a very considerable total of invisible receipts (shipping, freight, insurance, banking, financial and commercial transactions in the City of London, interest and dividends on capital invested abroad), the current balance of payments nevertheless showed a surplus which financed further exports of capital.

In 1935, however, this traditional set up had deteriorated and the current balance was slightly in deficit[1] (Table I). The trading deficit that year was more than half the value of exports. Equilibrium of the balance of payments at that time depended therefore on 'invisible' income from abroad. This financed nearly 30 per cent of goods imported.

Now between 1939 and 1945, more than £1,000m. sterling of capital invested abroad was liquidated to pay for indispensable war imports. And in addition our export markets in Latin America and Asia were voluntarily abandoned so that factories which served these markets might be turned over to munitions. During this same period the British merchant marine suffered heavy losses from sinkings. Finally, the Government had to incur heavy debts in North America and in other countries in the sterling area. The weakness of the balance of payments after the war was therefore very marked.

Post-war Recovery and its Shortcomings

In 1945 the British Government put at 50 per cent the increase in exports as compared with 1939 needed to finance a volume of imports no greater than pre-war without upsetting the current balance of payments.

Table I gives the figures for recovery over the subsequent years. In the period 1952–5, though the trading balance still remained in deficit, this deficit was less than 10 per cent of the value of exports. Thanks to the fact that exports increased more rapidly than imports, and also to some rebuilding of 'invisible' receipts, the current balance of payments showed an annual surplus of £140m.[2]

[1] But the economies of the principal Western countries were still feeling the effects of the world depression of the 1930s and international trade was hardly flourishing.

[2] Taking into account a very rough estimate of net current receipts not included into the current balance of payments and included under the head 'errors and omission'.

It might appear from the figures for 1956–9 in Table I that there was further improvement, since the balance of payments surplus more than doubled, with an annual average exceeding £300m., and since the visible trade figures were almost in balance. But it must be remembered that economic expansion was slight during this period so that demand for imports was slacker than it would have been if growth had been more rapid. Moreover, a fall in prices of these imports reduced their cost.

TABLE I

BALANCE OF PAYMENTS IN THE UNITED KINGDOM, 1938 TO 1963
(£ MILLIONS, ANNUAL AVERAGES)

	1938	*1952–5*	*1956–9*	*1960–3*
Exports (f.o.b.)	533	2,828	3,454	3,976
Imports (f.o.b.)	835	3,088	3,460	4,159
Trading balance	−302	−260	−6	−183
Private invisible receipts (net)[a]	+239	+425	+426	+498
Public expenditure abroad (net)	− 7	− 93	−194	−343
Current receipts under 'errors and omissions'[b]	—	+ 70	+ 70	+ 50
Current balance of payments	− 70	+142	+296	+ 22
Long-term capital balance	n.a.	−161	−182[c]	−105
Basic balance	n.a.	− 19	+114	− 83

[a] Including net payment of interest on inter-governmental loans.
[b] Estimated.
[c] Not including £236m. to the International Monetary Fund in 1959.
Source: Balance of Payments White Papers and National Income and Expenditure Blue Book.

The improvement in the current balance thus achieved was clearly precarious. After 1959 the surplus in the current balance was small—too small to finance a 'normal' amount of net capital exports.

In any case, during the last few years capital exports reached somewhat modest proportions, about £100m. a year average, compared with the figure (£185m.) for 1956–9. This can be accounted for by the fact that, to the no doubt temporary fall in British capital exports (especially for direct investments) there must be added an increase in long-term private investments in Britain coming from abroad and chiefly from the USA.[1] These changes

[1] It is possible that the prospect of the United Kingdom's joining the Common Market may have stimulated these investments.

explain why British net long-term capital exports were abnormally small between 1959 and 1963.[1]

The advantage which might have accrued to the steadiness of the balance of payments was much reduced by the very considerable parallel growth in Government expenditure abroad, especially for military requirements. Table I shows that this expenditure increased from under £200m. per annum in 1959–6 to nearly £350m. in 1960–3.

Further examination of the elements not only of the 'basic balance',[2] but also of the total balance, including movements of short-term capital and of reserves (Table II), reveals that, over the whole ten years following 1952, the British balance of payments was nearly steady, and that the net movements of reserves were slight.

TABLE II

ANALYSIS OF BALANCE OF PAYMENTS (£ MILLIONS, ANNUAL AVERAGES)

	1952–5	*1956–9*	*1960–3*
Basic balance[a]	− 19	+114	− 83
Sterling balances[b] held abroad	—	− 17	+ 24
Other short-term capital[c]	+ 38	− 48	+ 71
Sterling balances held by international organizations	− 38	+ 3[d]	− 20
Gold and currency reserves (+=increase)	+ 19	− 53	+ 8

[a] See Table I.

[b] Omitting those held by international organizations (chiefly the International Monetary Fund and, until 1959, by the EPU).

[c] Counting that part of 'errors and omissions' not included in the basic balance.

[d] Including £236m. to IMF in 1959.

Source: United Kingdom Balance of Payments White Papers.

It would, however, be wrong to assume from these figures that the balance of payments was satisfactory. For one thing the exports of capital and aid to developing countries did not reach the level that might have been thought desirable. For another, and this was much more serious for the British economy, the growth of the gross national product was slow, and if it had been faster it is doubtful whether the additional imports needed could have been paid for. The conclusion must therefore be drawn that the fragile state of the balance of payments during the 1950s was a permanent hindrance to British economic policy. It may be added that it was during this very period that Continental countries were able to increase their gold and currency reserves very substantially.

In Britain the total official reserves remained throughout around £1,000m. The smallness of these reserves must be borne in mind

[1] In 1965 the Labour Government introduced two measures which seem likely to reduce permanently the export of capital (see Chapter VI).

[2] i.e. Current balance of payments and long-term movements of capital.

when considering the annual fluctuations in the balance of payments, for it was a source of continual anxiety for demand management policy.

All the same, Britain has to some extent recovered her traditional role of creditor nation. The estimates published in 1964 by the Bank of England[1] show that the net creditor position of the country was £2,000m. sterling at the end of 1962.

TABLE III

STATEMENT OF THE CREDIT POSITION OF THE UNITED KINGDOM TOWARDS FOREIGN COUNTRIES AT THE END OF 1962 (£ MILLION)

Assets		*Liabilities*	
Short-term		*Short-term*	
(a) Public		(a) Public	2·5
Gold and currency reserves	1·0		
(b) Private	2·1	(b) Private	2·7
Long-term		*Long-term*	
(a) Public	1·0	(a) Public	2·6
(b) Private	8·0	(b) Private	2·8
(including direct investments 5·0)		(including direct investments 2·1)	
Situation relative to IMF		*Situation relative to IMF*	
UK payments	0·7	Sterling held by IMF	0·5
Total	12·8	Total	11·1

Source: Bank of England Quarterly Review, March 1964.

But the structure of assets and liabilities *vis-à-vis* other countries (Table III) is not always to the advantage of the United Kingdom. For example, although the private sector remains in general very largely on the credit side especially under the heading of long-term capital, the public sector is heavily in deficit. The long-term indebtedness of the State, £2,600m. at the end of 1962, represents the balance of debts contracted with North America during and immediately after the war.[2]

2. SHORT-TERM FLUCTUATIONS IN THE BALANCE OF PAYMENTS

The state of the balance of payments was the main reason why the British authorities since the war felt themselves obliged to curb

[1] The statistical basis of some of these figures is necessarily rather uncertain.

[2] The service of this debt costs about £70m. every year. By the end of 1966 national indebtedness towards foreign countries had very much increased, as will be seen in Chapter VI.

home demand from time to time. The trouble was mostly due to an excessive pressure of imports in relation to exports.

The graph shows variations from year to year between 1951 and 1961. Being annual variations, their full extent is sometimes obscured by the fact that a change of trend may have fallen in the middle of a year. It is nevertheless clear that after 1954 fluctuations were fairly frequent and that their extent was sometimes considerable. The maximum annual variation in the current balance since 1951 reached £500m., that is, a figure equal to half the total reserves of gold and currency in Britain.

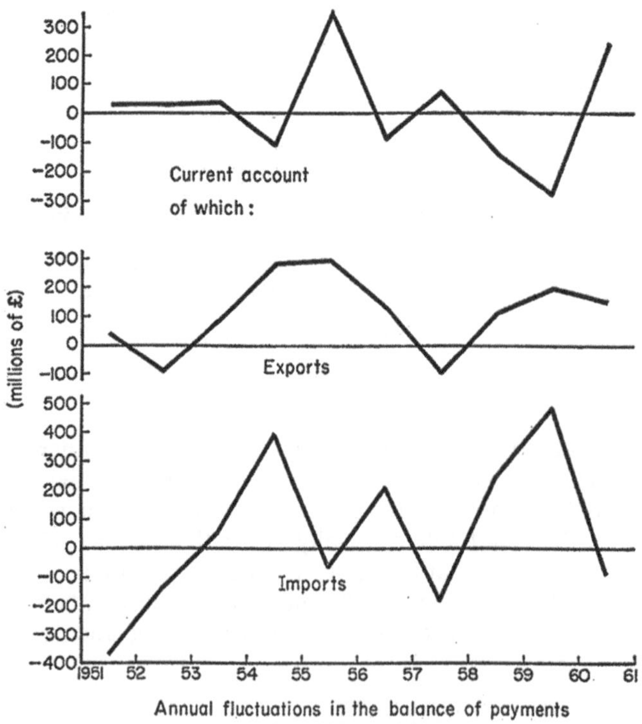

Annual fluctuations in the balance of payments from 1951 to 1961

Source: Economic Trends

In these circumstances it is easy to understand how small was the margin of manoeuvre at the disposal of British economic policy-makers. It is true that Britain could call on the International Monetary Fund to buttress its own slender reserves. But such remedies suggest a crisis situation harmful to confidence in the strength of a key currency like the pound. So, whereas a reduction in the reserves for the purpose of absorbing a temporary deficit in the balance of payments is for most countries a sensible policy which enables them to 'buy time' while taking the necessary measures to restore the equilibrium, Britain had to exercise the greatest care in making use of such a policy. So low were the reserves indeed that even a small deficit in the balance of payments could make serious inroads, with the risk of setting off speculative movements which would only increase the pressure on the reserves. This is one of the reasons why internal restrictions were sometimes both sudden and violent, as was seen in the preceding chapter.[1]

The fluctuations in the commercial balance, that is exports and imports, were the chief factor in the fluctuations of the current balance of payments.

Exports

The expansion of exports, which was very considerable immediately after the war, slowed down later just when imports were showing a marked increase, and this made it difficult to keep the balance of payments level.

The reasons for the low growth of exports fall into three categories: unfavourable structural conditions, a certain falling off in our competitive power, excessive pressure of home demand.

(a) Great Britain had to face somewhat changed conditions in her export markets after the war. Geographically other countries than those of the sterling area were assuming a growing importance in world trade, while various kinds of goods traditionally exported by Britain had fallen out of favour. In 1951, 51 per cent of British exports went to the other countries of the sterling area, 13 per cent to North America and 23 per cent to the continent of Europe. The first two of these markets expanded less rapidly in the 1950s than did the European market. This was a definite handicap for Great Britain, most of whose exports, went in directions where expansion was slowest. During the first half of the 1950s also the other countries of the sterling area were progressively relaxing the restrictions which, before and during the war, had hit goods of origin outside the area, thus reducing the preference previously allowed to British exports.

When exports are examined under their different categories, these also show unfavourable figures, especially for textiles (one-fifth of exports) which were to face intense competition from Asiatic manufacturers.

A big change in the geographical destination of British exports and in their commodity structure has taken place in recent years. Today

[1] This situation is strikingly illustrated by the events of 1964–6 described in Chapter VI.

more than one-third of British exports goes to Western Europe, whereas less than one-third goes to other sterling area countries. This is, of course, one of the reasons which led a section of public opinion to favour joining the Common Market. The analysis of the commodity structure of exports shows that textiles share has fallen to as low as 7 per cent.

There can be no doubt of the part played by these structural factors in the lack of dynamism of British exports, though opinions differ as to its precise details.[1] In any case these questions are no longer so vital now that a reorientation of trade has largely taken place and this is on the whole a good augury for the future.

(b) The importance of structural influences must not make us lose sight of another influence, the loss of competitiveness in British exports, linked with a more rapid rise in prices in England than abroad. After the devaluation of the pound in 1949, which was followed by nearly all the European currencies, British prices did indeed become competitive in relation to the dollar area, but subsequently both British and American prices lost their competitive power in face of exports from the larger European countries, and especially Germany.[2]

It is not easy to reach any firm conclusions, for we possess no valid data for export prices and can make use only of the indices of unit value.[3] These indices, apart from their statistical unreliability, give information only about the movement of prices of goods actually exported, whereas it is of prime importance to know the prices of goods which are not exported precisely because they are not competitive. However that may be, two studies by the International Monetary Fund[4] have noted that during the 1950s the increase in British export prices were, with those of the USA, the greatest among the chief industrial countries—except France. Some improvement in the competitive position of British exports had thus become

[1] Cf. for example the two articles published in the *Economic Review* of the National Institute in London (July 1960 and March 1961), the article which appeared in *The Board of Trade Journal* (March 11, 1960), and Wells, S. J., *British Export Performance*, Cambridge University Press, 1964.

[2] In France, the two devaluations in 1957 and late 1958 helped to correct a situation which, it must be admitted, was much worse than in Britain. In the case of USA the remarkable stability shown by prices for more than six years has now largely made good the loss of competitiveness in the 1950s.

[3] This lack has been filled for USA, cf. Lipsey, R. E., *Price and Quantity Trends in the Foreign Trade of the United States*, National Bureau of Economic Research, 1963.

[4] Cf. Romanis, A., 'Relative growth of Exports of Manufactures of the United States and other Industrial Countries', Staff Papers of the IMF, Vol. III, No. 2, May 1961. Cheng, H. S., 'Relative Movements in the Prices of Exports of Manufactures', ibid., Vol. IX, March 1962.

essential by the beginning of the 1960s if they were to expand. This improvement did not take place.

(c) The pressure of internal demand has something to do, too, with the limited expansion of exports, for it diverts a certain proportion of exportable goods away from foreign markets. This fact was brought out in the discussion of anti-cyclical policy,[1] and is fairly convincing. For example, in 1958 and 1960, at the time of the 'buying spree' in durable consumer goods, the British home market had priority over exports. But if prices are not sufficiently competitive in the export field, there is a great temptation for the manufacturer to concentrate on selling his products in the home market. It is for this reason that some observers have challenged the thesis that intense home demand has damaged exports. These observers could not fail to note that the years of slack home demand (between 1955 and 1958) corresponded with a reduction of exports (as can be seen also in the graph), while exports rose again in 1958–9 at the same time as the renewal of internal activity.

It seems certain that a very strong home demand may take up an excessive share of national production, but it does not by any means follow that a lessening of demand will encourage manufacturers to export. Some pronouncements on this question make too little distinction between the results to be expected during the time when the pressure of demand is slackening, and the quite different results when demand has settled down at a lower level. It is only while demand is decreasing that exports may reap some benefit, but nothing can guarantee the permanence of this result if prices and other selling conditions are not favourable. It remains true, however, that the influence of home demand on the current balance of payments shows itself more through imports than through exports.

Imports

The graph shows the extent to which changes in the level of imports of goods have influenced the fluctuations in the current balance of payments since the war. Essentially the variations in imports have been accounted for by the nature of commercial policy, by the influence of home demand, and by the inventory policy of manufacturers. In relation to these various explanations several remedies have been suggested.

(a) *The Explanations.* In the first post-war years, the United Kingdom, like the other European countries, kept strict control of imports, either by the imposition of quotas or by exchange control, or both together. But during the 1950s, trade within Europe shook off these hindrances within the framework of the European Payments

[1] Cf. Professor Paish, *Studies in an Inflationary Economy*, op. cit.

Union, and by the end of 1954 it had been 80 per cent liberalized, so far as Britain was concerned. At the same period imports from North America had been liberalized only to the extent of 50 per cent. But during the following years there was a marked speeding up in the liberalization of imports from the American continent in the United Kingdom; by 1959 three-quarters of them were exempt and the part that remained subject to quotas was quickly reduced. It must be admitted that, in 1959, there was little criticism of this bold policy of liberalizing imports at a time when the stability of the balance of payments was by no means assured. There were, on the contrary, some rather complacent attempts to minimize the effects of this policy on the grounds that many American prices were not really competitive.[1] Next year, however, in face of an increased deficit in the trade balance, the policy of removing restraints from international trade began to be challenged, especially in the light of British foreign trade statistics which showed that imports from USA had increased rapidly since the early years of the decade of the 1950s. For Sir Roy Harrod, for example,[2] there could be no doubt that this increase resulted from the policy of liberalizing trade, while other economists, like W. Reddaway[3] and the authors of an article published by the National Institute of London,[4] gave less importance to this policy.

In the atmosphere surrounding the balance of payments crisis in 1960 and 1961, too much weight was probably given to commercial policy. The deterioration in the balance was due also, and perhaps mainly, to other causes of a more general nature, and in particular to anti-cyclical policy and to the state of home demand. It must be remembered how vigorously, after three long years of slack industrial production, the authorities boosted demand at the end of 1958 and in 1959—the classic example of the 'go' policy. Now the passing of time has shown that the very suddenness of the expansion forced up the resulting imports more than ever. Faced with a rapid increase in demand, British industry took a little while to catch up.[5] Bottlenecks formed in key industries like steel. Hence imports became necessary to meet home demand.

The stockpiling policy of firms also had an effect upon imports. On the average, stocks represent 45 per cent of the gross national product and consist of 50 per cent imports. There are therefore close links between variations in stock levels and imports. At the beginning

[1] Cf. the article in the *Financial Times*, November 5, 1959.

[2] Cf. his book *The British Economy* already quoted and an article in the *Financial Times*, June 22, 1960.

[3] Letter to the *Financial Times*, March 20, 1961.

[4] *Economic Review*, May 1961.

[5] None the less, industrial production rose by 10 per cent between early 1959 and early 1960.

of a period of expansion, stocks tend to fall in order to satisfy the increased demand, while the gross national product grows. Thereafter, however, in order to restore the relationship to which they are accustomed between the level of production and of stocks, industrialists place abnormally high orders in order to stock up, and the level of imports rises rapidly.

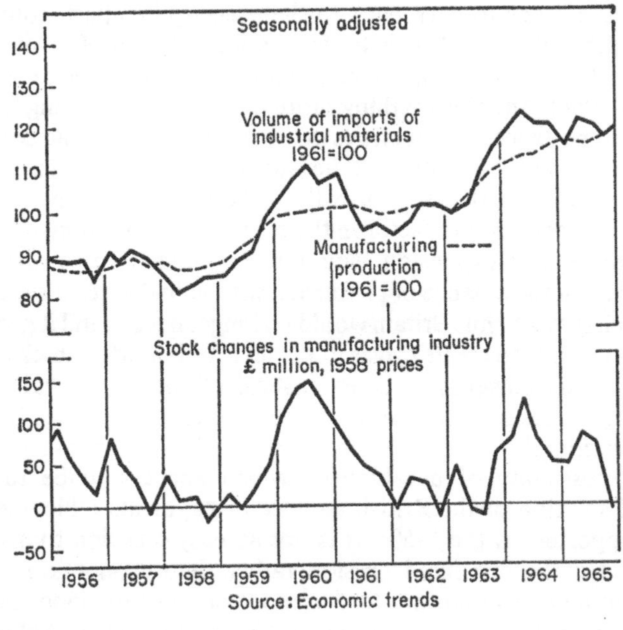

The graph shows this influence on imports. Of course, in a complete cycle the total cost of imports destined for stockpiling is the same as if the demand had increased in the ordinary way. But the consequences for the balance of payments are different. During a normal period of expansion, imports due to regular re-stocking are added smoothly to those which represent growth. 'Stop-go' encourages manufacturers to reduce imports for stockpiling during the phase of restriction of home demand—hence a noticeable but purely temporary improvement in the trade balance. This saving has to be paid for during the phase of expansion which follows, at the very moment, when in any case the commercial balance is subject to pressures tending towards unbalance.

(b) *The Remedies*. Not all those for whom the rapid rise in British imports was the result of a rash commercial policy wanted to withdraw some of the liberalizing measures of the 1950s. Nevertheless such a policy found an obstinate defender in Sir Roy Harrod[1] who asserted that, if the figures over a number of years showed that we had been more liberal in our imports policy than our resources permitted, we should reverse that policy and reintroduce certain restrictions. Chapter VI will show that such a policy was followed by the British authorities in 1964 when they applied a special tariff to imports of manufactured goods. Others believe that it would be of doubtful efficacy to hark back to the past—quite apart from consequent difficulties in British trade relations. C. McMahon[2] has remarked that only if import restrictions became more or less permanent would they be anything more than a way of playing for time.

It is to be expected that critics of 'stop-go' policy should seek additional ammunition in a study of the balance of payments. It is generally agreed today that the jerky growth of the British economy since the war was a contributory factor in the over-rapid expansion of imports. A more regular expansion would have avoided these alternating pressures on the balance of payments, with valuable results especially for stock levels.[3] Thus Britain would no longer have found it necessary, as again today, to create cycles in the level of imported stocks to save the gold and currency reserves, instead of the traditional practice of using the reserves to cushion import fluctuations caused by cycles of stockpiling.[4]

The possibility of devaluation, which appears to be the most radical solution of the British balance of payments difficulties, also had supporters in the 1950s. It is not an easy question to discuss in public. On the one hand passion rather than economic reasoning seems more often than not to determine support or opposition. On the other, in the case of a currency like sterling which holds a key position in international trade relations, speculative rumours about ultimate devaluation, which had serious consequences in the past, might prove still more serious in the future.

Statistical studies have, it is true, revealed a high degree of elasticity in the British demand for imports in relation to prices, a factor favourable to devaluation.[5] But this is not the only consideration which must be taken into account. A devaluation can stabilize the commercial balance only if a further rise in prices, which would cancel out the advantages of the operation, can be avoided. The

[1] Cf. *Financial Times*, June 22, 1960. See also his book *The British Economy*, op. cit., p. 147.

[2] *Sterling in the Sixties*, Chatham House Essays, 1964, p. 30.

[3] The analysis by Brechling and Wolfe in *Lloyds Bank Review*, January 1965, seems conclusive in this respect.

[4] Cf. McMahon, C., op. cit., p. 26.

[5] Cf. for example Scott, M. F. G., *A Study of United Kingdom Imports*, Cambridge University Press, 1963.

righting of the commercial balance following a devaluation thus needs internal deflation (this is shown by the example of France in 1959).

The National Institute for Economic and Social Research in London has rather consistently supported the view that British export prices are not conducive to a sustained growth of exports. In a study published under the auspices of the Institute in 1965 the idea was put forward strongly that 'there appears to be no substitute for rapidly rising exports as a means of ensuring confidence in longer-run demand prospects'.[1] The logical conclusion of this reasoning would appear to be the need for more competitive British prices for exports either through effective control of price level—waiting for inflation abroad to 'float-off' British exports—or through an exchange rate adjustment.

Such seem to have been the main ideas current in the 1950s about the right policy to strengthen the balance of payments.

3. THE POUND STERLING

The pound sterling is not only the currency of the United Kingdom it is also a key currency in international use. Changes that have come about since the war, both in the international payments field and in the structure of the British balance of payments, have led to a difficult period of readjustment for the pound sterling which made it even more arduous to keep the balance of payments on an even keel.

An examination of the consequences for the pound of being a key currency will help us to focus the problems raised by this fact in the 1950s.

The Pound, a Key Currency

During the last decades of the nineteenth century, the pound sterling assumed a dominant position in international monetary and financial relations. At that time the greatest number of international banking and financial houses were concentrated in the City of London. These firms provided credit facilities for more than half international trade, not only between British and foreign traders but also for third parties. The London basic products market fixed world prices. The *entrepôt* business attracted to London in this way was helped by a banking system peculiarly experienced in the financing of foreign trade, and by all the advantages afforded by the British merchant shipping and marine insurance companies like Lloyds.

As regards long-term capital loans, national States, local authorities and private firms, both in countries that were later to form the sterling area, and on the American continent and elsewhere, turned

[1] W. Beckerman, op. cit. Chapter II.

to London as a market specializing in the issue of foreign loans. This specialization reached such a pitch that, after the Second World War, according to a committee appointed to inquire into the monetary and financial machinery of the United Kingdom (the Macmillan Committee), it was easier for a foreigner to obtain money in London than for a British manufacturer to do so. In addition to all this, the possession of an immense Empire scattered over the globe gave Great Britain first place in commercial and financial transactions in her Overseas Territories.

This situation changed between the two world wars, not only because of the increased strength of the American economy, especially New York, in its capacity as a powerful international financial and monetary centre, but also because of the crisis of the 1930s which reduced the economic strength of London, and of the centrifugal tendencies growing within the Empire. It was after the 1931 crisis that an attempt was first made, in the documents dealing with the newly instituted exchange control, to define the countries belonging to what has since been called the sterling area, so as to keep a certain margin of freedom in trade and payments between London and the Empire.[1]

After the second war there were still more difficult problems of adjustment to be faced, owing to the deterioration in Britain's balance of payments and the changes which took place in world economic power relationships. But financial quarters in the City clung to the hope of a happier future when London would regain her erstwhile importance. This hope was given practical expression during the 1950s in the policy of a fully convertible pound sterling in which the Bank of England vigorously encouraged the Government. Before going over the various stages through which this policy developed, in rather different circumstances than had been anticipated after the war, we will consider one special aspect of the international position of sterling, linked with its function as a reserve currency.

In the nineteenth century the international currency reserves were in essence the creation of private banks, and the importance of the pound was partly due to the existence of sterling credits in London. After 1931 the sterling area functioned by having the area's reserves concentrated in London in the form of Government deposits. Since gold no longer passed between individuals, these reserves were composed of, on the one hand, various kinds of assets expressed in sterling—the sterling balances—belonging to countries of the sterling area outside Britain (assets which, of course, represented commitments for Britain) and on the other hand the British Government's

[1] Cf. Hackett, J., 'L'évolution des places de New York et de Londres depuis la guerre', *Economie Appliquée*, January–June 1956.

official gold reserves which were consequently available to the whole sterling area. To settle their trading account for Britain—and their trade preponderantly with this country at the time—the countries of the area needed only pounds, that is to say, their sterling balances held in London. If in their trade with other countries the members of the sterling area earned foreign currency or gold, they paid it into London in exchange for fresh sterling credits; if not, they bought the necessary foreign exchange or gold with their sterling balances in London. (It should be remembered that, as a rule, the sterling area countries except Britain ran sterling surpluses with the outside world.) The relationship between the gold held by the Government in London and the total of sterling balances was generally about equal between the wars. After 1945 it was near 1:4, as a result of debts incurred during the war by the United Kingdom to certain members of the sterling area, especially India and Egypt, to pay for military operations on the soil of these countries.

The burden of this debt was considerable, both because of the interest to be paid, and because of the ever-present possibility that repayment might be demanded and might easily over-tax Britain's resources. However, during the 1950s, it always proved possible to avoid over-hasty withdrawals.

During the same decade certain countries, such as India and Egypt—the latter having meanwhile left the sterling area—ran their sterling balances down almost to nothing in order to finance their own development. Others, often colonies not yet independent, increased theirs. As a result, the sum total of sterling balances remained more or less steady. At the end of 1961 sterling balances totalled about £4,000m., or much the same as ten years earlier.

TABLE IV

WORLD OFFICIAL GROSS RESERVES OF GOLD AND CURRENCY[1]
(USA $1,000 MILLION)

	1950	%	*1961*	%
Gold	33·8	71	41·2	67
USA Dollars	3·6	7	11·1	18
Pounds Sterling	9·8	21	7·8	13
Various	0·5	1	1·3	2
Total	47·7	100	61·2	100

[1] Excluding Eastern countries.
Source: International Monetary Fund.

After the war, as a result, sterling made little contribution to the growth of international liquid assets. This growth took place in the form of new gold and dollar balances, of which the latter represented

18 per cent of total world liquid assets in 1961 against 13 per cent for sterling balances, whereas in 1951 the figures were, respectively, 7 per cent and 21 per cent (see Table IV). London was not in a position to permit its sterling balances, i.e. its external debts, to increase at the same rate as those of the USA. The ratio of 1:4 between London's gold reserves and convertible currency on the one hand, and the short-term foreign liabilities on the other, was already too weak and the stability of the British balance of payments too uncertain. Moreover, after the war a number of countries in the sterling area began to build up their own gold reserves, thus immobilizing funds which would otherwise have been deposited in London. The private balances, representing more than one-fifth of the total (see Table V), have since 1945 suffered several times from speculative movements arising from fear of the pound being devalued.

TABLE V

STERLING BALANCES BY CATEGORIES OF HOLDERS (£ MILLIONS)

	1951 *(end of year)*	%	*1961* *(end of year)*	%
Total	4,143	100	4,513	100
of which:				
Official bodies in sterling area	2,252	54	2,097	46
Private holdings from within sterling area	333	8	534	12
Official bodies outside sterling area	659	16	440	10
Private holdings from outside sterling area	333	8	484	11
International bodies (chiefly IMF)	566	14	958	21

Source: Bank of England.

The Issue of the 1950*s*: *Convertibility*

The discussions in the 1950s about the future of the pound sterling took place with the prospect of an early return to full convertibility. It is now clear that the protagonists of this return had badly underestimated the difficulties. Furthermore, once the principle of a return to convertibility had been accepted, in 1952, by a Commonwealth conference, the methods of bringing it about led to confusion and misunderstanding, both in Britain and abroad. The resultant doubts about the real intentions of the authorities undermined the stability of the pound.

(a) *What form of convertibility should be adopted?* There are two kinds which do not necessarily coincide.

According to the Bretton Woods agreements in 1944, from which sprang the International Monetary Fund, those countries who were members of the Fund were to work towards restoring the convertibility of their currencies in their current dealings with other countries. Movements of capital could remain subject to exchange control.

The chief European currencies—apart from the Swiss franc which, like the United States and Canadian dollars, were convertible already in 1945—became in fact convertible only in 1958 (except the United Kingdom which, as will be seen, introduced *de facto* convertibility of sterling for non-residents in February 1955), and legally so in 1961. Meanwhile, all the European governments continued to operate exchange control, more or less rigorously, both over current and capital transactions. The pound was prepared for a return to monetary convertibility in the IMF sense during the 1950s by a progressive liberalization of trade in goods and services, at first between the countries of Europe and later with the dollar area. Without these liberalizing measures, tantamount to 'commercial convertibility', the monetary convertibility intended by the IMF would have remained a dead letter; it would have been useless for an importer to obtain an allocation of currency if he were at the same time refused an import licence.

In the United Kingdom, as compared with other European countries, the question whether monetary convertibility should accompany or precede commercial convertibility arose immediately in 1945. A decision had to be taken, not only as to when and how fully British residents should enjoy the fruits of convertibility, but also as to what rules should be applied to foreign holders of sterling balances. Were they, or were they not, to be allowed to convert their holdings into other currencies? In other words—and this is the point—could they convert them into dollars, in view of the world shortage of dollars after the war? If so, how would it be possible to prevent a massive conversion of sterling balances into dollars by the purchasers of goods from the dollar area? If not, how could one stop holders of sterling from selling it cheaply on the unofficial markets and thus undermining the official exchange rate of the pound? It is evident that the international monetary problems which the British authorities found themselves up against in 1945 were very knotty ones, and in no way comparable with those which beset Continental countries.

(b) *The stages of convertibility.* According to the conditions of the American loan to Britain in 1946, monetary convertibility, applying to sterling balances only, was to be brought in by July 15, 1947, at the latest. It was, in fact, adopted a little earlier. The result was not surprising. In spite of the Government's efforts to negotiate agreements with the principal holders of sterling balances to limit conversion into dollars, the losses of gold and currency reserves were enormous. As the crisis grew worse the experiment in convertibility was brought to an end on August 20, 1947, but not before \$3,600m. out of the \$5,000m. dollar loan advanced to the United Kingdom by USA and Canada the year before had melted away like snow. This experience left a deep mark on people's minds in Britain, but for all that it did not stop the question of a return to convertibility being raised again after 1952. In that year convertibility was included as one of the aims in the communiqué issued at the end of the Commonwealth Conference in London. Thenceforth there was tremendous activity in Government circles between those who, strongly supported by the Bank of England, stood for the rapid adoption of convertibility, and those who called for prudence, with the mishap of 1947 still in their minds.

This is not the place to go over all the details of the discussion. No irrevocable step was taken until, in 1955, the Bank of England was authorized to intervene in the money markets of Zürich and New York in support of 'transferable' sterling. This was the name given to pounds bought and sold by people not resident in the United Kingdom (such dealings being forbidden in London). The market was supported by holders of pounds, not resident in the sterling area, who wanted to exchange them for other currencies and especially dollars, despite the *de jure* inconvertibility of sterling. The buyers were people not resident in the area who needed to settle business transactions with the area and sought a cheap way of doing so. There was naturally a discount on transferable sterling in relation to the official exchange rate of the pound. The volume of this business grew greater and greater, drawing off a ever-increasing share of the normal receipts of the sterling area. It was to stop this drain that the Bank of England intervened in 1955. But although the discount rapidly dropped to about 1 per cent, the net profit for the gold and currency reserves was reduced by the cost in foreign currency of the Bank's intervention in Zürich and New York. All the same, a decisive step had been taken towards convertibility and, 'monetary' convertibility for people not resident in the sterling area was now an accomplished fact.

Animated discussions arose on the subject. For some, 'our liberty of choice as a sovereign nation in the field of social and economic policy is constricted by the views of a marginal holder of sterling in Zürich or some other foreign capital'.[1] For others, however, the bold action by the Bank of England intervened, perhaps in the nick of time, to preserve the integrity of the sterling area.[2]

Once this decision was taken, it seemed probable that it would be followed up by the much more importent step of declaring the pound legally convertible, as from a given date, accompanied perhaps by a variable exchange rate. Foreign opinion was already prepared for such action, for it was no secret that the British autho-

[1] Schonfield, A., *British Economic Policy since the War*, p. 269.
[2] Cf. Roy Harrod, *The British Economy*, op. cit., p. 137.

rities had been working on plans of this kind since 1952. But in 1955 serious difficulties, due to excessive home demand, upset the balance of payments. Coupled with rumours about convertibility, these difficulties caused a wave of speculation against the pound and the withdrawal of considerable sums from London. To dam the flow, the Chancellor of the Exchequer was obliged to make three statements to the effect that the British Government had no immediate plans for convertibility, nor for any modification of the policy of a fixed exchange rate. Again, in 1957, which saw the *de facto* devaluation of the French franc, together with anxiety in Europe about the regular very large surpluses in the German balance of payments, the air was full of new rumours, by no means unfounded, about the imminent adoption of a variable exchange rate for the pound. These set off a fresh and far-reaching crisis of confidence, in spite of the then satisfactory state of the British balance of payments. Faced by the rapid drain on the reserves of gold and convertible currency, the authorities decided to have recourse to the International Monetary Fund and postponed until 1958 the expansionist programme intended to revive the country's economy.

This was the last time there was any toying with the idea of a variable exchange rate. Thenceforth opinion, reflected in the report of the Radcliffe Committee, agreed in being 'strongly in favour of a fixed parity for sterling rather than a system of fluctuating rates'.[1]

The question of a return to convertibility of the pound was finally settled, in respect of 'commercial' convertibility, by a progressive liberalization of trade during the 1950s, only a very small proportion of trade in manufactures and 'invisible' transactions being still subject to restrictions. 'Monetary' convertibility was introduced *de jure* by Britain for UK residents at the end of 1958, at the same time as by the other chief European countries—and in February 1961, the countries of Europe adopted convertibility in accordance with Article 8 of the statutes of the International Monetary Fund.

So ends a chapter in the history of Britain's economic policy as regards the balance of payments. What have been the results? There was no precipitate or unilateral return to convertibility of the pound and attempts to achieve this proved costly. The discussions about convertibility took place in an atmosphere, abroad, of doubtful confidence in the pound, and at home, of regrets for past glories. All this did not help the working out of a balance of payments policy carefully thought out in all its aspects, especially in its relation to the growth of the economy and to the reserves and sterling balances.

[1] Cf., op. cit., paragraph 722.

CHAPTER IV

REGIONAL IMBALANCE

Uneven development as between different parts of the country is a characteristic that is not reserved to Great Britain. But Britain seems to have been among the first of European countries to take action, for the trouble was diagnosed as long ago as the 1930s when some attempts were made to find a remedy.

It is not surprising that England suffered in this way very early for the country was the first to feel the effects of the Industrial Revolution in the eighteenth century. The geographical unevenness of economic growth must be seen as a consequence of this revolution. In retrospect, until quite recently, the steps taken to correct this have been rather piecemeal and results have been incomplete and even disappointing. But regional development is one among the many problems to which fresh thought has been given in recent years. As a result there have been great changes in the whole conception and in methods of attacking the problem. We shall discuss the extent of these changes in Part II. But first, in the present chapter, we must study the facts of uneven regional development and the policy followed until quite recently (the Act of 1960, which will be examined later, marks the end of a period), and see how matters then stood.

1. THE FACTS

The basic facts are historical. In fairly recent times they have become both more marked and more set, thus giving rise to the twin phenomena of highly prosperous regions alongside depressed ones and of urban congestion.

The Legacy of History

It is no paradox to say that Britain is paying the price of having been the pioneer of industrial development. This development was based upon a source of energy, coal, and certain key industries, textiles and shipbuilding, which were highly concentrated in well-defined areas—the North-west for textiles, the North-east and South Wales for mining, Scotland and Northern Ireland for shipbuilding.

Since 1914 coal has had to face ever-increasing competition from other forms of energy, electricity and oil—and indeed nowadays atomic energy too—which are much less concentrated geographically because they can be easily transported over long distances.

The old-established industries began fairly early to show signs of latent stagnation which was accentuated by the economic crisis in 1930 and, after the Second World War, by the appearance of new techniques, especially those of artificial textiles. Employment in these industries grew therefore at a slower pace than in the newer industries and even fell (Table I). The table also shows that employment in agriculture, a major activity in Scotland and Northern Ireland—two problem areas—has also fallen considerably.

TABLE I

PERCENTAGE RISE OR FALL IN TOTAL NUMBERS EMPLOYED IN THE PRINCIPAL GROUPS OF INDUSTRIES 1952–62

Professional and scientific services	+ 43
Distributive trades	+ 34
Insurance, banking and finance	+ 32
Mechanical and electrical industries	+ 24
Paper, printing	+ 20
Building trades	+ 19
Various services	+ 8
Motor manufacture	+ 8
Metal industries	+ 7
Chemical industry	+ 6
Gas, electricity, water	+ 4
Bricks, pottery, glass, cement	+ 3
Food, drink, tobacco	—
Woodwork, furniture	− 2
Public administration	− 3
Transport and communication	− 4
Clothing and footwear	− 7
Leather and skins	− 10
Textiles	− 14
Shipbuilding	− 15
Mines and quarries	− 18
Agriculture, forestry, fisheries	− 25
Total	+110

Source: Ministry of Labour Gazette.

Predominantly agricultural areas and those depending on the older industries have thus suffered from persistent unemployment at a figure well above that for the country as a whole. At times of economic crisis, and especially round 1930, this tendency became particularly strong, and although it was less noticeable during the second war, it emerged again with the end of hostilities.

Since 1950, for example, unemployment in Northern Ireland has been three times the national average; in Scotland it has been 70 per cent above the average, in Wales 65 per cent and in Northern England 45 per cent.

Table II shows unemployment figures in the depressed areas from 1950 to 1961 compared with those for the whole country.

TABLE II

UNEMPLOYMENT RATES (MONTHLY AVERAGES)

Year	*Northern Ireland*	*Scotland*	*Wales*	*Northern England*	*United Kingdom*
1950	5·8	3·0	3·5	2·8	1·6
1951	6·2	2·5	2·6	2·2	1·3
1952	10·3	3·3	2·9	2·6	2·1
1953	8·2	3·0	3·0	2·4	1·8
1954	7·0	2·8	2·5	2·2	1·5
1955	6·8	2·4	1·8	1·8	1·2
1956	6·4	2·4	2·0	1·5	1·3
1957	7·3	2·6	2·6	1·7	1·6
1958	9·1	3·7	3·8	2·4	2·2
1959	8·8	4·5	3·8	3·4	2·3
1960	6·8	3·6	2·7	2·8	1·7
1961	7·5	3·1	2·6	2·4	1·6

Source: Ministry of Labour Gazette.

Moreover, personal incomes have always been lower in areas of high unemployment than in the rest of the country. Thus in Northern Ireland the average personal income in 1959–60 was £200 lower each year than in the London area.

If areas which depend largely upon old-established industries show up badly in relation to the national average, both for unemployment and for income, the reverse is true of those areas where new industries have grown up together with a greatly expanded service sector generally—insurance, banks, trade, etc. In contrast to the older areas, these are activities for which it is no longer essential to be near sources of power and mineral deposits and where the important considerations are, for example, being within reach of a large domestic market, good communications, easy contact with the ports. The areas which are more prosperous than the average are the Midlands and the South generally, but especially the South-east with its great conurbation of London.

Differences in the industrial structure of various areas do not fully explain why employment has grown more quickly in some than in others. According to a study made by the National Institute of Economic and Social Research,[1] to which we shall frequently have

[1] Hemming, M. F. W., 'The Regional Problem', *National Institute Economic Review*, No. 25, August 1963.

occasion to refer, the fact that employment in the same industry has grown more, or has decreased less, in some areas than in others must also be taken into account.

Consequences

There has sprung from all these factors a two-fold imbalance of which the closely interwoven parts are noted separately here only for convenience of study.

Internal Migration from 1951–61

(a) *Drift to the South.* The coexistence in a country of 'two nations',[1] one in this case being the depressed areas with a considerable labour

[1] The term has been frequently used in the Press; it was coined by Disraeli who used it as the title of a book on the social problems in England in the nineteenth century.

force unemployed and with low incomes, and the other the areas of intense economic development holding out great opportunities for new jobs, has given rise to internal migration, what is known as the 'drift' from the North to the South, as shown in the map (p. 79).

Already well under way before the war, the tendency has continued since. Between 1951 and 1961 there were the following changes in area population due to migration (Table III). Between these same dates the number of jobs in the North fell by 260,000 and rose in the South East by 400,000.

TABLE III

CHANGES IN POPULATION DUE TO MIGRATION, 1951 TO 1961

Regions	*Numerical variations*
East	+455,000
South	+237,000
South West	+ 78,000
Midlands	+126,000
Wales	− 49,000
North	− 86,000
Yorkshire, East and West Ridings	− 98,000
North West	−124,000
London	−183,000[a]

[a] The fall in population in London is explained by migration to towns in the Home Counties.

Source: The Times, November 14, 1963.

These migrations, though brought about mainly by uneven economic development, are also due in part to the attraction of great urban centres like London or Birmingham. Nor must one neglect more general factors, not necessarily economic but sometimes climatic or aesthetic. For example, it is warmer in the South than in the North, the urban setting is often pleasanter and life easier. If one used, says Alan Day, 'an index including temperature, sunshine, absence of rain, and absence of strong wind, I have no doubt that the South would show up extremely favourably . . . In our somewhat sybaritic age . . . in so far as the drift occurs because many people find the South inherently a more attractive place in which to live—and can choose to do so in an age of greater geographical, social and educational mobility—it would be short-sighted for any to try to fight the trend.'[1]

(b) *Urban Concentration.* One of the chief characteristics of the spread of population in Britain is the concentration of people in towns. Two-fifths of the total population live in seven urban agglo-

[1] Day, A., 'Planning the Face of Britain', *The Political Quarterly*, April–June 1964, p. 163.

merations (known as 'conurbations'): Clydeside, Tyneside, West Yorkshire, South East Lancashire and Merseyside with Manchester and Liverpool, the West Midlands with the metropolis of Birmingham, the London area.

This urban concentration goes back, like other area peculiarities, to the beginning of the industrial revolution—see Table IV, which shows changes in population (as percentages of the total) between 1801 and 1931.

TABLE IV

CONCENTRATION OF POPULATION IN GREAT BRITAIN 1801–1931

	Population per cent of total		*Area per cent of total*
	1801	*1931*	
London and Home Counties	18·0	28·4	6·8
Lancashire	6·4	11·2	2·1
West Riding, Notts, Derbyshire	8·5	11·0	5·3
Staffs, Warwickshire, Worcs, Leics, Northants	8·1	9·6	5·2
Northumberland and Durham	3·0	5·0	3·4
Central Scotland	3·7	5·9	2·1
Glamorgan and Monmouthshire	1·1	3·7	1·5
Total	48·8	71·2	26·4

Source: Barlow Commission Report, Table I, p. 22 (more about the Report below), reprinted by the *National Institute Economic Review*, August 1963, p. 44.

There are three newer aspects of this long-standing phenomenon of concentration.

One is the general decrepitude of the urban equipment in the depressed areas. Based on coalmining, these areas in the nineteenth century witnessed the growth of the 'black towns', where could be found the horrifying industrial conditions described by many writers at that time and where many slum dwellings were little more than hovels. This past history is one of the handicaps to development today. Existing building is so old that reconstruction would usually mean starting again from the beginning.

Another aspect is the increasing tendency to urban concentration in the economically highly developed areas, i.e. the Midlands, London and the Home Counties.[1] If the figures in the table above had been worked out up to 1961, they would show that the population has continued to grow both in London and the Home Counties

[1] Bedfordshire, Buckinghamshire, Essex, Hertfordshire, Kent, Middlesex, Surrey.

(25·1 per cent of the total in 1961), and in the Midlands (10·5 per cent in 1961). There is nothing surprising in this, in view of the attractions offered by these agglomerations in geographical situation, communications and commercial outlets. But this state of affairs, though by no means recent (in the sixteen years ended in 1937 the London area was swollen by half a million people and now has more than 8 million inhabitants), is a cause of grave concern for the future. In the light of the foreseeable growth of the population in Britain over the next forty years (reckoned at 19 million), and taking account of the increasing marriage and birth rates, the two areas—the Midlands and London—which cover only one-eighth of the country will have to absorb 10½ million new inhabitants.

TABLE V

EXODUS FROM MAJOR CITIES, 1851–1961

	Increase/Decrease	
	Numbers	*Per cent of population*
LANCASHIRE		
Manchester	− 42,041	− 6·0
Liverpool	− 43,348	− 5·5
Other county boroughs	− 63,758	− 4·0
Remainder	+162,940	+ 8·0
WARWICKSHIRE		
Birmingham	− 7,034	− 0·6
Remainder	+168,653	+22·5
LONDON AND SOUTH EASTERN REGION		
Greater London conurbation	−176,121	− 2·1
Remainder	+363,064	+14·2

Source: Preliminary Report of the 1961 Census of Population, reprinted in the *National Institute Economic Review*, August 1963, p. 45.

Present-day urban concentration shows another characteristic, the growing tendency for people to live at some distance from their work. This habit was already noticeable at the beginning of the century. In 1921 about a quarter of the 2 million people working in the County of London—many in central London, the City and Westminster—lived in the neighbouring counties. The tendency has become more and more marked. On the one hand town centres have been increasingly forsaken as places to live in in favour of the outer suburbs, as Table V shows. On the other hand the number of jobs in the centre of large towns has gone on growing, especially in London, where 15,000 new office posts are created each year. As a result there are serious 'commuter' problems between home and work, such as the organization of rush-hour transport, to say nothing of the time and energy lost in travel.

Such are briefly the essential facts which must be taken into account in any policy of regional development.

2. THE CHOSEN POLICIES

Before the Second World War the problem of the depressed areas had already received public attention, and the economic crisis of 1929–30 which made unemployment in Britain so much worse marked a turning point. In 1934 an Act of Parliament officially recognized the existence of Special Areas, particularly hard hit by unemployment, where economic development must therefore be encouraged. These areas were four in number: North East Coast,[1] West Cumberland, Central Scotland, South Wales and Monmouthshire. Northern Ireland with its heavy unemployment was not included in the special areas but had regulations of its own.

The Act of 1934 provided for the nomination of two Commissioners whose main task in the special areas was to attract light industry from the Midlands and the South.

With this in view they encouraged the setting up of non-profit-making bodies to purchase land and build factories which would be offered on attractive leases to industry (the trading estates). An Association for the reconstruction of the special areas was created with power to give grants guaranteed by the Treasury. In 1937 the Treasury itself was authorized to make loans and grants.

By 1938 much had been achieved. £21m. had been spent or promised and ten trading estates had been started, giving employment to 12,000 people. Nevertheless, unemployment persisted in the special areas (about 300,000 workless).

In contrast, and again before the Second World War, the over-population of certain areas, in particular London, had also given rise to thought and study, and in July 1937 the Government decided to charge a Royal Commission, under the chairmanship of Sir Montague Barlow, with the task of examining the main aspects of the problem. The Report,[2] published in 1940, recommended the setting up of a National Industrial Board to organize the dispersal of industry from over-developed areas, and to supervise urban development, decentralization and the balance of industry. The Board was to have regional offices and its approval would be required for the construction or extension of all industrial buildings. A minority report wished to replace these proposals by much more far-reaching measures: the setting up of a new Ministry to control the location

[1] i.e. Tyneside, Haltwhistle and most of County Durham.

[2] Report of the Royal Commission on the Distribution of the Industrial Population, Cmd. 6153, 1940.

of industry throughout Britain, and to undertake national planning having regard to the needs of industry, agriculture, housing and leisure occupations. The war put an end to the proposals, both of the majority and of the minority of the Barlow Commission, but the proposals were novel at the time and it is interesting to remember them because a number of them have been revived today (see Chapter VIII).

Up to a point the Second World War, with all its economic consequences, was for a time to reduce the seriousness of the double problem of regional development and industrial decentralization, mainly owing to the opening of munitions factories in the special areas and to the dispersal of many others, to avoid the risk of total destruction of over-concentrated industrial centres. The same practice was employed in other countries, especially France, Germany and the Soviet Union. The result in the old depressed areas in England was a reduction of unemployment from 18 per cent in 1937 to $1\frac{1}{2}$ per cent in 1945 (compared with the national figures of 10 per cent and 1 per cent respectively).

But this method of fighting unemployment was obviously only a temporary expedient and once the war was over it became necessary to work out a new policy for dealing with uneven regional development, an evil the causes of which, as we have seen, are structural.

It is this policy which must now be examined in its application to two chief sectors, the towns and, more generally, regional development as a whole.

The Towns

We have chosen rather arbitrarily to treat the urban problem separately because of the very characteristic forms taken, after the Second World War, by the policy underlying the 'New Towns'. The New Towns Act of 1946 has given Great Britain twenty-one new towns either completed or under construction. The intentions which inspired the Act and the whole idea of these new towns deserve examination.

(a) *The Intention.* The idea of providing for urban expansion by means of completely new towns was one of the measures intended to combat the double scourge of population growth in urban agglomerations and the insufficient development of certain areas owing, among other causes, to the run-down nature of their urban environment. It is, then, the two schemes of decentralization and development which are, once again, linked in the New Towns Act.

It is therefore convenient to distinguish new towns built to absorb an excess of urban population—such as, in England, the eight destined to receive the 'overspill' of population from Greater London, Basildon and Harlow in Essex, Hemel Hempstead, Stevenage,[1] Hatfield and Welwyn in Hertfordshire, Crawley in Sussex, Bracknell in Berkshire, and the three new towns in Scotland performing the same function for Glasgow (East Kilbride in Lanarkshire, Glenrothes in Fife, Cumbernauld in Dunbartonshire)—from towns built to serve as centres of attraction and growth in predetermined areas, such as Corby in Northamptonshire, Aycliffe and Peterlee in Co. Durham, Cwmbran in Monmouthshire, Skelmersdale in Lancashire, Livingstone in West Lothian.[2]

(b) *The Conception.* The Committee set up under the chairmanship of Lord Reid in October, 1945, set its sights high, describing the plan as an essay in civilization, an opportunity to work out and put into practice the means of securing a happy and full life for the benefit of future generations.

The new town is conceived as a group of residential communities each of 3,000 to 10,000 inhabitants. Each community is relatively self-contained, having its own shops, schools and churches, its cafés and sports grounds. The largest residential areas have also a community centre and a public library. The new town consists of three or four communities of this type, and so the average size will be around 20,000 inhabitants. Its core consists of a commercial and cultural centre with a number of secondary schools and technical colleges: on the outskirts stretches an industrial belt of varying size and sometimes a second linked to it. There is thus no real separation between where people live and where they work, as is so often the case in the old-style big industrial towns.

The location of new towns is decided in principle by the Ministry of Housing and Local Government. The building is under the supervision of a Development Corporation with power to acquire sites by negotiation or by compulsory purchase. The capital outlay is covered by a loan from public funds, and when building is completed the corporation is wound up and its assets and liabilities transferred to a central agency created in 1961. The new town now passes under the control of a local authority in the normal way.

The practical working of the new towns policy is thus coloured by the existence of a special legal status and by the part played by local authorities. These two questions will appear again when we examine the steps taken by the authorities between 1945 and 1960 to encourage regional development as a whole.

[1] The first of the new towns, built in 1946. However, before the war, two garden cities had been built, Letchworth in 1903 and Welwyn Garden City in 1930.

[2] Another recently completed is Dawley in Shropshire.

Steps taken towards regional development

The policy followed between 1945 and 1960 falls into three stages, each marked by an Act of Parliament (1945, 1947 and 1960). The first two were introduced by the Labour Party, the third by a Conservative Government.

(a) *The Distribution of Industry Act of 1945* continued that of 1934. The idea of backward areas was kept, though the name was changed to 'development areas'.[1] Several more areas were added to the four pre-war ones, Wrexham and South Lancashire in 1946, Merseyside and the Scottish Highlands in 1949, North-East Lancashire in 1953. The commissioners of the 1934 Act were replaced by a directorate for the location of industry under the Board of Trade, and it was the directorate which acquired sites and built factories to lease to industry in the development areas. The method of aid originally introduced in the 1934 Act was thus continued.

Financial aid in the form of grants and loans still came from the Treasury, and was even extended by the 1958 Act to include non-industrial activities and areas of high employment other than the development areas.

(b) *The Town and Country Planning Act of 1947*, the first of a series of Acts, did not replace the 1945 Act but covered a number of new regulations in quite distinct fields. The regulations were of two main types: planning powers conferred on local authorities, and the right to scrutinize the location of industry given to the Board of Trade.

The 1947 Act obliges local authorities to draw up development plans and to co-ordinate proposals from unofficial bodies and private persons in the light of regional development as a whole. If local authorities possess land they may change the use of it, but with certain exceptions may not build factories or office blocks. In principle, development plans must be harmonized by the Ministry of Housing and Local Government.

Besides giving local authorities planning powers as regards regional development, the 1947 Act gave the Ministry a powerful arm to oppose the concentration of industry in certain areas to the detriment of others, the Industrial Development Certificate. According to the Act, one of these certificates must be obtained before any construction or extension of industrial buildings with an area of 5,000 square feet or over may be carried out. The certificate is issued by the Board of Trade. Only industrial buildings are concerned; the Act does not apply to commercial buildings. Despite this limitation

[1] The changed terminology was the indication of the intention to implement a much more active policy than pre-war.

the powers at the disposal of the Board of Trade are very considerable.

(c) *The Local Employment Act of 1960* superseded the 1945 Act except for those of its regulations which were incorporated in the Town and Country Planning Acts of 1947 and subsequent years, and was a new and important step forward in regional development policy. It introduced a fundamental reform in the conception of assistance towards development by replacing development areas, relatively few in number but large in size, by development districts in far larger numbers (165 at the beginning) but of limited size. The Act did not apply to Northern Ireland which has its own series of Industries Development Acts approved by the Northern Ireland Parliament to give more generous treatment, on the whole, than does the British legislation.

The Act laid down what is to be understood by a development district and the methods by which assistance shall be given.

The development district is defined as an area which Board of Trade returns show to have a persistently high rate of unemployment. The whole idea of the district is thus closely linked with unemployment. The average unemployment rate in the United Kingdom in March 1960 being 2 per cent, the Board of Trade decided that a 'high' rate should be taken as 4·5 per cent or over. There was nothing rigid about this figure, for the Board of Trade, in agreement with the Ministries of Labour and Transport, has excluded certain places with an unemployment rate above 4·5 per cent while including others with a lower rate. Nor was there anything final about the list of development districts. It was changed by the Board of Trade two or three times a year in the light of current employment figures. Table VI shows the average unemployment rates in development districts for the months of April and December during 1960–2, together with the highest and lowest rates in industrial districts.

A number of development districts were within the former development areas, but some did not appear previously, for example, in the South-West.

The methods of assistance are not very different from those introduced by the Acts of 1934 and 1945—building of factories that are then leased (generally for 21 years) at favourable rents or sold on deferred terms, capital grants made directly to the industrialist building a factory in a development district, loans for acquiring working capital or equipment. The Government departments can also assist local authorities financially when derelict sites are cleared or basic services improved.

The industrial estate companies, controlled by the Government and which had been set up under the Distribution of Industry Acts, were

TABLE VI

WHOLLY UNEMPLOYED IN THE DEVELOPMENT DISTRICTS
(PERCENTAGES)

	1960		1961		1962	
	April	*December*	*April*	*December*	*April*	*December*
ALL DISTRICTS						
High	9·4	11·5	8·7	10·5	13·6	16·9
Low	1·7	2·5	2·2	2·3	1·8	2·3
Average	4·4	4	3·8	4	4·4	5·7
Great Britain	1·7	1·1	1·4	1·6	1·8	2·3

Source: Ministry of Labour Gazette (Table reprinted by the *National Institute Economic Review*, August 1963, p. 47).

replaced under the 1960 Act by three Industrial Estate Management Corporations (one each for England, Wales and Scotland) financed by, and under the control of, the Board of Trade whose role in the administration of regional development policy was thus increased.[1]

3. THE BALANCE SHEET

The balance sheet of the policies which have been tried, in spite of the by no means negligible results on the credit side brought out by statistics, reveals a certain number of shortcomings, not to say gaps, which tend to throw doubt on the whole philosophy of the system.

The Achievement

This may be considered under the two main heads of the exercise, urbanism and regional development.

As regards the building of new towns, £310m. of public funds were advanced to the Corporations between 1946 and 1963 and 18 towns were built, housing more than 500,000 people. In addition, under the Town Development Act of 1952, 29 'expanded towns' were created, each with 5,000 inhabitants or more. But the problem of urban congestion has not really been solved, since most of the new or expanded towns are in highly developed areas, like the periphery of Greater London, so that they do nothing to lessen the problems of the less-favoured areas in the north of the country.

Following the Acts of 1945 and 1960, the Treasury disbursed £12m. in loans and grants over 15 years from 1945, and the capital outlay of the Board of Trade for the purchase of sites, building of factories, etc., came to £78m. By the end of March 1960, 45·6 million square feet of factory space had been leased to 1,095 manufacturers employing 20,000 people, 2·8 million square feet had been sold and 2·2 million square feet were being brought into use.

[1] This change had already been foreshadowed in the Distribution of Industry (Industrial Finance) Act of 1958.

The assistance envisaged by the 1960 Act has remained on the whole limited, in spite of some spectacular successes like the steel rolling mills opened in South Wales and Scotland, and the new motor factories in the same areas and on Merseyside.[1] In the first three years after the Act came into force the Board of Trade spent about £81m. (£29m. on the building of factories and £52m. on direct financial aid), and this help brought about the creation of 90,000 new jobs. The building of factories is an important part of the assistance. Between April 1960 and the end of December 1962, twelve were built for sale bringing in £17m. In 1962 two building programmes of what were called 'advance factories' (i.e. factories of which the tenants are not known in advance) were adopted for the erection of ten factories in areas affected by the closing down of pits, and nine others destined to be the core of new development in areas suffering from unemployment, such as Sunderland, the Hartlepools and Dumbarton. By the beginning of 1964, six new factories had been completed in the north

TABLE VII

REGIONAL DISTRIBUTION OF NEW JOBS FROM INDUSTRIAL DEVELOPMENT CERTIFICATES (COMPARED WITH POPULATION AND UNEMPLOYMENT)

Regions	*Population 1961*	*Unemployment March 1962*		*Extra jobs attributable to IDC 1/4/60–31/3/62*	
	%	*('000)*	*% of GB*	*('000)*	%
Northern	6·3	34·9	9·9	20·7	9·6
East and West Ridings	8·1	20·4	5·8	10·7	4·9
North Midland	7·1	16·0	4·5	15·6	7·2
Eastern	7·3	15·2	4·3	26·4	12·1
London and South-Eastern	21·6	54·2	15·4	25·6	11·8
Southern	5·5	13·3	3·8	16·7	7·7
South-Western	6·6	18·9	5·4	17·2	7·9
Midland	9·3	28·4	8·1	13·0	6·0
North-Western	12·8	53·4	15·2	27·1	12·5
England	84·7	254·7	72·4	173·0	79·7
Wales	5·2	25·4	7·2	18·3	8·4
Scotland	10·1	71·8	20·4	25·7	11·9
Great Britain	100·0	351·9	100·0	217·0	100·0

Source: Ministry of Labour Gazette, Board of Trade Journal and Seventh Report of Estimates Committee, session 1962–3, reprinted by the *National Institute Economic Review*, August 1963, p. 49.

[1] Nevertheless, the geographical location of two rolling mills in Wales and Scotland met with some criticism.

of England, and fourteen more were under construction, one in Wales, nine in Scotland and four in England.

The outcome of the policy of industrial development certificates introduced by the 1947 Act and continued in the 1960 Act is also only partly satisfactory. Although between 1945 and 1947 the strict control of the location of industry through building permits resulted in 50 per cent of new buildings being in development areas, the proportion fell to one-sixth after 1947. Moreover, even when development certificates succeeded in attracting industries to backward areas, they could not always even out the disparities in unemployment between these areas and the development areas. For example, if development certificates gave Scotland, between April 1960 and March 1962, the same number of new jobs as London and South-Eastern England on a population of half the size,[1] the number of unemployed still remained higher. In most of the other areas the number of new jobs corresponded roughly with the number of unemployed, except in the East and the South where the creation of new jobs was much larger. Table VII shows these facts.

TABLE VIII

EXPENDITURE UNDER THE LOCAL EMPLOYMENT ACT (£ MILLIONS)

	1961–2	*1962–3*
Provision of land and buildings	11·0	7·0
Loans to undertakings	20·1	12·6
Grants	1·7	4·3
Total	32·8	23·9

Source: Seventh Report of Estimates Committee, Sessions 1962–3, reprinted by the *National Institute Economic Review*, August 1963, p. 49.

The combined effect of the various measures taken did not really reduce unemployment, which, although slight in Britain as a whole, remained high in the development districts and had even a tendency to rise. But, paradoxically enough, expenditure under the Act went down between 1961–2 and 1962–3. This is one of the questionable aspects of the 1960 Act which leads to the result that the total of request for assistance sent to the central Government varies inversely with the employment situation. The Board of Trade has itself con-

[1] A special inducement was given to the motor industry to encourage it to settle in Scotland (thus the Rootes Group at Linwood) which was the chief beneficiary of the 1960 Act during the first two years of working, when it received 60 per cent of the total of aid.

demned this arrangement. 'We spend most when the country is prosperous and least when it is depressed.'[1]

From some date, therefore, which is difficult to determine exactly, but which falls about 1961–2, the policy began gradually to be challenged.

The outcome of this reconsideration was not the immediate working out of a genuinely new doctrine (the distinction between the two parts of this work will lead us to examine this doctrine in the second part). It gave rise rather to a mass of criticism from many different quarters which will now be considered.

The Criticisms

They stem mainly from regional organizations, trade unions and research centres.

During the 1950s, certain private organizations found themselves more and more actively preoccupied with problems of regional development, and were thus led to study the short-comings of existing regulations and work out proposals for improvement. One of the most dynamic of these is undoubtedly the North-East Development Council, under the chairmanship of the former MP George Chetwynd, which published two important reports between 1961 and 1963.[2] In the same way in Scotland and Scottish Council (development and industry) was formed, one of whose most notable achievements was the setting up of a committee of inquiry to study problems of regional development in Scotland and suggest reforms. The report[3] of this committee, under J. N. Toothill, deserves special attention as it is the basis of present policy in that region.

Regional problems in Northern Ireland were also the subject of special study in 1961, a study which in this case took on virtually an official character since the working party responsible were all civil servants. This is perhaps why the recommendations of the report,[4] which was published in October 1962, were moderate and contained few innovations.

As the problems of regional development began to be more and more discussed in the Press and in reports, and public opinion was stirred, it was to be expected that employers' organizations and trade

[1] Seventh Report of the Estimates Committee, op. cit., p. 82.

[2] North-East Development Council First Annual Report, 1961–2. North-East Development Council Second Annual Report, 1962–3.

[3] Inquiry into the Scottish Economy, 1960–1 (Toothill Report).

[4] Report of the Joint Working Party on the Economy of Northern Ireland (Hall Report, from the name of the Chairman, Sir Robert Hall), Cmd. 446. HMSO, October 1962. Note that regional development in Northern Ireland is covered by special legislation, the Capital Grants Acts, the Industries Development Acts.

unions would come to be involved. On the employers' side the Federation of British Industries took up the study and published its conclusions in May 1963, under the title 'The Regional Problem'.[1] Similarly, various articles written from the trade union, or more often the Labour Party point of view, were devoted to regional development.[2] In the early 1960s a number of research organizations began critical studies of Government policy, of which we shall note particularly the one published by Political and Economic Planning (PEP) under the title 'The Location of Industry'.[3]

These various studies build up into a body of criticism of, on the one hand, the Local Employment Act of 1960—and these are the greater number—and, on the other, of various points dealing with individual aspects of regional development and industrial decentralization.

(a) *Criticisms of the 1960 Act.* They are directed against the geographical units laid down by the Act, the criteria according to which assistance is given, and the method and nature of such assistance.

There have been very many reservations about the definition of development districts under the 1960 Act. These, it will be recalled, were to be of limited area, and it thus became possible to designate for assistance localities which were unsuitable to manufacturers because of their very smallness and sometimes also because of their isolated situation. Examples can be quoted both in the South-West and in Scotland. Further consequences follow. To the extent that the Act achieves its object, it tends to 'freeze' the location of industry and of work in a way that is sometimes unsatisfactory. It is thus possible for industries to be led to establish themselves on inadequate sites when an entirely new situation would have been much more suitable. In the motor industry, the British Motor Corporation (BMC) was in this way, under moral suasion from the Government and tempted by large grants, sent to Bathgate in Scotland, a district where surplus labour appeared to be available and where unemployment was high. But many of the local unemployed proved to be unsuitable for motor car production and the company had to recruit labour over a wide surrounding area. They were also obliged to bring their materials from 500 miles away in the South, because the Scottish factories around Bathgate turned down BMC's request to make this material. In contrast, another plan also affecting the motor industry

[1] A Study of the Areas of High Unemployment.

[2] See the Fabian Society pamphlet, 'More Power to the Regions', D. Steele, March 1964; Peter Hall's article 'Regional and Urban Planning' in *Labour's New Frontiers*, 1964; and the Labour Party programme, *Signposts for the Sixties*, October 1961.

[3] PEP, *Location of Industry*, October 29, 1962.

and intended to regroup various motor concerns on Merseyside turned out to be much more viable because the transfer of industry was more extensive and the selected area much larger and less isolated. The 'compulsory' location of industries thus presents problems of profitable returns and running costs.

On the other hand, when an industry is established in a locality of limited area, the industrial development so artificially expanded runs the risk of complete collapse if the industry in question quickly becomes exhausted or if the firm changes its development plan and decides to close down. This is not just a hypothetical case, but one which may frequently be met with in modern conditions where abrupt changes in technique or in the economy may come about. In the PEP study, for example, the decision by Imperial Chemical Industries (ICI) in June 1962 to concentrate geographically their production of ammonia is examined. As a result, two factories were closed. One, at Dowlais, in a remote Welsh valley, employed 500 workpeople for whom the disappearance of their jobs had serious consequences. The other, at Prudhoe, was near the great conurbation of Newcastle which could luckily offer the 400 factory hands the possibility of alternative employment. PEP therefore draws the conclusion that 'the attempt to bring employment to all the remoter and smaller centres will create communities which survive only at the mercy of circumstances.'[1]

There was not the same objection to the older scheme for much larger development areas. For this reason, the North-East Development Council preferred a single area to cover the whole region to the designation of a number of development districts.

The criterion governing the allocation of assistance to the districts, under the 1960 Act, is the degree of unemployment. Many people have challenged this *a priori* negative attitude, for it does indeed seem strange to have to wait until unemployment has grown before the threatened locality or area can benefit from regional development assistance. Here is what E. G. W. Allen, director of the industrial development association for Lancashire and Merseyside has to say on the subject. 'Unemployment, on its own, should never be the only factor to be taken into account, for it is the product, not the cause, of situations such as now exist in many parts of the North. Post-war distribution of industry policy, particularly the Local Employment Act, 1960, has touched only the fringe of the problem.'[2]

These criticisms led to the suggestion that the choice of development areas should be based, not on unemployment, as for the districts, but on the possibilities of future expansion in an area,

[1] PEP, op. cit., p. 347.
[2] Quoted in *The Times*, November 14, 1963.

having regard to such resources as available sites, communications and labour. Moreover, the relevant factors must not only be economic, for one of the grievances against the 1960 Act is that it takes no account of social necessities which are highly relevant in the setting up of new industries. The employers, through the FBI, have been among those who have drawn attention to such questions. 'We believe that the improvement of road, rail, air communications and dock facilities is vital to the attraction of new enterprises to areas of high unemployment. Of equal importance is the need to encourage the building of comfortable hotels and social amenities which are now taken for granted in more favoured districts. . . . There is evidence that the dreary and bleak appearance of some urban areas, and the absence of attractive modern housing suitable for senior executive and administrative personnel, constitute a forceful discouragement to firms which would otherwise be disposed to move into industrial districts such as the North-east Coast.'[1]

These arguments led to the idea of action of greater scope than what the Board of Trade can do by itself, to the conception of regional growth points round which a certain number of firms would settle. Thus the FBI 'strongly supports the views on Growth Areas contained in the NEDC report and urges that the aim should be to offer a wide choice of location to the investor so as to build up industrial complexes where firms dependent upon each other's products or services can develop and expand'.[2]

The method of assistance equally did not escape critical examination, and was often accused of being too restricted. It depended of course in the first place on the number of requests which industrialists present to the Board of Trade, but it was also affected by conditions laid down by the Government. One of these is the rule that an industrial development is considered 'reasonable' (i.e. suitable for assistance) if the expenditure on labour is not in excess of £1,500 per head. The validity of this figure has been challenged because it takes no account of economies which would result from the creation of new jobs, such as reductions in grants in aid and in unemployment. Another condition is that proposals must be approved by the Board of Trade Advisory Committee, which tends to take more account of the financial status and economic soundness of the proposer, and of the commercial possibilities of the proposal, than of its value in the interests of regional development. As a result the Committee's attitude is said to be unduly rigid; thus between

[1] FBI, op. cit., p. 5.

[2] FBI, op. cit., p. 4. The reference to the NEDC is to the report *Conditions Favourable to Faster Growth*, HMSO, April 1963, that is discussed in Part Two of this book.

April 1960 and the end of January 1963, 603 out of 649 proposals were turned down.

The uncertainty inherent in the assistance offered to manufacturers under the Act has also been deplored, since development districts have not been fixed once and for all but may at any time be added to or cancelled. In addition, the amount and the conditions of loans for the lease of sites and buildings are not laid down definitely, and the delay (sometimes as much as two years) between receipt of the original proposal from the manufacturer and final approval by the Board of Trade makes industrialists hesitate about taking long-term decisions.

Finally, there has been criticism of the scope of assistance as being both too narrow and too wide—too narrow in that it does not cover commercial firms (the Toothill report took this line)—too wide in that assistance has sometimes been granted to firms which cannot claim to be increasing employment nor to be seeking a new site.

(b) *Other Criticisms.* Apart from the numerous writings called forth by the 1960 Act, the attention of reformers turned towards other aspects of regional development.

One such is the Industrial Development Certificates, which have been criticized for excluding commerce. The comment has also been made that the officials of the Board of Trade are often insufficiently briefed to do justice to a request for a certificate. It is not difficult for a businessman to prove to them that he can expand his industry efficiently in the place which he has chosen himself, and that any other solution would reduce the profitability of the undertaking. He may even threaten that, if he is not given permission to expand where he wants to, he will not expand at all. In practice, therefore, decisions taken with regard to Industrial Development Certificates are governed by factors which have nothing to do with the needs of regional development, such as the size of the industry in question, the persuasive powers of industrialists, the stubbornness of Board of Trade officials. For this reason some people—for example, the FBI which suffers particularly from the constraints of the certificates—have gone so far as to suggest the abandonment, at any rate in part, of the procedure introduced by the 1947 Act.

There have been reservations, too, about other aspects of the Act which deal with the part played by local authorities in regional development. The study conducted by PEP shows that local authorities have little active power since they are not allowed to build. They can only purchase sites, which is an expensive procedure and therefore little used (PEP quotes the case of the City of Birmingham which, up to July 1959, had bought only fourteen industrial sites).

So gradually there came into being the idea of reconstituting the powers of local authorities and of increasing their size, especially in urban areas. The Labour Party has shown itself in favour of the suggestion and indeed ready to go much further than the relatively modest reforms proposed by the Local Government Commissions set up by the Government in 1958–9. 'The real urban unit of Britain in the 1960s and still more of Britain in the 1980s', in the words of the Labour writer Peter Hall, 'is a much wider urban region, of which the conurbation will form only the core.'[1]

The case of London and its administration is only one special aspect of the whole question of local government. We shall be returning to this.

The new towns, also, have in practice not escaped some criticism, especially their somewhat artificial character. There is too great a concentration of the younger age groups with a lack of older people; there have been difficulties in the social integration of young married households: and many people have commented on the teen-age problem. A new sickness has been invented called the New Towns Blues. In spite of criticisms it is a matter for regret that more of these new towns have not been built. The Labour Party attacked the Conservatives for this, and, according to Peter Hall,[2] one of the first measures taken by a Labour Government would be to 'announce an extended new-towns programme'. We shall return to this point later.

As regards the 'philosophy' of regional development there are several rival lines of thought. Is it, or is it not, right to create employment where workpeople are available or it is better to promote the mobility of labour and the migration of workers from depressed areas to more prosperous ones? All post-war legislation has tended towards the former solution which incidentally enjoys the support of the employers.[3] Others, mainly from the Labour Party, have wanted the economic attractiveness of the South to be recognized and this natural tendency to be encouraged. 'What we are witnessing today is the developing of new areas, and to interfere basically with this would certainly have adverse repercussions through the whole economy,' writes G. Parker. 'It is therefore in the general interest—as opposed to regional interests—that industries should in principle be located in the most favoured areas at any given time, and not be forced to locate themselves elsewhere.'[4]

[1] Hall, P., 'Regional and Urban Planning', *Labour's New Frontiers*, p. 106.

[2] Op. cit., p. 108.

[3] 'While mobility of labour between different firms, skills and even industries is a desirable objective of economic policy, we do not consider that large scale movements of population from the depressed areas to the congested Midlands and South-East should be encouraged.' Cf. FBI, op. cit., p. 2.

[4] Parker, G., in *Socialist Commentary*, June 1963, p. 16.

These arguments could be studied indefinitely, but their chief interest is that they are evidence that, by the early 1960s, England was thinking seriously about the regional problem. Up to then the approach to the problem in England had been piecemeal, but progressively the whole question has been rethought and the idea of 'development' discussed in this chapter has given place to the much wider one of regional re-structuring which will be examined in the second part of this book.

For the time being let us be content with a provisional conclusion which looks forward to the future: 'Perhaps the most important need of all is that we must, all of us, re-examine many of our basic attitudes and be willing to accept and work with, not against, much more rapid changes in economic and social matters than have been experienced for many decades.'[1] This judgment was formulated mainly with the problems of the less developed areas of the United Kingdom in view. But it will serve as an epitome on the economic history of the decade of the 1950s and as a conclusion to Part One of this book.

[1] PEP, op. cit., p. 360.

PART TWO

NEW TRENDS

INTRODUCTION

After 1961 the student of the British economy cannot fail to note a change of atmosphere. It is not always easy to say precisely what the change is, but its existence cannot be denied. We have come to the end of a period of which the achievement, while far from wholly negative, has nevertheless the major defect of offering too little scope for future development. So the need for far-reaching changes is now generally admitted, especially in industry, but also among some officials and labour leaders. The most tangible sign of the new climate of opinion is to be found in a proposal by the Conservative Government, put forward at the height of the balance of payments crisis in July 1961, to institute a medium-term system of economic planning. Such a proposal at that time meant a marked shift in the Party's traditional position and cut right across the economic policy of the last ten years. As far as practical results went, this attempt by the Conservatives to quicken the expansion of the home market was wrecked once again on the external payments position. But if the record of the years 1961–4 show the weight of this failure on the liabilities side, we must not overlook the importance of the changes in the approach to, and in the method of handling, economic policy issues that occurred during that period. It seems therefore appropriate to devote the first chapter of the second part of this work to the experiment in planning by the Conservative Government between 1961 and 1964 (Chapter V).

It is natural enough that the Labour Opposition should have ideas about planning different from those of the Conservatives, if only because, traditionally and on principle, this Left-wing party is inclined to favour a more deliberate orientation of the economy through greater State control. In the event, however, Labour do not seem to have worked out any very definite doctrine before 1961, at the time when their political opponents put forward the idea of a development plan. The system of controls which they used between 1945 and 1950 bore little relationship to the economic problems of the 1960s, both as regards the use of a wide range of direct controls and the nationalization of the basic industries. The ideas of the Labour Party on the planning of a modern, developed economy for the most part gradually took shape as the experiment carried out by the Conservatives after 1961 worked itself out. This perhaps explains why, when Labour returned to power in 1964, the changes brought about by the new Government in the system of planning, though considerable, hardly touched basic principles. This Labour experiment since 1964 will be dealt with in Chapter VI.

In the list of obstacles to a rapid and at the same time well-balanced growth of the British economy, it was clear, in 1961, that prices were among the most fundamental. Indeed without prices sufficiently stable to keep exports competitive, it was useless to work out ambitious schemes for the expansion of home demand. We have already noted in Chapter II ('stop-go' policy) how ineffective the traditional weapons of anti-cyclical policy proved in dealing with this problem in the 1950s. The ground was therefore prepared for the idea that it must be approached from a new direction, that of a prices and incomes policy. If it is still too soon to pass judgment on the results of this new policy, some knowledge of events in this field since 1961 is certainly essential for an understanding of the prospects of the British economy. This subject will therefore be studied in Chapter VII.

It was inevitable that, once national planning came into being, the piecemeal efforts, studied in the first part of the book, in Chapter IV, to deal with uneven development in the regions should be viewed in the light of the development of the economy as a whole. The launching of the national plans was just what was needed to breathe new life into the policy of regional development which, as we have seen, was judged to be increasingly unsatisfactory. This new approach is sufficiently different from the earlier one for the change to be characterized by a new name, 'territorial re-structuring', a name which covers more numerous and more varied elements than 'regional development' (Chapter VIII).

As we have said elsewhere about planning experiments in Western market economies: 'The Plan is a way of providing permanent arrangements for a collective and systematic reflection on the problems and prospects of the economy with a view to action'.[1] What we meant by this, among other things, was that planning must be much more than a collection of techniques to produce a quantitative picture of the future evolution of the economy as a whole. It must also consider by what means the objectives set may be attained. In this connection, the partial failure of the attempt begun in 1961 to secure a faster and more sustained expansion of the British economy may

[1] Hackett, J., and A.-M., *Economic Planning in France*, Allen and Unwin, 1963, p. 363.

perhaps be attributed to insufficient weight having been given to certain basic obstacles linked with the very structure of the economy. The structural weaknesses have been discussed in the first part of this book. Chapter IX, on the other hand, will attempt to make clear the new thinking in recent years.

CHAPTER V

THE FIRST PLANNING EXPERIMENT: THE CONSERVATIVES AND THE NATIONAL ECONOMIC DEVELOPMENT COUNCIL

Economic planning as practised by some of the advanced countries of the West is a complex phenomenon that is not easy to reduce to a few clear-cut principles. That this should be so is not surprising. The details of this type of planning were worked out with a view to meeting urgent problems of economic policy, and Western planning still bears the mark of the consequent empiricism. In Britain, for example, the decision taken in July 1961 by the Chancellor of the Exchequer to invite representatives of the employers and the unions to discuss with him the setting-up of a planning mechanism arose essentially from a general and growing dissatisfaction, especially among industrialists, with a situation which the traditional instruments of economic policy had shown themselves incapable of controlling. For this reason the plan was which proposed was flexible and based upon no preconceived ideas.

Nevertheless, after the Chancellor's statement, certain questions of principle about the form of the plan became the subject of a continuing debate that is indeed still going on.

The chapters in the second part of this book will seek to show how deep and far-reaching are the repercussions brought about by planning in the most varied aspects of social and economic life. In the present chapter the British plan will be analysed under three heads: 1, preliminary questions; 2, the solution adopted in 1961; 3, its partial failure.

1. PRELIMINARY QUESTIONS

In the choice of what form of planning should be adopted the Government had first to consider a number of questions grouped under what, following French terminology, can best be called a 'concerted' economy.[1] Or, in other words, what would be the role of

[1] Cf. Fr. Bloch-Lainé: *A la recherche d'une économie concertée*, Editions de l'Epargne, 1959.

the representatives of the private sector? Once it had been decided that representatives of the private sector and of the trade unions should take part, these had to make up their minds about their attitude to the experiment and how far they would be prepared to go to achieve the aims which would be decided on. There were also various problems to be solved about the internal organization of the plan. We shall consider these themes under the headings of the Government's proposal and the reactions of employers and unions.

The Government Proposal

This contained no surprises, for it had been possible to foresee it from the Government's attitude for several months. No doubt, however, the balance of payments crisis in July 1961 hastened a decision.

Among the urgent steps taken to ward off the crisis an allusion by the Chancellor of the Exchequer, Mr Selwyn Lloyd, to longer-term measures of the nature of a plan passed almost unnoticed.[1] Yet twice in January 1961 the Chancellor had described planning as a 'not unattractive idea'.[2] In April of the same year an important conference in London, under the aegis of the National Institute for Economic and Social Research, had brought together M. Pierre Massé, head of the French plan, several of his colleagues, British businessmen and economists, and representatives of the Treasury[3]—the latter already well primed with documents about a medium-term plan for Britain.

Realizing that his proposal had to some extent been overshadowed by the announcement of urgent short-term measures, the Chancellor returned to it more explicitly the following day in the House of Commons. With regard to existing means of consultation with the private sector he declared, 'I say frankly that I want something more purposeful than that. I envisage a joint examination of the economic prospects of the country stretching five or more years into the future. It would cover the growth of national production and distribution of our resources between the main uses. Above all, it would try to establish what are the essential conditions for realizing potential growth.'[4] 'I have deliberately not been specific about machinery,' the Chancellor said in reply to criticisms of vagueness in his speech, 'because, for the Government to lay that down beforehand is not, I think, the best way to get full co-operation' from the private sector.[5]

The Government, then, was proposing to collaborate with in-

[1] An article published in *The Times* the day after the speech made no mention of it.

[2] Address to the Liverpool Chamber of Trade, January 10, 1961. See also the speech at a gathering of the National Union of Manufacturers, January 17, 1961.

[3] See the report, *Economic Planning in France*, PEP, 1961.

[4] *Hansard*, July 26, 1961, Col. 439.

[5] *Hansard*, ibid.

dustry, and this, given the habits of British administration, was something of a revolution. The reader may be reminded of what was said in the first chapter about the rigid frontier which had hitherto divided consultation between Government and private enterprise from the domain of administration and decision. The offer of collaboration made to the representatives of private industry in July 1961 was a real break with that tradition.

The Federation of British Industries and the Trades Union Congress received identical letters from the Chancellor on August 8, giving details of how the Government's proposal would work out in practice. The Chancellor tried to set at rest the fears of some employers and union leaders that the new organization would become yet another 'talking shop', pointing out how experience had shown the need for a closer link between Government and industry in order to create a climate favourable to expansion and allow effective action to correct the weaknesses of the economy. Such a link would provide the representatives of private business with better opportunities for helping the Government to work out its economic policy. The Government had thus come out clearly in favour of what the French called a concerted 'economy'.

The Chancellor's proposal envisaged the setting up of a two-stage organization: a representative council, the National Economic Development Council, with a technical bureau attached to it, the National Economic Development Office. But the final details were only worked out progressively in the course of discussions with both sides of industry. What was fairly clear from the start was that the Conservative Party was not anxious to use discriminatory State control to attain the aims of the plan, and in this their views differed radically from those of the Labour Party. The Labour chief, Mr Harold Wilson, made no bones about it when he told the annual congress in October 1961 that 'a party which does not believe in controls cannot believe in planning'. He felt that the Conservative Party were merely setting up 'a bureaucratic system to reconcile and correlate the industrial targets of individual firms and industries and the production of myopic documents to convince the unions that a wage increase could not be afforded'.[1] But, in 1961, the solution adopted for the NEDC/NEDO was pretty well what the employers' and workers' representatives envisaged.

The Attitude of the Employers' Organizations

Certain sections of industry played a decisive part in the creation of NEDC. Pressure from them had begun to be felt in 1960, before the

[1] Cf. *Financial Times*, October 3, 1961.

Government's invitation, and was to continue throughout the preparatory discussions.

Before 1960 a few isolated voices in private industry had spoken up in favour of planning.[1] But the most striking manifestation of the growing dissatisfaction with the results of the economic policy of the 1950s showed itself in the conference organized by the FBI in 1960 under the revealing title 'The Next Five Years', and attended by more than 100 leading industrialists. The discussions brought out that 'the Government and industry might see if it would be possible to agree on an assessment of expectations and intentions to be placed before the country as a framework for economic effort during the next five years'. They maintained that studies industry-by-industry could contribute to a better growth performance: 'studies might be attempted on an industry basis, as had been done with some success by the steel industry, of plans and demands for five or ten years ahead'.[2] After this conference working parties continued to meet to develop these ideas.

And so the warmest welcome to the Chancellor of the Exchequer's speech on July 25, 1961, came from the FBI. The very next day the Federation issued a statement in which they expressed their disappointment at the paucity of comment on the Chancellor's very important utterance and assured him that they readily accepted the invitation to join in consultations.[3] This goodwill was nevertheless accompanied by reservations about the dominant position the State might have in the organization set up under the plan.

It was not easy to satisfy the double wish of the employers to see an efficient system of planning launched while enjoying a certain degree of independence from State interference. The entirely independent organization suggested in 1961 by the Council on Prices and Incomes (called the Heyworth Committee after its Chairman)[4] was abandoned by the FBI in favour of a council with Ministerial participation, so that the Government also would be bound by the decisions of NEDC and so that Ministers could be more directly influenced by the representatives of private industry. As it was put by an industrialist who later became one of the employers' representatives on NEDC, the plan should be prepared and published *for*, but

[1] Cf. the statement in 1957 by Sir Ivan Stedeford (Chairman of Tube Investments) in favour of a central organization which would attempt to forecast several years in advance the nation's investment needs—quoted in PEP, 'Growth in the British Economy, London', 1961.

[2] Federation of British Industries, 'The Next Five Years', report on a conference, November 1960.

[3] *Financial Times*, July 27, 1961.

[4] Council on Prices, Productivity and Incomes, Fourth Report, 1961, cf. Chapter VII.

not *by*, the Government, for whom it should be as much a guide as for the private sector.[1]

This distrust of the State, natural enough on the part of private industry, was a fairly widespread feeling in Britain which found voice in the view that the record of the 1950s certainly did not show the bureaucrat in Whitehall to know better than anyone else what should be done to improve economic performance. Indeed the post-war nationalizations in Britain had not been the success that their advocates had hoped. Again, the competence of the administration in the co-ordination of public investment had been much criticized.[2] The British Treasury has been attacked for being by its nature on the side of those who have an instinctive fear of too-rapid expansion because of its excessive preoccupation with short-term financial objectives.[3] Such criticisms overlook of course a number of real problems, not always well understood by the partisans of expansion; since the Treasury's responsibilities cover a wider field than that of growth, the demands of expansion must be considered in relation to the sum total of economic policy. This very fact, it is true, made it seem even more desirable to some observers that the machinery of the plan should be kept quite separate from the Treasury. But this solution was not tried until Labour came to power in 1964 and even then not as completely as had been suggested nor very successfully.

The Attitude of the Trade Unions

Though attacked by some for associating themselves with the work of NEDC, the general council of the TUC won a large majority in favour of participation at their congress in 1962. Mr George Woodcock had launched a forthright appeal to the doubters: 'Are you so scared that you are not prepared to stand by your experience, by your competence and your ability? Are you so modest in all these things that you reject every challenge and reject every opportunity? I would rather be a dog and bay the moon than such a trade unionist.'[4]

If the support of the unions for the idea of taking part in NEDC had not been won without difficulty, this was due much more to the circumstances in which the Chancellor's invitation was sent than to any

[1] M. R. Geddes (Managing Director of Dunlops), quoted in the *Financial Times*, August 9, 1961.

[2] The system of control of public investment introduced by the Treasury after the war has often been considered too negative in its action and too indifferent to economic criteria. See, for example, the study by Beer, S. H., 'Treasury Control', Oxford, 1957, and the *Report of the Select Committee on Nationalized Industries*, HMSO, 1957.

[3] Cf. for a full-scale attack on traditional Treasury methods: S. Brittain, *The Treasury under the Tories*, Pelican, 1964.

[4] Congress of TUC, September 1962, p. 390.

fundamental disagreement. In an attempt to achieve the rapid righting of the balance of payments, the Government had proposed, among other measures, a 'pause' in wage increases in both the private and the public sector,[1] and in fact for several months they systematically refused every wage increase even when sponsored by an arbitration tribunal. It was obviously very awkward for trade unionists, even those who were willing to discuss planning with the Government, to formulate a constructive reply so long as the wages pause remained one of the main themes of anti-cyclical policy. For this reason the official acceptance by the TUC was held back till February 1962, and was the outcome of numerous interviews with the Chancellor and a promise of flexible handling of the pause.

The ideas of the TUC about the form planning should take seem to have been similar to those of the employers. Though the speech of July 1961 had come as no surprise to the FBI, since a number of their members had been pressing the Government to take such a step, it was something of a bombshell to the unions. Neither the Labour Party nor the unions had devoted a great deal of thought to the idea of planning, though at the end of July 1961 the general council of the TUC had stated that they were quite prepared to take part in a joint examination of 'how Britain's great potential can more effectively be harnessed to the service of its people'.[2] Already some of the more far-sighted members of the union movement, who felt the lack of real opportunities for the TUC to take part in discussions on economic policy with the Government, whatever its political hue, had realized that the substitution of more deliberate control of the economy for the free working of natural forces was bound to bring about changes in attitude and structure in the unions themselves.[3] This 'participationist' view was expanded and its implications recognized in a pamphlet by the TUC on planning published in 1963: 'We believe that the development of economic planning on a consultative basis will help us to secure our other main objectives—a greater share in decisions about the industries in which our members work and more influence over national economic and social policies which affect our members as workers and citizens'.[4] This document was the first attempt by the secretariat of the TUC to get Congress to discuss planning in a modern, peacetime economy.

This willingness to take part, fundamentally no less genuine than

[1] Cf. Chapter VII.

[2] *The Times*, August 10, 1961.

[3] Cf. an article by the late Sir Alan Birch, one-time chairman of the Economic Committee of the TUC, 'Structure of the British Trade Union Movement', Manchester Statistical Society, 1957, p. 35.

[4] TUC, *Economic Development and Planning*, 1963, p. 6.

that of the FBI, did not prevent the TUC, like the employers, from voicing suspicions about a planning body which was too much under the thumb of the Government. George Woodcock noted with satisfaction in September 1962, in the light of several months' experience as a member of NEDC, 'We have a planning office which so far has shown . . . every sign of becoming what we want it to be, a part of the NEDC and not an arm of the Treasury. That was one of the dangers that had to be avoided. . . .'[1] George Woodcock has also been a consistent supporter of the idea that planning, if it is to be effective, must essentially be founded on consent; the more the representatives of industry, both employers and workpeople, at all levels are involved in the working out of the plan, the more they will feel obliged to help carry it into effect. The steps in planning ascribed to George Woodcock as 'discussion, agreement, commitment' sum up this view.

From the fact that they accepted a 'concerted economy' as a general framework for planning, it is clear that the British unions looked upon their participation in the plan as permanent and not as something that would alter according to the fluctuations in the political colour of the Government. The employers took the same view and experience since 1964, and the return to power of Labour shows that the institutional arrangements for planning set up after 1961 had at least the great virtue of inserting the planning concept as a permanent feature into economic policy-making.

2. THE SOLUTION ADOPTED IN 1961

As we have already said,[2] from one point of view the whole economic policy of the United Kingdom today has been influenced by the period of re-thinking whose clearest manifestation seems to us to be the adoption of a system of planning. For this reason our answer to the question 'What is meant by planning?' would be to say that the traces of the impact of the planning experiment are to be found in practically all aspects of economic policy-making in Britain today. For the moment, however, let us limit our examination to the structure of NEDC/NEDO tandem and to the tasks which the Council set itself.

Structure

At the beginning, in 1962, there existed only the Council (NEDC) and its technical office (NEDO). The Economic Development Committees (the 'vertical' committees) dating from 1964 are nevertheless an essential part of the whole structure, which we shall be in a better position to appreciate in the next chapter.

[1] Report of TUC Congress, 1962, p. 369.
[2] Introduction to Part Two.

(a) *The Council.* The representatives of the employers affiliated to the Federation of British Industries had agreed to take part in NEDC in the summer of 1961, but the negotiations with the unions were more difficult, as has been seen. When therefore the director of the Office (NEDO), Sir Robert Shone, was appointed in December 1961, the Council itself was not yet fully constituted. In February 1962 the Chancellor of the Exchequer proposed that the Council should consist of twenty members, six from the employers, six from the unions, two from the nationalized industries, two independent members, plus the director of NEDO and three Ministers. The names of the members were published immediately, except for the six union representatives. The TUC formally agreed to take part on March 5, 1962, and the Council, now complete, held its first meeting two days later.

The composition of NEDC was sufficiently notable to deserve attention, and it was not just empty words when, at the first meeting, the Chancellor of the Exchequer, Mr Selwyn Lloyd, described the occasion as 'a major step in Britain's economic history'.[1] Indeed never before had twenty men, bearing such heavy responsibilities and so widely representative of English economic life, met together on a permanent basis in one organization. And it must be remembered that during the preliminary discussions both employers and unions had insisted that the Council must have real powers; the assurances then given by the Chancellor were reiterated at the first meeting.[2]

The employers' representatives consisted, not of members of the 'Establishment'[3] but of men known for their dynamic support in the FBI, of new thinking about economic policy and directors of important firms in the forefront of technological progress. This was equally true of the two representatives of the nationalized industries. Both of them, though their background was very different, had recently taken

[1] *Financial Times*, March 8, 1962. In view of the changes that were introduced into the planning machinery in 1964 (and which are described in the next chapter) it is interesting to recall here the view of the present Director-General of the NEDO on the importance of the NEDC experiment as it illustrates, it seems, the fact that, beyond differences of approach when specific machinery is being set up, there is a fundamental purpose that the Council is able to fulfil in British economic life: 'If powerful national figures are made responsible for doing something that the country wants and some of the ablest men in Government service are re-deployed to help them, then a new centre of power has been brought into being in the national decision-making process and major national decisions will, from then on, have a different bias.' H. F. R. Catherwood in *The Times*, May 3, 1966.

[2] 'I do not want this to be a body which just listens to Government decisions, and is merely asked for its comment. I want it to have an important impact on Government policy during the formative stage, and upon the economic life of the nation. I believe it can.' *NEDC, History and Function*, London, October 1962.

[3] Cf. Chapter I.

over with a mandate from the Government to carry out far-reaching reforms, which they were in process of achieving. In the list of trade union representatives on NEDC appeared the names of George Woodcock, whose outstanding role in the renewal of the ideas and methods of British trade unionism we have already noted, R. Smith, one of the younger generation of union leaders, H. Douglass, at the head of one of the unions which has most successfully adapted itself to modern industry, the steelworkers.

All the trade unionists had been nominated by the general council of the TUC explicitly as their representatives, but the employers' who sat on the NEDC in the early years were in no sense delegates of the FBI or any other body. Difficulties very quickly arose over the representative function of these members in connection with the incomes policy and today the employers have adopted the same system of representation as the unions.

The Council, then, consisted of men of the same calibre as the 'neo-realists'[1] as they have been called in France and who have done so much to restore their country's economy. 'The members of this group were not exactly technocrats, but rather those that drew from the catastrophe [of the Second World War] the conclusion that France must be a responsible nation and who tried to act, each in his own sphere, towards that end. Let us call them the Neo-Realists.' If these men in Britain have been given more scope since 1961 for their action it seems we have the NEDC to thank for it.

(b) *NEDO.*[2] The National Economic Development Office had a small personnel; the administrators with technical qualifications (in economics or other subjects) numbered only forty. In recruiting them the wishes of both employers and unions to have a wholly independent body of administrators had been respected. The number of civil servants seconded to NEDO did not exceed two or three, they were mostly scientists and not economists, and none came from the Treasury, the others came from the private sector.[3] Thus the director, Sir Robert Shone, had long been in charge of the Iron and Steel Board.[4] His two chief assistants, Sir Donald MacDougall and Mr

[1] *France: Change and Tradition*, a set of essays prepared by the Centre for International Affairs of Harvard University, Gollancz, 1963, p. 343.

[2] The structure and role of NEDO were considerably modified in October 1964 (see next chapter). Here only the pioneer model will be discussed.

[3] This solution was of course radically different from the French arrangements where the departments of State are strongly represented in the staff of the Commissariat Général du Plan. Cf. J. and A.-M. Hackett, *Economic Planning in France*, ibid.

[4] Unofficial organization set up, after denationalization, by the steel industry in 1953 and given powers of supervision and co-ordination especially in respect of investment and prices.

T. C. Fraser had been, respectively, a professor of political economy who had held important Government posts during the war, and director of the central organization of the wool industry.

The work of NEDO fell into two divisions, each under its own director. One dealt with general economic problems and the other with industrial questions. The economics division consisted mainly of economists from the universities, private research institutes or industry. The industrial division employed chiefly scientists and engineers.

The legal status of NEDO, whose staffing and general expenses were borne by the Government, has been compared to the secretariat of a royal commission. But just as the council to which it was attached was something new in English public life, so NEDO had its own peculiarities which distinguished it from the traditional secretariat. It is of course true that the council was supreme and that NEDO existed only to serve it. It is equally true that a body of twenty members needed to be briefed and provided with topics for discussion. Thus Professor H. Phelps Brown, one of the two independent members of NEDC, compared the relationship between the council and NEDO with that existing in private industry between the board of management and the board of directors which meets only occasionally.[1] Experience has shown that NEDO has proved a stimulant and a catalyst to NEDC.

The wish for a very clear distinction between Government departments, especially the Treasury, and NEDO caused a certain number of difficulties, which the changes introduced by the Labour Government since its return to power in the autumn of 1964 were intended to remedy. The working out and launching of the first programme of expansion for example threw up disagreements between the expansionists centred on NEDO and the Treasury. This was neither surprising nor unhealthy and closer collaboration between the two would have enabled them, if not to settle these disagreements, at least to see clearly where they lay. These teething troubles could, no doubt, have been overcome in time and appropriate adjustments in methods of work made.

In 1962, an internal reorganization of the Treasury was carried out which, in any event, had the result of focusing this department's work more than previously on longer-term issues.[2] Thus systematic, and comprehensive, 'forward looks' several years ahead for public

[1] Cf. Phelps Brown, H., 'The National Economic Development Organization', *Public Administration*, Autumn 1963, p. 243.

[2] This reform arose out of the work of an interdepartmental committee (the Plowden Committee), the essence of whose findings was published as a White Paper: *Control of Public Expenditure*, Cmd. 1432. Then the forward estimates of public expenditure, *Public Expenditure in 1963–4 and 1967–8*, Cmd. 2235, published in 1963 attested to this new approach by the Treasury.

expenditure were instituted. A new administrative unit, called the National Economy Group, inside the Treasury, received the mandate to analyse the impact of the public sector's activities upon the balance of real resources in the economy in the medium-term and to include in its scope the work of the NEDC. The group was subsequently transferred, at the end of 1964, by the Labour Government, to the newly-created Department of Economic Affairs (see Chapter VI).

But it must be admitted that, during the period 1961–4, the NEDO staff tended not only to be independent of the Treasury—which had been intended by the Government and the representatives of both sides of industry—but to be cut off from any contact with the Treasury and the other Government departments—which had certainly not been foreseen.

(c) *The Economic Development Committees.* Perhaps it was partly owing to the pressure of work that the third branch of the British planning system—the Economic Development Committees—did not appear until December 1963. With the benefit of hindsight, this time-lag appears as the major shortcoming of the NEDC experiment.

In a Press announcement the NEDC recorded its decision to set up economic development committees in a number of industries with the following terms of reference:

'1, to examine the economic performance, prospects and plans of the industry and assess from time to time the industry's progress in relation to the national growth objectives, and provide information and forecasts to the council on these matters;

'2, to consider ways of improving the industry's economic performance, competitive power and efficiency, and formulate reports and recommendations on these matters as appropriate.'[1]

Thus although these committees had no mandatory authority over the firms in their industry, they were given very wide powers.

The director of the industrial division of NEDO to which the economic development committees were attached has expressed the opinion that 'planning cannot take place in a vacuum, but needs to be anchored to the realities of industrial life. The industrial committees provide this essential link.'[2] With this in view he assigned them four tasks: to analyse progress made and note divergences from the plan; to help in the preparation of a new plan; to examine certain special problems such as the expansion of exports, the competition of imports with British industry, firms' inventory policy; to study all questions connected with the achievement of growth objectives,

[1] Reproduced in the *Board of Trade Journal*, December 13, 1963.

[2] Cf. Fraser, T. C., 'Economic Development Committees', *FBI Review*, July 1964.

for example the availability of capital and qualified manpower. These tasks remain in force today, as the next chapter will show; but up to the end of 1964 a start had been made in implementing this mandate in only a few sectors.

By August 1964, nine committees had been set up and had held their first meeting. An Economic Planning Advisory Council for the Construction Industries had already been formed in 1963 with the support of NEDO; except in name it resembled an economic development committee.

One of the reasons for the slowness in setting up these committees was the lengthy negotiations needed to work out the list of members. Thus for the committee for mechanical engineering on the employers' side alone there had to be several preliminary meetings attended by the representatives of more than forty associations, while on the workers' side one union would not readily agree to be represented by another. This kind of difficulty forced both industrialists and unions to create larger and more representative groups than those hitherto existing.[1] These sometimes laborious wrangles had at least the good result of giving the committees a well qualified membership capable of tackling successfully the tasks awaiting them. Consisting for the most part of chairmen and managing directors of firms, and, on the unions' side, of general secretaries or high officials; each committee has also one or two independent members and official representatives. The chairmen of the committees are elected by the members; so far they have been industrialists or representatives of nationalized industries.

The absence of trade unionists from chairmanships is apparently due, not to any reluctance on the part of the unions, but to the somewhat technical nature of the work. Indeed the unions have continued to show a great interest in the committees. The document by the TUC on planning, approved by the 1962 Congress, looked forward to the time when these bodies 'might become a focus for co-operative research and marketing activities or, in time, accumulate or be entrusted with funds for promoting industrial rationalization'.[2] In 1963, in order to help those of its members who might be called upon to sit on the committees, the TUC took steps to widen its own economic services and to arrange meetings with TUC delegates on NEDC. One of these declared at the 1963 Congress that the committees would 'offer new opportunities to trade unionists to influence developments in their own industries. Trade unionists will now be able to move from the role of critics after damage has been done to the role of architects when developments are being planned'.[3]

[1] Cf. Chapter IX. [2] Op. cit., p. 11.

[3] Cf. H. Douglass, president of the Iron and Steel Trades Confederation and member of NEDC, at the congress of the TUC, September 1963, p. 384.

The institutional arrangements for planning just described were short-lived. Set up in the course of the second half of 1961 and early 1962, they were modified substantially in the autumn of 1964 when the Labour Party secured a majority in Parliament (see Chapter VI). The approach to planning institutions adopted by the Conservatives had therefore too little time to show its worth. It does appear, however, that the delay in setting up the Economic Development Committees was regrettable as was the excessive concentration, in 1963, of the NEDC on reaching agreement on the principles for a policy for prices and incomes (discussed in Chapter VII). The criticism has been made that the NEDC suffered from the fact that, in their approach to planning, both sides of the private sector—but particularly the trade unionists—saw themselves as engaged in a process of bargaining between powerful interest groups with the Government as the 'honest broker'.[1] But it seems that Western-type planning can hardly avoid something of this kind happening. True there had been an unfortunate tendency for the Office of the NEDC and the Treasury to work in watertight compartments; but it appears unlikely that the drawbacks of this situation would not have been perceived and corrective action taken.

The Tasks

To decide on targets, and then on the means to attain them, was the main work of NEDC in 1962 and 1963. It was no doubt to be expected that the first part of this programme should prove much easier to accomplish than the second.

(a) *The Targets 1961–6.* In October 1962, that is, less than eight months after the first meeting of NEDC, the Office was in a position to submit to the Council, an outline plan for the development of the economy as a whole up to 1966.[2] The scheme was published in its definitive form in February 1963.[3] An analysis of this '1966 model' shows that the aims it set were sufficiently ambitious to call for fairly considerable changes in the past trends of the British economy.

The 1966 model was constructed, as is customary in France and in other countries using the same type of planning, within the framework of the national accounts. No allowance was made for any probable or desirable annual changes between the starting year (1961) and the final year (1966). The lack of time and of statistical information, and the novelty of this kind of exercise both for business and for Government departments, explain why this model contained

[1] A. Schonfield: *Modern Capitalism*, Oxford University Press, 1965, p. 153.

[2] This is a very short period of time. Usually, much more is required. Thus the French plan demands more than two years' preparation for example.

[3] *Growth of the United Kingdom Economy to 1966*, NEDC, HMSO, February 1963.

nothing very original or profound as to methods.[1] But the very fact of tackling the problem was a sign of progress. Planning is a long-term task, a kind of continuous weave, in which the future learns from the experiences of the past.

The methods used were based, on the one hand, on a macro-economic analysis of the principal structural relationships in the British economy, and on the other hand, in order to check the results so obtained by comparing them with the concrete experience of industry, on an inquiry made during the summer of 1962 by NEDO among the representatives of seventeen branches of industry. An econometric model was not used, because the only one which would have been of any value[2] would have raised too many problems, statistical and others, at that stage. Nor was any use made of an 'input-output' table which would have linked up the projections of the different categories of demand with the demand for each sector of industry.

The procedure followed was thus not dissimilar from the 'iterative' method that is common in the working out of medium-term plans. But the very short time available did not make it possible for the firms consulted in the inquiry to receive in advance much in the way of an outline for the final year of the overall plan or of details directly concerning the demand for their own products. The construction of the macro-economic model and consultation with industry had to be carried on more or less together. As regards the labour force, it became evident that the available statistics were far from complete and ill suited to the requirements of a medium-term plan. In order to fill this lack, the Ministry of Labour created in March 1963 a new service for the collection and analysis of all statistics relating to the labour force and suitable for the working out of a programme of economic growth.[3] This is a good example of the way in which planning can encourage improvements in statistics.

The main projections of the utilization of resources for 1966 are shown in Table I. The key figure is the rate of increase of the gross domestic product (4 per cent per annum, that is 22 per cent at a compound rate for the five years 1961 to 1966). This rate was based on a forecast of available manpower increasing at 0·8 per cent per annum between 1961 and 1966, and an annual increase in productivity of 3·2 per cent per person employed. The most solid basis for the 1966 projection was provided by the NEDO inquiry in the summer of 1962

[1] The council itself called it a 'trial run'.

[2] This is the model worked out at Cambridge University by Professor Stone and his colleagues. Stone, V. R., *The Model and its Environment. A Progress Report*, Chapman & Hall, 1964.

[3] The Manpower Research Unit.

TABLE I

USE OF RESOURCES FROM 1961 TO 1966

	£ millions at 1961 prices		*Increase from 1961 to 1966[a]*
	1961	*1966*	*Annual percentage rates*
Available resources			
Gross domestic product at market prices	26,835	32,650	4·0 (4·0)
Imports of goods	4,013	5,050	4·7 (4·0)
Net imports of services[b]	26	50	–
Total	30,874	37,750	4·1 (4·0)
Use of resources			
Consumer spending	17,531	20,930	3·6 (3·5)
Public consumption	4,574	5,445	3·5 (3·5)
Fixed investments	4,582	5,935	5·3 (5·2)
Stocks	304	450	–
Exports of goods	3,883	4,990	5·1 (5·0)
Total	30,874	37,750	4·1 (4·0)

[a] Some of the figures in the initial plan published in 1963 were revised the following year. The initial estimates are shown in brackets.

[b] Military expenditure abroad, payments on shipping, travel, etc., less receipts from abroad under the same heads.

Source: The Growth of the Economy, HMSO, 1964, and *Monthly Digest of Statistics.*

held in seventeen branches of industry covering about 40 per cent of the gross national product and of total employment, 40 per cent of exports and more than 50 per cent of total investment.[1] According to the replies received, the firms consulted saw no real difficulty in achieving a total rate of expansion of 4·8 per cent per annum up to 1966 as regards production, and of 4·1 per cent for productivity per employee. As these figures were better than what was needed overall (4 per cent for production and 3·2 per cent for productivity), NEDO fixed the effort to be required in the sectors not covered by the inquiry at a lower figure. (See Table II.) If the estimated growth in productivity per person employed is compared with the achievement of the recent past, the figures show that a considerable improvement was expected during the period 1961 to 1966. (See Table III.)

NEDC thus took an optimistic view of the future acceleration in the rate of increase of productivity. The figures in Table III do not even show the full extent of that optimism, for by 1961 total productivity had not yet reached an annual rate of increase equal to the 3·2 per cent estimated for the period 1961–6. Towards 1966 therefore it would become necessary for this rate to be exceeded in order to

[1] Not including housing construction.

TABLE II

PRODUCTION, EMPLOYMENT, PRODUCTIVITY ANNUAL INCREASE FROM 1961 TO 1966 (PERCENTAGES)

	Production	*Employment*	*Productivity*
17 branches of industry	4·8	0·7	4·1
Rest of the economy	3·5	0·9	2·6
Gross domestic product	4·0	0·8	3·2

Source: National Economic Development Council.

achieve an average of 3·2 per cent over the whole period. NEDC justified its view by reference to the improvement noted in the 1950s in the annual growth of productivity (Table III), and maintained that this improvement was now even less likely to fall off as, since about 1959, there had been very considerable investment in industry. NEDC was also counting on the beneficial effects of the 1961–6 plan on productivity, on greater stability of demand and on certain favourable structural changes.[1]

Domestic consumption would absorb the largest part of the increased production forecast by the 1961–6 programme. It would take in all 50 per cent of the increase in resources. But the most rapid rate of annual increase was reserved for investment.

A 3·6 per cent annual rate of growth in total domestic consumption (Table I) would be equivalent to a rate of 2·9 per cent per head from 1961–6 compared with only 2·1 per cent over the previous five years. It was therefore possible to foresee a marked improvement in the standard of living. Nevertheless the estimates foresaw also larger savings, since the rate of increase in consumption per head of the population (2·9 per cent) was less than the rate of increase in productivity (3·2 per cent per person employed and 3·3 per cent per head of the population). Over the last five years household consumption had risen slightly faster than the gross national product, but in future it would increase less rapidly (3·5 per cent compared as with 4·0 per cent). It was therefore of fundamental importance for the

TABLE III

ANNUAL INCREASE IN PRODUCTIVITY PER PERSON EMPLOYED (PERCENTAGES)

	1953–7	*1957–61*	*1961–6 (estimated)*
17 branches of industry	1·8	2·8	4·1
Rest of the economy	1·8	2·0	2·6
Gross domestic product	1·8	2·5	3·2

Source: National Economic Development Council.

N.B. The figures given in Tables II and III are taken from two publications, *Growth of the United Kingdom Economy to 1966* (1963) and *The Growth of the Economy* (1964). Between these two publications certain data were revised.

[1] *Growth of the United Kingdom Economy to 1966*, op. cit., paras 160–4.

equilibrium which it was hoped would be achieved by 1966 that incomes and their increase should not exceed the targets thus fixed. This point will be developed in Chapter VII on incomes policy.

It was necessary to moderate incomes, in spite of a more rapid rise in the domestic standard of living than in the past, because it had been decided to increase the proportion of the gross national product to be devoted to investment and also because it was essential to improve the balance of payments position. NEDC put at 5·3 per cent per annum the rate of growth required for investment expenditure, which was to increase from 17 per cent of the gross national product in 1961 to more than 18 per cent in 1966. This overall growth was the outcome of various trends corresponding to different kinds of investment. Thus for the manufacturing industries the overall increase in investment expenditure during the five years of the plan was calculated to be a little less than 7·5 per cent, a rather low figure, influenced by the fact that the steel industry had already completed a big investment programme between 1959 and 1961. If this industry is not counted, the manufacturing sector forecast an expansion of investment of 23 per cent between 1961 and 1966, a percentage about equal to the rate of growth of the gross national product. In firms other than the manufacturing industries investment was to grow a good deal faster—43 per cent over the period 1961–6, expansion in the electricity supply industry (+93 per cent), the General Post Office (+79 per cent) and the distributive trades (+44 per cent) being particularly vigorous.

The calculations of NEDC with regard to the balance of payments for 1966 are shown in Table IV. Let us first look at those two heads in the forecasts of resources and their use shown in Table I from which it is possible to link the national accounts with the balance of payments, the heads being imports and exports which, with invisible receipts, constitute the current balance of payments.[1] Later we shall analyse the capital balance.

The annual percentage increase in imports (4·7 per cent), only slightly larger than that of the gross national product, is perhaps the key figure in NEDC's forecast for 1966. For this estimate to become fact a fairly considerable change in trend would have been necessary compared with past years in which imports had grown decidedly more rapidly than the gross national product. The later part of this chapter will show that the optimism of the members of NEDC in 1962, when they banked on an improvement in the competitive strength of the British economy compared with other industrial countries, was not justified in the event.

[1] As the figures in Table I are worked out according to the definition of the gross national product, the total of invisible receipts is lower than in Table IV.

This situation is closely connected with the serious problems which the experts of NEDC had to face during the period when the 1961–6 plan was being worked out. In 1962 the experts were entitled to believe, in estimating the conditions governing world trade up to 1966, that before that date the United Kingdom would have joined the Common Market. The negotiations which were then in progress in Brussels had the support of many people in Britain who thought that the impact of increased competition following the entry of the country into the Common Market would provide a salutary shock which would make easier the indispensable modernization of the economy. Therefore in its first outline for 1966 NEDO had forecast a more rapid expansion of both imports and exports. It was only after the failure of the Brussels negotiations at the beginning of 1963 that the forecasts were revised as shown by the figures in Table IV.

TABLE IV

BALANCE OF PAYMENTS, 1961–6 (£ MILLIONS AND PERCENTAGES)

	1961	*1966*[a] *(at 1961 prices)*	*Increase from 1961 to 1966 (annual per cent)*
Imports (f.o.b.)	4,013	−5,050 (4,890)	4·7 (4·0)
Exports and re-exports (f.o.b.)	3,883	+4,990 (4,955)	5·1 (5·0)
Visible balance	− 130	− 60 (+ 65)	
Invisible balance	+ 120	+ 285 (+285)	
Current account balance	− 10	+ 225 (+350)	
Balancing item[b]	− 14	+ 50 (+ 50)	
Current account balance plus balancing item	− 24	+ 275 (+400)	
Long-term capital movements			
official	− 45	− 275 (−200)	
private	+ 89	(−150)	
Overall balance	+ 20	0 (+ 50)	

[a] The figures in brackets are the initial estimates adjusted so as to include modifications in the balance of payments statistics (see note ([b])).

[b] In the initial estimates for 1966 the average annual total of net current receipts included in the 'balancing item' was calculated at £100m. Improvements in the statistics of the balance of payments made it possible to identify some £50m. of net credits falling under the head of invisible balance, so that the net positive total of the 'normal' balancing item could be calculated at £50m. and the invisible balance was increased by £50m.

Source: The Growth of the Economy, HMSO, March 1964.

Essentially the target fixed for the expansion of exports of manufactures between 1961 and 1966 (5·1 per cent per annum) was less an estimate of probability than a calculation, based on the other objectives of the '1966 model', of the effort required to reach the balance of payments target for 1966. The NEDC put forward arguments in support of this figure. It was calculated that external demand would remain very strong, that the commodity structure of British exports would not present the same difficulties as in the past, that industrial productivity would benefit from the more vigorous growth of the economy and that British prices would become increasingly competitive. Nevertheless NEDC described as 'formidable' the task represented by an annual increase of this magnitude.[1] Exports had indeed never yet surpassed an increase rate of 3 per cent over any long period and, according to the results of the industrial inquiry held by NEDO to which reference has already been made, businessmen in their estimates did not foresee any increase in the rate in relation to the previous period. The hypothesis that the terms of trade in 1966 would be largely the same as in 1961 might also be thought excessively optimistic as events after 1961 soon showed.

With regard to the capital balance, the United Kingdom is an industrial country which has been traditionally a net exporter of capital to less developed countries either as official grants and loans or as private capital (direct investments and portfolio investment). Equilibrium of the current balance of payments is therefore not enough to ensure the health of the balance of payments as a whole. There must be a surplus in order to finance the export of capital unless a net capital import from other developed countries is postulated. This surplus was first estimated at £400m., but in 1964 the figure was reduced to £275m. (cf. Table IV).

(b) *Necessary Conditions for Achieving the 1966 Target.* At the third meeting of NEDC in June 1962, the growth target of 4 per cent having been fixed at the previous meeting, the Council decided that, at the same time that a programme of expansion was being worked out, they should study the obstacles in the way of its fulfilment. It was in this connection that the members of the Council were to meet their first serious disagreement. The following chapters will deal in detail with the subjects discussed and the results obtained; it will be sufficient here to indicate the topics which arose.

A report issued in April 1963 deals with the conditions favouring expansion.[2] It first discusses a number of human elements which influence growth. On the subject of education, whether scientific and technical, the systematic training of future leaders of industry or the training of skilled workmen, NEDC echoes the criticisms which were heard in Britain throughout the 1950s. Resistance to technological change and the limited mobility of the labour force were thought to restrict the adaptability of the economy and to call for vigorous intervention especially by the Ministry of Labour. A much more energetic policy was called for in dealing with uneven regional

[1] *Growth of the United Kingdom Economy to 1966*, op. cit., p. 52.

[2] *Conditions favourable to faster growth*, NEDC, HMSO, April 1963.

development. Attention was given to the question of how far participation in the planning experiment was likely to entail changes in the methods and structure of government, the employers' organizations and the trade unions. On anti-cyclical policy, a particularly delicate subject discussed with some reticence because of the presence of trade unionists, the report comments that experience has shown that when the margin of unemployed capacity is being rapidly absorbed, or has already been reduced to a very low level, conditions are favourable for price increases and an excessive growth of imports.

The report recognized that the balance of payments was the Achilles heel in the achievement of the programme of medium-term expansion 1961–6. The 1966 model could only be completed by banking on a relatively high rate of growth of exports of manufactures. It was thus proper to consider a certain number of means which could be used to hold the balance of payments position if this forecast did not come true or if the expansion of imports was too rapid. Consideration was therefore given to such measures as restrictions on the movement of capital and on imports, financial help to exporters, consolidation of sterling balances; there was even an indirect reference to devaluation. This list is interesting, especially because several of the suggestions it contains are to be found in the economic policy followed by the Labour Government since the autumn of 1964 in countering the balance of payments crisis.

Finally, on the question of price stability, NEDC notes that in future, if the forecasts of foreign trade are to be realized, the rise in money incomes will have to be decidedly slower than the annual average of from 5 per cent to 6 per cent recorded in the past.[1] Such a statement by a tripartite organization of the weight of NEDC is clearly more than an exercise in style. We shall come back to it in Chapter VII which deals with the incomes policy.

3. THE PARTIAL FAILURE OF THE 1961–6 PROGRAMME

In 1962 the Government began to introduce expansionist measures, thus ending the period of restrictions inaugurated in 1961. This new policy of expansion took for its target the 4 per cent rate of growth used by NEDC in its plan for 1961–6. Home demand, both for investment and for consumption, responded quickly to these measures, to the extent that at one moment the 4 per cent rate was surpassed. But in 1964, that is, very soon after, new balance of payments difficulties arose and it became apparent that the attempt to put the economy into an orbit of rapid and sustained growth could not be brought to fruition.

[1] Op. cit., paragraph 213.

The Expansion of 1962–3

Between the reduction of the Bank rate from 6 per cent to 5 per cent decided in March 1962 and the budget of April 1963 there was a series of measures intended to re-stimulate demand. The budget of April 1962 was relatively neutral in its effects on total demand, although the purchase tax on cars was reduced. But in June there was considerable easing of the credit conditions laid down for hire purchase and the restrictions on the banks' liquid assets through the special deposits introduced in 1961 were removed. These measures for liberalizing credit were strengthened during the winter and a new easing of credit for consumption, together with reductions in indirect taxation, came into force. In the autumn of 1962 it was decided to increase expenditure on public investment and investment by private industry was encouraged by considerable tax relief.

The Government's policy on expansion of demand was laid down by the Chancellor of the Exchequer in the debate on the Finance Bill in April 1963: 'The purpose of this budget can be clearly stated; it is to do the Government's part in achieving the rate of growth broadly described as the 4 per cent target which we have accepted in the National Economic Development Council.'[1] With this in mind, new tax reductions were announced and these, added to a substantial increase in Government spending, brought about a budget deficit of £687m. for the fiscal year 1963–4 against £66m. in the previous year.

Later in the year the authorities took a new step by publishing for the first time targets for increase in official expenditure over a period of five years.[2] According to this document 'the Government are aiming at a rate of growth of the gross national product of 4 per cent a year on average', and the calculations of official expenditure were intended to 'establish a pattern for the future development of the public services which is properly related to the prospective needs of the community and is consistent with, and supports the growth of, the nation's resources'.[3]

The Government therefore followed the recommendations of NEDC not only by adopting a rate of overall growth of 4 per cent, but also in the field of public expenditure. In particular the effort demanded by NEDC in the direction of social investment found a place in the official investment plans as published. The plans for investment in the generation and distribution of electricity—which NEDC thought might prove a bottle-neck—were also stepped up. It should however be noted that a number of outside observers thought

[1] *Hansard*, April 3, 1963, p. 455.
[2] *Public Expenditure in 1963–4 and 1967–8*. Cmd. 2235, December 1963.
[3] Op. cit., paragraph 36.

these expansionist measures still too timid,[1] which, in the light of the 'overheating' that developed in 1964, shows how difficult it is to calculate accurately the true impact of expansionist measures on demand.

The political situation in 1964 was, of course, rather unfavourable to the energetic pursuit of the NEDC/NEDO experiment as the prospect of imminent general elections began to colour the thinking of the three participants on the Council—the Conservative Ministers, the employers and the trade unionists.[2] As a result, a lot of the steam went out of the NEDC's drive—particularly after the failure to reach agreement on an incomes policy—and the putting in hand of the structural reforms that, in the last analysis, were the only means by which reflation of demand as practised in 1962 and 1963 could be crowned with success, began to show signs of flagging. An assessment of the NEDC/NEDO experiment from 1961 to 1964 must, it seems, give some considerable weight to these 'extra-economic' considerations.

The 'Overheating' of 1964

That the boost given to total demand during this period was too violent is shown by the rapidity with which the economy reached both a state of 'overheating' in 1964 and an adverse balance of payments which recalled the experience of 1961.

In 1963 the spearhead of expansion was private consumption, whereas the following year it was investment, both official and private, which developed most.

The increase in the gross national product between the fourth quarter of 1962 and the fourth quarter of 1963 was 7 per cent in volume, a figure much greater than the 'normal' growth in the productive potential, even supposing that this had been as high as the 4 per cent rate postulated by NEDC in its 1961–6 programme. Such an increase was of course only possible because of the unused resources available at the beginning of the period. In 1964 expansion slowed down considerably (4 per cent), partly because export demand began to fall off while imports increased very rapidly, but also because available resources were beginning to be fully utilized. Private consumption, which rose by more than 4 per cent in 1963, grew rather less the following year. But the slowing down was chiefly the result of an increase of more than 3 per cent in retail prices, nominal incomes

[1] Cf. for example the very influential National Institute Economic Review, April 1963.

[2] This point is given particular stress by Dr Mitchell in her book: *Groundwork to Economic Planning*, Secker and Warburg, 1966, Chapter V. The whole of this chapter may be consulted with profit on the questions dealt with here.

having risen by 7 per cent. Investment expenditure in private industry grew by 16 per cent in 1964, housing by 25 per cent (this unusually large figure was due to bad weather during the winter of 1962–3 which brought about inflated percentage figures for the following year), and public investment (not including housing) by 15 per cent. To these increases must be added a growing demand for stocks. These figures were much higher than had been estimated in the 1961–6 plan and revealed a growth which was too rapid to be maintained. It was not surprising therefore that by 1964 the unemployment rate had fallen below 1·5 per cent and the trade balance was moving in a strongly adverse fashion.

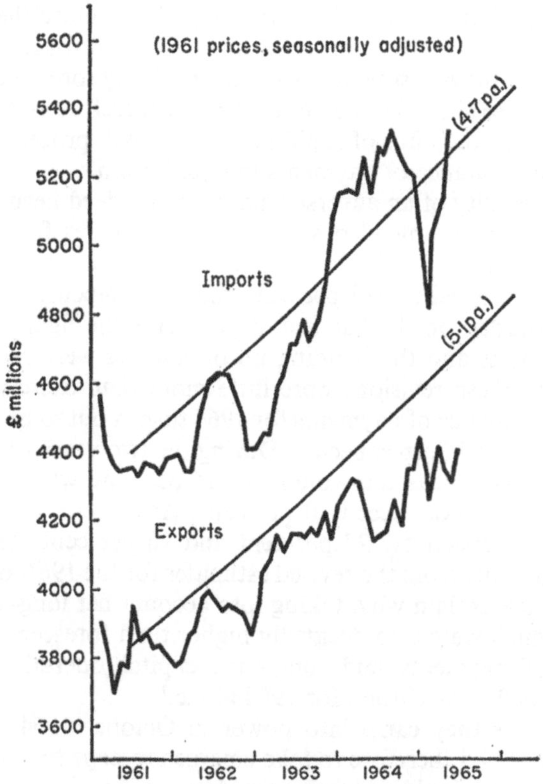

Volume of imports and exports
(plan targets and achievements)

Source: Sir R. Shone in Moorgate and Wall Street Review

In 1962, the starting years of the new phase of expansion, the balance of payments was already in a rather weak position, with a surplus of only £90m. It had been foreseen that the opening of the campaign to stimulate home demand would cause a deterioration of the balance if only because of the increase in imports brought about by expansion. In the event the increase in exports in 1963 was faster than average (more than 7 per cent), with the result that, in spite of considerably increased imports, the surplus on the current balance of payments in 1963 was almost the same as in 1962. But this was no longer true in the following year when there was a deficit of £374m., that for the trade balance alone being £553m. This was the largest deficit since the Korean crisis in 1951. The merchandise balance was made worse by an unfavourable movement in the terms of trade, the rise in prices of imports being greater than that of exports. By an unfortunate coincidence the year 1964 showed a very large development of net long-term capital exports (£200m. more than in 1963), due partly to an increase in direct investments abroad, but also to a reduction in the investments made in Britain by foreign countries.

The balance sheet for the period 1961–4 therefore was disappointing as regards the aims of rapid internal growth proceeding hand in hand with a balance of payments in equilibrium.

The possibility of an adverse balance had indeed been foreseen by NEDC when they amended some of the estimates for 1966 at the beginning of 1964. As Table IV shows, the estimate of 4 per cent for imports was raised to 4·7 per cent, and to compensate this supplementary burden on the balance of payments the figures relating to capital exports and the building up of reserves were revised downwards. But these revisions were little more than exercises in arithmetic. The balance of payments for 1964 turned out to be much more adverse than had been expected. During the two years 1963 and 1964 alone imports increased in volume by 16 per cent, whereas the figure for exports did not exceed 10 per cent. At current prices these increases are respectively 27 per cent and 16 per cent. These results depart markedly from the revised estimates for the 1961–6 model (see graph). They explain why, taking into account net long-term capital exports which were also decidedly higher than foreseen, the current balance of payments and long-term capital operations together showed a deficit of £813m. for 1964 alone.[1]

As soon as they came into power in October 1964 the Labour Government had therefore to take emergency steps to stop the drain on the reserves of gold and foreign currencies. As will be shown in the next chapter, the precarious condition of the balance of payments still weighs heavily upon the new Government's freedom of action in achieving economic growth.

[1] Assuming that the moratorium granted at the end of the year in the service of the debt arising from post-war loans from USA and Canada is counted as a financial operation.

CHAPTER VI

LABOUR AND PLANNING

By its very nature planning has to deal with the medium and long term. Therefore, since the plan worked out by the Labour Government was published in September 1965, to analyse British planning policy under Labour at the present time is really to note administrative changes and schemes for the future, even hopes, rather than to list targets already reached. This all the more as general demand restraint has been the order of the day since 1966 and has numbered among its victims the production and investment targets up to 1970 that were written into Labour's Plan.

The position of the new Government in 1964 was not without its dramatic side. Elected on a programme of economic expansion they had to face the fact that the efforts of their predecessors since 1961 to create the conditions for rapid and sustained growth had been frustrated by a large balance of payments deficit. Such a situation called for measures of deflation, not an expansionist policy. It was therefore decided to abandon the 1961–66 plan and work out another for the period 1965–70.

The novelty, from certain points of view, of the methods used and the importance which the Labour Government attaches to them will justify an examination of the present structure of the planning organizations. Then we shall pinpoint the aims which the Government set itself for 1970 and the present impediments to their realization.

1. THE MACHINERY OF THE PLAN

Labour had never concealed its view that the Conservative experiment with a 'concerted' economy lacked muscles.[1] This feeling

[1] Cf. the comment by Mr Wilson on the Conservative's plan quoted in Chapter V, p. 105.

Professor Balogh, at present personal economic adviser to the Prime Minister, sketched out in 1963 planning machinery differing widely from what NEDC had produced in 1961. According to him the working out of the plan should be entrusted, not to an organization outside the Government, like the secretariat of NEDC, but to a Minister of Planning, who would be independent of the Chancellor of the Exchequer. The reader will note that the Labour Government's first thoughts on these matters did follow Professor Balogh's ideas fairly closely. Cf. *Planning for Progress*, Fabian Society 1963.

suffices to explain why Labour brought the plan more into the orbit of the Government. The decision to entrust planning matters to a new Government department—the Department of Economic Affairs—rather than to the Treasury was to be expected in view of the Labour Party's frequent criticisms of the Treasury's handling of economic policy. The nature and extent of the power given to the Department of Economic Affairs (DEA) have naturally affected the role played by the different parts of the existing planning machinery that were described in Chapter V. However, the fact that in 1966, after the return to power of the Labour Party with a vastly increased parliamentary majority, it was thought necessary to make some adjustments in the initial planning set-up suggests that we are still in a period of experimentation.

The Department of Economic Affairs

When the creation of the Department was announced in the Economic Statement of October 26, immediately after the election, it was entrusted to Mr George Brown, No. 2 in the Labour Party hierarchy who, with his title of First Secretary of State, had precedence over all his Cabinet colleagues, including the Chancellor of the Exchequer. Mr Brown himself set the tone for the new Ministry[1]: 'Our intention is to take up the work already done by the NEDC: expand it, strengthen it, and produce, in consultation with both sides of industry through the council, a plan for the next five years.' Setting aside the fears of greatly increased State control expressed by both unions and employers, the Secretary of State added, 'although this planning will be concentrated in the Government, the planning processes must and will be co-operative'.[2]

The field of action of the Department of Economic Affairs was initially very wide, for it was responsible for the working out and execution of the National Plan, for prices and incomes policy and for regional planning.[3] But, in 1966, day-to-day responsibility for prices and incomes policy was handed over to the Board of Trade and the Ministry of Labour respectively.

The internal structure of the Ministry corresponds to these various functions. At the head, the Secretary of State is assisted by two Ministers of State, one of whom is responsible for regional development policy. During the first eighteen months the Secretary of State was assisted by a personal adviser, a specialist in industrial questions brought in from private business and who sat on the

[1] Quoted in *The Times*, November 5, 1964.

[2] Same article.

[3] These two aspects of its function are studied separately in Chapters VII and VIII.

NEDC with Mr Brown who became chairman of the council. Mr Stewart replaced Mr Brown in August 1966 at the DEA and Mr Catherwood is now the Director-General of the NEDO. The DEA has no executive responsibilities like the Board of Trade or the Ministry of Labour. Its primary role is in co-ordination. It thus lays great stress on relations with private industry and a group of industrial advisers—all drawn from the private sector—representing the DEA on the 'Little Neddies'. Co-ordination of policy as regards industry is the task of the Industrial Policy Division. For planning at the macro-economic level the Ministry includes an Economic Planning Division whose work is the main responsibility of the Director General of the Department (Sir Donald MacDougall), the former director of the economic division of the Office of NEDC. The original nucleus of the staff of the DEA was drawn mainly from NEDO economic division and from members of the medium-term study group who moved over from the Treasury, part of whose Economic Section staff dealing with short-term forecasting moved to the DEA as well. A special function of the DEA is regional planning, in particular maintaining liaison with the new regional planning machinery that is described in Chapter VIII and it took over the Board of Trade's Regional Development Division for that purpose. Finally, the DEA staff have to deal with overall policy questions relating to prices and incomes. Starting from scratch in the autumn of 1964, the present staff of the Department numbers about 500 and, unlike any other Government department, a not insignificant number of them come from the private sector.

Relations with the Planning Machinery set up before October 1964

This machinery continued to exist in part, but the creation of the Department of Economic Affairs raised problems of competence and co-ordination which have not all been solved.

As far as NEDC is concerned, the existence of the new Ministry took away its direct responsibility for the preparation of the medium-term plan.[1] According to Mr Brown it was to become something more like a forum for the discussion of plans prepared by the Department and of questions of economic policy relevant to the plan.[2] It has, for example, been given the task of considering the general development of prices and incomes policy, the study of concrete

[1] Mr Crosland, at that time Minister of State of the Department for Economic Affairs, said in November 1964 that the task of preparing detailed statistical plans for the different sectors of the economy was being withdrawn from NEDC.

[2] 'There is clearly a continuing need for an outside body on which the representatives of industry and commerce can discuss the Government's plans at various stages of their formulation, and can contribute to their formulation.' Quoted by *The Times*, November 5, 1964.

cases being reserved for the National Board for Prices and Incomes. But, as a later chapter[1] seeks to show, it is the latter that has played the most significant role in practice.

The ascendancy of the Department of Economic Affairs explains why its Minister replaced the Chancellor as chairman of the NEDC. The council now includes the Ministers of Labour and Technology and the President of the Board of Trade as well as—until the spring of 1966—the personal adviser to the Secretary of State. The number of members from the private sector remains unchanged. As before six seats are reserved for the employers and six for the TUC. The employers are now delegates from the new single employers' organization[2]—a fact which is worth noting. With the ministerial and other official representatives and the independent members the Council has 21 members (20 previously).

The secretariat of the council, once it was deprived of its economic division, consisted only of the industrial division which, after 1963, had begun to form a network of 'vertical' committees under the plan for different branches of industry.[3] But since the Department of Economic Affairs is directly represented on each of these committees which form the channel of communication between the Government and the representatives of private industry, the function of the industrial division of the industrial division of NEDC was much reduced; the same was true of the NEDC itself.

In 1964, as regards the relations between the Department of Economic Affairs and the Ministries dealing traditionally with economic issues, the outstanding question was obviously the relationship with the Treasury which had hitherto held first place among the economic departments and also in public administration as a whole. In economic affairs its field of action was, for the first time, laid down in a restrictive manner. The Chancellor of the Exchequer was to be responsible for budgetary policy, monetary policy, external payments, for the control of official expenditure and for the administration of the Civil Service. All questions concerning planning including prices and incomes policy and regional planning, were to become the province of the Department of Economic Affairs. But as public expenditure is the most powerful weapon at the disposal of the State for attaining the targets of the plan, the functions of the Treasury and of the Department of Economic Affairs are bound to overlap so long as the Chancellor of the Exchequer is responsible for the budget. In this connection it is significant that it was the Chancellor who announced in the House of Commons in February 1965,

[1] Chapter VII.
[2] Cf. Chapter IX.
[3] Cf. Chapter V.

the Government's intention to limit the growth of official expenditure between 1966 and 1970 to 4·25 per cent per annum. With regard to anti-cyclical policy, which must for a time[1] take precedence over plans for medium-term economic growth, the initiative seems still to lie with the Treasury.

In sum, the setting up of the Department of Economic Affairs constituted a major innovation, in the British system of Government departments. This being the case, it is hardly surprising that it has not yet found its real place in the regular departmental process. We are still in a period of experimentation and of adaptation in this regard.

Changes introduced in 1966

In the spring of 1966, the Labour Party was returned to power after the General Election with a considerably larger parliamentary majority. But this does not seem to have been the determining factor behind the adjustments that were made in the planning machinery following the elections. Before March 1966, there had already been signs that the experiment initiated at the end of 1964, when the DEA was set up, had shown the need for changes. These took the form of an increased emphasis given to the NEDC and of a lightening of the responsibilities of the DEA in the day-to-day carrying out of the plan.

It is difficult to pinpoint the precise moment after October 1964 when a certain dissatisfaction, notably among the industrialists on the NEDC but not confined to them, with the role of the Council began to manifest itself. Already 1964, up to the October elections in that year, had not been a very happy period for the Council after its failure to agree on basic guidelines for a prices and incomes policy. For some months after October 1964 the principal representatives of both sides of industry on the Council were very actively concerned once more in discussions with the DEA on this same issue, as is described in Chapter VII. Subsequently, however, the steam seems to have gone out of the drive to keep the Council in the centre of things. The new Director-General of the Confederation of British Industry[2] went on record as saying: 'Things began to go wrong towards the end of last year [1965].'[3] The proposed Industrial Reorganization Corporation and the investment incentive schemes —discussed later in this chapter—seem to have provided the occasion

[1] Cf. the last section of this chapter.

[2] Cf. Chapter IX.

[3] He added: 'The Government started behaving as if they thought consultation was simply a matter of telling us what they were going to do, and we just had to lump it.' *Financial Times*, April 20, 1966.

for a concerted move by the employers' representatives to put their views on the role of NEDC to the Government. About the same time it became known that the Director-General of the NEDO (Sir Robert Shone) wished to devote himself to academic life.

The appointment, in April 1966, of Mr H. F. R. Catherwood—who had been Mr Brown's chief industrial adviser at the DEA and a member of the NEDC—to succeed Sir Robert Shone is likely to have removed some of the obstacles to better communication between the Council and the DEA. It is also in keeping with the publicly expressed views of Mr Catherwood that the Council should have a real role to play in policy formation and implementation.[1] As the main driving force behind the setting up, during 1965, of a number of Economic Development Committees, Mr Catherwood's appointment should also serve to bring the Council back more closely into touch with the grass roots of industry after a period of divided control during which the main channel of communication with the Committees appears to have been the DEA rather than the NEDO.

As for the DEA itself, the experience of events during 1965 had showed that it was in danger of accumulating a probably excessive burden of administrative responsibilities, especially as regards the working of the prices and incomes machinery, to the detriment of its broader functions of conception and co-ordination. In April 1966, it was announced that, henceforth, the DEA would shed the day-to-day administration of prices and incomes policy on to the Ministry of Labour, the Board of Trade, the Ministry of Agriculture and other appropriate departments. The DEA is to continue to have a general co-ordinating function in this field.

More generally, the respective roles of the DEA and the Treasury in the planning process continue to be a subject for discussions as the apparently tidy delimitation of the Treasury's functions made in 1964 has proved to raise more complex issues than appeared at first sight. It is not only that the unrelenting urgency of demand management matters since 1964 has kept the Chancellor of the Exchequer continually in the forefront where economic policy-making is concerned. The practical application of the targets in the National Plan regarding expenditure in the public sector—targets which are, after all, the backbone of the plan—has remained the domain of the Treasury.

[1] 'The Government, the TUC and the CBI accept that a council which includes the Government cannot, as such, be "independent" of Government in its collective statements. The independent role of NEDC must be exercised by the Director-General and the Office whose public statements do not commit the Government. On the other hand, one of the functions of NEDC is to advise the Government on the economy and on industry, and the members representing both sides of industry will want to see that its advice is as influential as possible.' H. F. R. Catherwood, quoted by the *Financial Times*, April 27, 1966.

Notably the new procedures and techniques for calculating the aggregate of public sector expenditure and for allocating shares to spending departments together with precise targets for 1966–7 and forward estimates for 1969–70 were presented to Parliament in February 1966 by the Chancellor.[1] This situation gives added force to the comment by a senior Treasury official that: 'The Government's instrument in the planning of the public sector is the Treasury's control of public expenditure.'[2]

As for the implementation of the objectives of the plan in the private sector two departments—the Board of Trade and the Ministry of Labour—have, since 1961, and even more so since 1966, inherited vastly increased powers and their Ministers sit on the NEDC. Thus the Board of Trade's responsibilities are as multifarious as they are far-reaching. the operation of controls on building and the distribution of industry, the application of legislation on monopoly and restrictive practices, company law, the organization of censuses of production and distribution, the collection and publication of a vast amount of statistics, approval of grants and aids in favour of development areas. Experience in other countries—and in particular France where planning has a longer history behind it than in Britain—has shown that bringing the activities of such Government departments to bear fairly and squarely on the task of implementing the development plan is not to be achieved overnight. There seems no reason to expect that events in Britain will belie this conclusion.

2. PROSPECTS OF GROWTH, 1965–70

Published in September 1965, the Labour plan,[3] a thick volume of some 500 pages, contains many statistics relating to the growth of the economy from now to 1970; it lists the changes in emphasis which are judged necessary and the means of carrying them out. The figures used in the paragraphs that follow are those in the Plan; but, as the precise targets for the growth of output, investment, exports and imports have now had to be abandoned they now only serve to illustrate the initial trends in Labour's thinking.

The plan prints the Press communiqué issued by the National Economic Development Council at the end of its meeting on August

[1] *Public Expenditure: Planning and Control*, Cmd. 2915, HMSO 1966.

[2] Sir Richard Clarke, a Second Secretary at the Treasury, in a lecture to the Royal Institute of Public Administration, quoted by the *Financial Times*, November 30, 1965. He went on to add that: 'One's imagination must boggle at the situation which could arise if [the Treasury and the DEA] were pulling in opposite directions. . . .'

[3] *The National Plan*, Cmd. 2764, HMSO, September 1965.

5, 1965, where the Council noted that the target of 'a growth in the national product of 25 per cent between 1964 and 1970 . . . is within the nation's capacity, but given the situation likely to exist over the early years of the period it is clear that the achievement of this objective will require a major national effort'.[1] This note of caution echoes the opinion expressed by Mr Brown in the preface to the publication that the objective 'may seem an ambitious aim at a time when balance of payments considerations limit the short run possibilities for expansion'.[2] Subsequent events have borne this out.

The welcome accorded to the plan by the employers' representatives confirms the hope for 'co-operative planning'[3] between the administration and private industry. At a quinquennial conference held in 1965 by representatives of the private sector on the theme 'The Next Five Years', no criticism of planning in principle was recorded, even if the earlier enthusiasm of the previous conference in 1960—which had had a decisive influence on the adoption of planning in 1961[4]—was tempered by a more realistic attitude towards the difficulties to be surmounted. The day after the publication of the Labour plan the Confederation of British Industries acknowledged that it had the merit of making a real contribution to the working out of national economic policy.[5] Since then, as we have just seen, industrialists have voiced their criticism of some aspects of planning, notably the role of the NEDC after 1964—criticism to which the Government has not remained deaf.

But from the political point of view the 1965–70 plan shows up much keener differences of opinion between Labour and Conservatives than did the earlier plan; so that although the Government have insisted on the co-operative nature of the plan, a change of political majority would in any event have led to a revision of some aspects of Labour's plan, just as Labour revised the first Conservative plan. That this should be so is not surprising. It is to be expected—and is desirable—that a medium-term plan should express the major policy intentions in the economic field of the party in power. Although there is obviously a great deal of common ground between the intentions of the Labour and Conservative Parties in this respect—more than the public utterances of their leaders might suggest—it is a healthy development that alternative policy intentions should find their expression in the framework of the medium-term plan. It is perhaps not too far-fetched to imagine that, in this way, the worst

[1] Op. cit., p. v.
[2] Op. cit., p. iii.
[3] Op. cit., p. 3.
[4] Cf. Chapter V.
[5] *British Industry*, September 15, 1965.

influences of political demagogy on economic policy can be avoided precisely because of the intellectual effort involved in presenting alternative policies in accordance with the internal logic of the development plan.

In the event, the election campaign in the spring of 1966 showed that the principle of economic planning was not seriously questioned by any political party just as there was a general agreement about the urgent need for reform in certain definite fields,[1] if hopes for faster growth were to be confirmed.

We shall begin with a general view of the growth of the economy as foreseen by the new plan (1965–70), despite its theoretical character at present when the most important results may be expected in specific fields that are dealt with in later chapters.[2] We shall concern ourselves here only with the part to be played by Government and by the economic development committees, now in full swing, in the execution of the plan.

The Plan 1965–70

From the point of view of method, there were few important innovations in the working out of the 1965–70 plan. But the objectives were different in a number of respects from those of the first plan (1961–6) as was inevitable after the latter's partial failure.

(a) *Questions of Method.* Up to the present, at any rate, the method is the same as that utilized for the first plan and practised in other Western countries. It is 'iterative', it does not work by applying a complete economic model[3] and it uses both macro-economic analysis and the results of an Industrial Inquiry. As the last chapter dealt with these general methods adopted in constructing the first plan we shall confine ourselves here to certain selected aspects of the preparation of the new plan.

NEDC was told in February 1965 of the Government's intention to aim at a 25 per cent rate of growth of the gross national product for the six years 1965 to 1970, that is, a little less than the 4 per cent per annum that was the target in the first plan.[4] The council seems to have been informed of the Government's views without being given the supporting data about the growth of supply and demand that had

[1] Some of these will be mentioned in this chapter, but also in other chapters of this second part.

[2] Prices and incomes policy (Chapter VII), regional planning (Chapter VIII), structural modernization (Chapter IX).

[3] It is true that Professor Stone's team, that had constructed such a model at Cambridge University, were consulted in the working out of the plan. Cf. Chapter V.

[4] At compound rate.

been used to determine the choice of 25 per cent, so it could do no more than signify its approval. Indeed, in the early months of 1965, it is likely that the suggested growth target was mainly a well-informed guess of the likely future growth potential.

Subsequently the council was several times consulted, not about the plan as a whole during its preparation (it did not exist as a whole before the summer of 1965 anyway), but about particular aspects of the work, such as investment, the labour force and foreign trade. The fragmentary nature of the consultation was probably due to the shortness of the time (less than a year) allowed to the technical services of the Department of Economic Affairs for the preparation of the plan.

Consultations with private industry were also made a little more difficult owing to the pressure of time. Each Economic Development Committee received a long questionnaire in February 1965, to be returned before the end of March, about the prospects of expansion in its branch of industry, and the achievement of recent years. Where a committee did not yet exist the professional association of the branch acted as intermediary. Similar information was asked from the nationalized industries.

The purpose of the questionnaire[1] was to discover what volume of production would be reached by each branch of industry on the basis of a hypothetical growth of the gross national product of 25 per cent for the years 1965–70, sales in the home market being kept separate from exports. It was also designed to show requirements for raw materials, purchases of fuel being kept separate from other materials owing to the shortage in the United Kingdom of natural sources of energy other than coal. Other questions dealt with forecasts of requirements in manpower by professional categories and according to geographical location,[2] and also the volume of investment required by a 25 per cent growth rate of the gross national product. But it did not prove possible to supply guiding figures—as is done in France for example—to enable each branch of industry to place its own growth in relation to the overall rate of 25 per cent.

The analysis of the statistical targets of the plan is conducted systematically in 'constant prices', no examination of price movements which might be expected being attempted. Also the analysis in the National Plan of the relations between savings, investment and financial flows is only cursory, the view of the authors of the Plan being that: 'The result of the examination indicates that in 1970 the

[1] Reproduced in Annex C of the National Plan, Cmd. 2764, September 1965.

[2] The work done by the Manpower Research Unit of the Ministry of Labour (cf. Chapter V) was useful in this connection in supplying improved data concerning the labour market.

total of savings by persons and companies and of the current surplus of the public sector as a whole, implied by the assumptions made, is likely to be broadly in line with investment requirements.'[1] It may be expected that a more detailed exploration of these complex issues will figure in later versions of the plan.

(b) *The Objectives.* The experience of the years 1961–4 suggests two crucial questions before considering the objectives which were decided on. Could the rate of growth be as high as was fixed for the first plan, but which—as we have seen in the preceding chapter—could not be reached? What policies should be adopted with regard to the balance of payments, the correction of which is today the 'central challenge'[2] for Britain?

In proposing a rate of growth of the gross national product of 25 per cent in six years, or 3·8 per cent per annum,[3] the Labour Government had slightly lowered the targets as compared with the 4 per cent of the first plan (1961–6). Nevertheless, when the very substantial decrease in the estimates of the growth of available manpower from now to 1970 is taken into account, the new growth target was even more ambitious than the first plan as regards the rise in productivity. The figures in Table I illustrate this.

TABLE I

GROWTH IN OUTPUT, OUTPUT PER HEAD AND MANPOWER (ANNUAL PERCENTAGES)

	1961–6 Targets of first plan	*1960–4 Rate actually achieved*	*1965–70 Targets o second plan*	
Gross domestic product	4·0	3·4		3·8
Output per head	3·2	2·7	(3·55)[a]	3·4
Manpower	0·8	0·7	(0·25)[a]	0·4

[a] The figures in brackets take no account of an increase in available manpower due to energetic regional planning.

Source: The National Plan.

The marked change which is expected in the curve of growth of available manpower would not have made it easier to attain the objectives fixed for the gross national product. Instead of the annual increase of 0·8 per cent envisaged by the first plan (0·7 per cent in fact between 1960 and 1964), more recent estimates give a figure of only 0·25 per cent. If this figure proved to be correct in practice, it would probably be illusory to expect a 3·8 per cent per annum increase in the gross national product, for in that case there would have to be an

[1] *The National Plan*, p. 163.
[2] Ibid., p. 1.
[3] At compound rate.

average growth in output per head of 3·55 per cent during the period 1964–70. Although the medium-term tendency of output per head is rising—and this is one of the most encouraging observations currently to be made for the British economy—the authors of the new plan calculated the present rate of increase at only about 3 per cent, a figure much below the 3·55 per cent in question. But the plan is counting on the effect of regional planning policy[1] to bring work to some 200,000 extra workers who would otherwise be unemployed. This supplementary manpower would make it possible to foresee a total availability of manpower increased by 0·4 per cent per annum from now to 1970 and thus to reduce the required increase in output per head to 3·4 per cent. Despite this statistical juggling this last figure, even if it is taken as an average over the period 1964–70, still implied an improbably large improvement in productivity.

These forecasts explain why the plan insists so strongly on measures both to improve productivity in industry, and to increase mobility and skill in the labour force.[2] They provide also, in part, the *raison d'être* of the 'selective employment tax' introduced in the May Budget in 1966. Levied at three rates,[3] the tax treatment of employers varies according to whether they are in one or the other of the following groups: (a) distribution, service industries, extractive industries (the National Coal Board is in group (c)) or construction, (b) manufacturing industries, (c) central and local government, nationalized industries, transport undertakings and agriculture. Employers in group (b) receive refunds of the tax plus a premium equal to about 30 per cent of the tax. Those in group (c) are compensated directly by the Government, for example in the case of agriculture in the annual price review. In presenting the new tax to Parliament, the Chancellor of the Exchequer referred to the rapid growth in employment in the service trades, distribution and construction (over 1,000,000 between 1960 and 1965) compared with that in manufacturing (142,000). In the Government's view, the fact that the service trades, until then, bore little indirect taxes tended to accentuate the already powerful trend for consumers to spend a rising share of their incomes in these sectors. By changing price relationships, the changes in consumer demand should produce induced modifications in the demand for labour. This result is only achieved to the extent that the tax is passed on to consumers, in which case it conflicts with the aim of price stability. Conversely, to the extent that the tax is not passed on, it provides an incentive to employers to economize labour. Though it

[1] Described in Chapter VIII.

[2] Cf. Chapter IX.

[3] 25s a week for adult male workers, 12s 6d for women and boys, and 8s for girls; the tax is paid at the same time as National Insurance contributions.

may not be easy for any notable transfer of manpower from taxed sectors to those that are tax-free to take place, it may be that the future growth of demand for labour in the former will be inhibited.

The selective employment tax provides a substantial new source of revenue to the Exchequer, of some £240 million in the fiscal year (1966–7). It also carries the British fiscal system further in the direction of a bias in favour of indirect taxes. The wider implications of the new tax were drawn by the Prime Minister when he noted that it was a first step 'to concentrate our taxation less on industrial profits and more on industrial costs'.[1] The Prime Minister added that the possibility of introducing a tax on value added (TVA) was to be studied again. This idea had been rejected in 1964. Its adoption would have the advantages of broadening the tax base, of making possible rebates for exports, and of bringing British taxes closer to that of the Common Market countries.

The prospect of a shortage of manpower in the medium-term does not however prevent a reduction of tensions on the labour market at the present time. The rise in unemployment since the summer of 1966 may, as is hoped, shake out labour from less productive uses. It is more important in marking a drastic revision of thinking on the appropriate level of unemployment if 'overheating' is to be avoided.[2]

The balance of payments is the second direction in which the future of the British economy is mortgaged. One of the principal architects of the plan expressed the view that the success or failure of the plan would depend upon the success or failure of the strategy chosen to obtain expansion of production and at the same time a consolidation of the balance of payments position.[3] This view is confirmed by the forecasts for the balance of payments in 1970, as shown in Table II.

It is evident that the improvement assigned to the balance of payments is very considerable—nearly £1,000m. sterling. About half this sum was expected to come from a reduction in the deficit on the commercial balance. £300m. are reckoned to come from a reversal in the movements of private long-term capital; Britain would thus exchange her traditional role of net exporter of private capital for that of a net importer. More than £100m. are to come from an increase in net invisible receipts. Certain economies are expected in the mass of

[1] Speech to a Press Gallery luncheon at the House of Commons, reported in the *Financial Times*, May 12, 1966.

[2] Cf. Chapter II, p. 56.

[3] Cf. H. F. R. Catherwood, in the *Review* of the Confederation of British Industry, June 25, 1965.

TABLE II

BALANCE OF PAYMENTS, 1964 TO 1970 (£M. AT 1964 PRICES)

	1964	*1970*
Balance of visible trade	−534	− 45[b]
Government expenditure (current invisibles and capital) net	−555	−510
Other invisibles, net	+561	+680
Private long-term capital, net	−228	+ 75
Balancing item[a]	+ 35	+ 50
Total	−721[c]	+250

[a] Cf. Chapter III.

[b] Allowing for 3 per cent improvement in the terms of trade.

[c] There was a waiver on the North American loans in 1964 (cf. the last section of this chapter).

Source: The National Plan, p. 83.

official expenditure abroad. If all these projections proved correct, the United Kingdom would be in a position to show a surplus of £250m. in its balance of payments in 1970, this sum being required for the repayment of debts incurred abroad.[1]

The rate of increase laid down for imports (4 per cent) is the same as for 1960–4 in spite of the more rapid growth forecast for the gross national product (cf. Table I).[2] A slowing down of purchases of manufactured and semi-manufactured goods is still expected as in the first plan. A more vigorous development of British agriculture is contemplated to encourage the replacement of some growing imports of foodstuffs. Finally, there is expected to be some reduction in the growth of imports of fuels which have been exceptionally heavy in recent years. The plan does not attempt to minimize the effort which will be required in order to obtain these import targets.

As regards exports, the objective (5·2 per cent) remains as high as that set in the first plan (5·1 per cent) which, as we have already seen, was far from being attained (3·1 per cent).[3] It is true that replies from manufacturers giving their export forecasts were fairly optimistic and anticipated a good deal more rapid growth than in the past. But apart from the fact that similar replies had been given to the same question in 1962, the conditions of world trade, even though they remain basically favourable, are not such that the new British objective can be achieved without a radical change in present export trends. On the other hand the plan contains no hypotheses about

[1] Cf. the last section of this chapter.

[2] When adjustments have been made to counteract the influence of an exceptionally high level of imports in 1964, the target is somewhat higher ($0·5 per cent to 5 per cent).

[3] Cf. Chapter V.

possible modifications resulting from a move by the industrial countries of the West towards freer trade, or changes brought about by Britain's joining some enlarged European economic community. Given all these elements of uncertainty, the objectives of the British plan may well need considerable revision. For the most part, hopes of a more rapid rise of British exports are based, on the one hand, on an improvement in their competitive level brought about, in particular by a more successful stabilization of prices than in other industrial countries and, on the other, by improved exporting techniques, more rapid technological change and the improved export credit facilities that were introduced in 1966.

TABLE III

FOREIGN TRADE, 1961 TO 1970 (ANNUAL PERCENTAGE INCREASES IN VOLUME)

	1961–6 Targets of first plan	*1960–4 Actual achievement*	*1965–70 Targets of second plan*
Exports	5·1	3·1	5·2
Imports	4·7	4·0	(4·5–5·0) 4·0[a]

[a] Rate adjusted to eliminate the effect of an exceptionally high level of imports in 1964.

Source: Table I of Chapter V and *The National Plan*, Chapter VII.

Even without these uncertainties surrounding the future of exports it would be vain to expect from merchandise trade alone a large enough contribution to put the balance of payments back into equilibrium; hence the importance of the expected modifications in private investment, in invisible and in Government expenditure. The reduction in private investment is expected to come essentially from the strengthening of exchange control and the new tax arrangements for companies.[1] Such a change of policy for Britain, traditionally a net export of private capital, has far reaching effects.[2] Considerable savings are still expected in military expenditure abroad, and the plan quotes the Prime Minister's statement that the Government 'are determined to achieve a saving of £50m. to £100m. in overseas military expenditure'.[3] The plan also makes it clear that it will not be possible in the short run to make any increase in British aid to developing countries.

After this discussion of the two fundamental aspects of the

[1] Cf. the last section of this chapter.

[2] The figures in Table II give perhaps an exaggerated idea of the hoped-for change. In 1964 the net long-term exports of private capital were abnormally high; the average figure over the last ten years was £85m. per annum.

[3] Op. cit., p. 75.

National Plan, productivity and external payments, let us consider the objectives for the internal use of available resources from now until 1970 (Table IV).

TABLE IV

USE OF RESOURCES, 1964 TO 1970

	£m. at 1965 prices		*Percentage annual increases*	
	1964	*1970*	*1960–4 Rate achieved*	*1965–70 targets*
Gross domestic product	32,847	41,060	3·4	3·8
Current balance of payments[a]	226	275	—	—
Consumption expenditure	21,334	25,790	3·1	3·2
National Defence	1,930	2,045	1·2	1·0
Other current official expenditure	3,481	4,405	3·0	4·0
Gross fixed capital formation	5,802	8,018	6·6	5·5
Stockbuilding	526	530	—	—

[a] Less net transfers abroad £186m. in 1964.
Source: The National Plan and *Economic Trends.*

The very considerable improvement in the balance of payments position which is called for will of course for the time being restrict increases in expenditure at home.[1] On the average over the whole period 1965–70 private consumption can increase at the outside by 3·2 per cent per annum, that is much less rapidly than the gross national product (3·8 per cent); moreover, 'the rate of increase is likely to be slower than this in the early years of the period',[2] a slowing down which was expected to be made up later on. The events of the summer of 1966 now make this catching up impossible.[3]

Public expenditure,[4] which does not include the investment programmes of the nationalized industries, will grow more rapidly than the gross national product (4·25 per cent per annum on the average). The Government intend to stabilize military expenditure at approximately its present level. This decision makes it possible to increase other categories of expenditure. The plan includes programmes for the social services and the health services, education and housing (with emphasis on house building by industrialized methods).[5] Since comparisons with the past are not possible owing to the lack of statistical data, it is not easy to decide how far the new programmes

[1] *The National Plan*, p. 163.
[2] *The National Plan*, p. 164.
[3] See the concluding section of this chapter.
[4] Including that of local authorities.
[5] But the estimated increase in housing building will be slower than between 1960 and 1964.

show a change of emphasis as compared with the quite ambitious plans advanced by the previous Government.

The future will to a considerable extent to determined by the development of productive investment, in view of the effort required to improve the infra-structure and the efficiency of industry. In the nationalized sector of electricity and in the distributive trades, as in other services, investment expenditure is expected to rise more slowly than in the past. On the other hand there is likely to be much increased investment in manufacturing industry and in transport and communications. Manufacturing industry, all of it in private hands, is at the heart of the problem which the plan sets out to solve. The authors of the plan were aware that economic trends in Britain since 1964 were not too favourable to private productive investment but they counted on the stimulus provided by the publication of the plan and on the economic development committees to keep up the optimism of the private sector.[1]

The plan also said the Government were 'currently examining the whole question of fiscal incentives for investment'.[2] The new investment allowance procedures introduced in 1966 are designed to implement this policy.

The system of investment allowances was described in Chapter II where the criticisms of its use during the 1950s as a demand management weapon were noted. From 1966 onwards these allowances have been abolished and replaced by a new system of cash grants. These grants are paid by the Exchequer to firms at a rate of 20 per cent of the cost of new plant and machinery for use in manufacturing and extractive industries.[3] It is estimated that this system will cost approximately the same as the old one would have done under the corporation tax régime.

It is likely that in deciding to replace an allowance deductible from profits for tax purposes by payment by the Exchequer of a cash grant, the Government were influenced by a number of findings showing that industrialists tended not to allow fully, in their calculations of rates of return, an investment expenditure for the effect of investment allowances.[4] But the fact that the new corporation tax, also introduced in 1966, would have reduced the fiscal advantage of the investment allowances anyway has attracted some criticism from in-

[1] *The National Plan*, p. 9, and the last section of this chapter.

[2] Op. cit., p. 9 and p. 64.

[3] *Investment Incentives*, Cmd. 2874, HMSO, 1966. Thus the service and construction industries are excluded from the scope of the grants scheme whereas they are to pay the new selective employment tax.

[4] See, for example, *Investment Appraisal*; National Economic Development Council, HMSO, 1965.

dustry that, according to its own inquiry among businessmen, would have preferred a free depreciation scheme. The new scheme may not provide a marked overall stimulus to private investment in manufacturing and the extractive industries though it should be noted that, in principle, the grants will be received more promptly by firms than the tax credits under the investment allowances. Its impact on the level of investment in the development areas will no doubt be greater as the rate at which grants will be paid to firms in those areas is double the standard rate, 40 per cent.[1]

The Public Sector in the Execution of the Plan

The Labour 'philosophy' is set out in the opening pages of the National Plan. Here it is stated that the very extent of public spending in the economy gives it a decisive influence on events; that being so, the Government 'intend to use this influence to secure faster growth and national solvency'.[2] The spontaneous working of the private sector is not necessarily in the national interest, for example with regard to the export drive, increased productivity and investment. Since 'both Government and industry have to plan several years ahead, it is desirable to co-ordinate the forward estimates of both' to their mutual advantage. Although many projections are liable to a wide margin of error, they should help firms and industry 'to take more informed decisions than if they were left in the dark about other people's intentions and beliefs' in view of the much greater knowledge which would be at their disposal. Projections are also useful as a method of checking: 'if an industry falls below projection it will be valuable to discover why'. The reason may be just a miscalculation calling for no intervention by the State; but it may also be 'a useful warning signal for action by industry, by Government, or by both in co-operation'.[3]

Government action may take several forms. We have already seen that, in regard to the balance of payments, taxation of exports of private capital and the replanning of official expenditure abroad are expected to account for nearly half the improvement from now to 1970. Apart from this, short-term demand management policy has played a major part since 1964 in re-establishing external equilibrium and will continue to do so in future if the lessons of experience with 'go' as well as 'stop' policies in the 1950s, which were described in Chapter II, are taken to heart.

Official expenditure is to be tailored so as 'to strike a reasonable balance between the essential but non-productive needs of defence and support of external policy, the provision of services such as

[1] Cf. Chapter IX. [2] Op. cit., p. 2. [3] Op. cit., p. 3.

roads and ports, support for industry and advanced technology and the improvement of regional balance, and the extensive and growing network of social services'.[1] The programmes of public spending must nevertheless be kept flexible and in step with economic progress as it actually develops in future years. With this in mind, annual revisions of official expenditure are to be carried out.[2] These points raise a number of crucial issues for the implementation of the plan and thus merit some detailed consideration.

The projections of public expenditure worked out by the Conservatives for the period ended 1967–8 were thought by the new Government to be unbalanced and out of step with the priorities required by the economic and social objectives. 'The Government next examined the prospects for public expenditure and receipts of all kinds. They found here a lack of balance and absence of proper social and economic priorities; nor did they find sufficient faith in the possibility of long-term economic growth or adequate recognition of all that it involves.'[3] Since the investment targets of a 'social' nature from now to 1970 were fixed in the new plan, restrictions have been imposed on local authority expenditure as part of the deflationary measures taken since 1965. This type of conjunctural measures which, it will be recalled, had attracted heavy criticism during the 1950s when it was used to dampen home demand, finds its justification no doubt in the gravity of the balance of payments situation and in the continued buoyancy of the economy during 1965 despite the restrictive measures taken earlier (and which are described in the concluding section of this chapter). Consequently, despite the good intentions just noted, there is at present no medium-term perspective for public expenditure. A major task in 1967 will be to set fresh goals in the framework of new procedures for the control of public expenditure to which we now turn.

Already in 1965 the Government had announced its intention to limit the growth of public expenditure to 4¼ per cent a year, a target that was included in the National Plan published in September.[4] The details of this decision had then to be filled in by defining the pro-

[1] Op. cit., p. 177.

[2] Op. cit., p. 177.

[3] 'The Economic Situation.' A Statement by HM Government, October 26, 1964, paragraph 9.

[4] *The National Plan*, p. 176. Public expenditure is defined for this purpose as: 'the sum of central and local government capital and current expenditure, with the exception of debt interest, and includes the gross outgoings of the national insurance funds and the investment of new town corporations'. The capital investment programmes of the nationalized industries, and Exchequer advances to those industries, are excluded.

cedures by which it was to be implemented. This was done in February 1966 in an important White Paper on Public Expenditure—planning and control.[1] The recommendation of the Plowden Committee in 1961[2] in favour of five-year 'forward looks' in respect of public expenditure led to the publication in 1963 for the first time of such estimates.[3] A new stage has now been reached where, on the one hand, the overall target rate of increase in public expenditure over the next five years is made part of the allocation of total resources available to the economy as it results from the medium-term plan and, on the other, precise techniques are being evolved for ensuring that the allocation of public expenditure to specific purposes is consistent with the overall target and corresponds to an efficient use of resources. This approach to the control of public expenditure, compared with practice during the 1950s, represents a revolution. Yet, in the context of modern economic policy-making, it appears rather as an indispensable minimum, the only real cause for surprise being that it did not happen earlier.

The idea of having a medium-term target for the growth of public expenditure such as 4¼ per cent a year is, in any case, a useful one in the context of the procedures just described although 4¼ per cent is too high in present circumstances. It has at least the merit of introducing a barrier to the growth of public expenditure that, otherwise, as the experience of the 1960s has shown, runs a serious risk of getting out of hand, thus making emergency, *ad-hoc* cuts inevitable.[4] Such a ceiling also implies that the need for choice emerges more clearly; if more expenditure is decided in one direction it has to be compensated by economies elsewhere.

The Government intend, henceforth, to elaborate the estimates for public expenditure for the coming year in the framework of a new five-year 'forward look'. In the words of the White Paper: 'The survey of public sector expenditure is an annual one, and the 1966 operation will decide what aggregate increase over the level established for 1969–70 will be practicable for 1970–1, and how this is to be

[1] Cmd. 2915, HMSO, 1966.

[2] *Control of Public Expenditure*, Cmd. 1432, 1961.

[3] *Public Expenditure in 1963–4 and 1967–8*, Cmd. 2235, 1963.

[4] Many observers have not been slow to point out that this target implies that GNP is itself growing at the rate fixed by the National Plan, which is far from being the case at present. Also, the practice of estimating public expenditure in volume—as, indeed, all the targets in the National Plan—raises problems notably as it tends to underestimate the growth of public expenditure compared with other types of expenditure due to the heavy share of wages and salaries in the former. Eventually, no doubt, it will become necessary to make estimates in current prices as well as in volume as is done in the French development plan, for example.

allocated between the main programmes. This is how part of the National Plan will roll forward another year, with guidelines for the development of the main services for a further year ahead. At the other end of the time scale, decisions will be taken on the limits for 1967–8, which will again be the basis for the work on the Estimates in the autumn of 1966.'

Departmental programmes were divided between 'basic' programmes for the development of individual services already in train and 'additional' programmes for improvements if extra resources became available. They were examined by an inter-ministerial group —chaired by the Chancellor of the Exchequer—and 'in the light of this examination, the group recommended the adoption of specified limits for each of the main programmes of expenditure both for 1966–7 and for 1969–70'.

The nationalized industries—whose activities are related mainly to the general growth of the economy and for whom a fixed ceiling for expenditure is not deemed appropriate—are excluded from the procedures just described. It may be expected, however, that the need for a more systematic approach to the surveillance of plan implementation in this important sector of the economy will make itself felt before long. The White Paper contents itself, for the time being, with recalling the need for an improved return on capital in a number of nationalized industries. In these industries, and in the public sector generally, it is clear that attempts to control by new methods the allocation of public expenditure will call, in future years, for a deployment of the new cost-benefit techniques that are now becoming available—and are already in use abroad, notably in the United States.

Side by side with the influence exerted by the public sector upon the private sector, the improvement in efficiency of nationalized undertakings is an urgent problem for Britain. Here Labour have inherited from their predecessors schemes which are already in force, though they have ideas of their own on the subject.

It will be sufficient at this point to mention the plan to renationalize the iron and steel industry. This industry was nationalized by the Labour Government in 1945 and denationalized in 1952 by the Conservatives. Its renationalization always forms part of any Labour Party programme. Though no Bill to carry it through appeared during Labour's first term of office after October 1964, it figured in the legislative programme in the spring of 1966 and the Bill was presented in the summer. Such a Bill will have little immediate effect on the steel industry. But, even in the absence of legislation, the authorities are by no means deprived of control over the plans of the steel firms for, when the industry was denationalized in 1952, an Iron and

Steel Board was set up whose function is to review prices and to prepare quinquennial development plans.

Transport, including the docks, lends itself more readily than iron and steel to the study of problems of administration and efficiency, because the reforms which need to be carried out run less risk of being politically coloured. Indeed it was the Conservatives who took the revolutionary step in 1952 of calling in a businessman, Dr Beeching, to become head of British Railways, with the task of taking in hand the critical financial situation and carrying through essential modernization. Dr Beeching put forward a two-fold proposal: to recast the railway system by closing unprofitable lines with no hope of improvement; to modernize the remaining lines and launch a plan to regain at least some part of the business lost to road transport since the war. By 1964 already, the putting into effect of the proposals had brought about a marked improvement in the financial position. Travellers on British Railways in recent years could not fail to be struck by the efforts being made to improve services. Diesel engines are now in general use, comfort and service are definitely better, there are 'business trains' running to a carefully contrived time-table, and many stations have been modernized. Now, despite the suspicions of the railwaymen, the Labour Government have agreed to the launching of 'liner trains' to give a much improved goods service, as suggested by Dr Beeching in 1964.

Before the election there had been proposals for recasting the Beeching plan and incorporating it in a plan of much greater scope covering road transport as well as the railways. For the Labour critics the Beeching proposals suffered from the disadvantage of being too limited in conception, and so in 1965 the Minister of Transport nominated a personal adviser[1] to co-ordinate a communications policy. It is doubtful, however, whether his powers are sufficient to carry this task through successfully. The guidelines to Labour's transport policy were set out in a White Paper published in July 1966, a document that gives only a few concrete details of how policy will be applied. The Beeching plan of rail closures is to be brought to a halt and the rail net-work will be 'stabilised' at a higher mileage figure. The consequent need for State subsidies to the railways is recognized and it is proposed to hive off in the accounts the cost of such 'social 'expenditure. A National Freight Authority is to come into being to take over the general merchandise and sundries traffic of British Railways and the Transport Holding Company. The present licensing system for private road hauliers is to be reviewed and it is likely that this review will have implications for the

[1] Lord Hinton, formerly at the head of the nationalized Central Electricity Generating Board.

size of the private sector in transport. Part of the solution here will depend upon the Government's success in persuading the railway unions to allow a development of the 'liner trains' first mooted by Dr Beeching. The White Paper also notes the Government's intention to set up 'conurbation transport authorities' in major towns to review the policy of London Transport and to proceed to nationalize the docks.[1]

In the dock world the year 1965 seems likely to have marked the beginning of a programme of modernization which had been on the stocks for a long time. In July 1965, the National Ports Council, created in 1964 by the previous Government to advise the authorities about the re-development and modernization of the docks, issued an interim report.[2] It recommends that expenditure on the improvement of ports should be doubled (the present figure is £20m. per annum) over the next five to seven years. The authors of the report make no attempt to minimize the gravity of the present situation, especially as the United Kingdom must, as we have seen, step up its export drive. The report concludes with the statement that the interim plan thus proposed 'carries no danger of excessive provision of facilities. The arrears are so large and the present physical fabric of the docks so unsatisfactory that the proposals do not constitute a threat of over-investment'.[3] In the summer of 1966, perhaps in view of the magnitude of this task, the nationalization of the docks was announced.

A feature of the Labour Party's economic policy *vis-à-vis* the private sector is, as was to be expected, a willingness to use State action in a deliberately selective manner so as to achieve particular objectives. We have already seen examples of this as regards the employment tax and the new investment grants. A potentially more far-reaching project in this connection is the setting-up of an Industrial Reorganization Corporation in 1966.[4] But before discussing this project two, more traditional, forms of intervention concerning the aircraft industry and shipbuilding should be noted.

A committee was set up in 1964 under the chairmanship of Lord Plowden 'to consider what should be the future place and organization of the aircraft industry in relation to the general economy of the country'. It reported in February 1966. The Committee took the view that: 'The business of aircraft requires a partnership between Government and industry.'[5] The heavy demands of the Government

[1] Transport Policy, Cmd. 3037, July 1966.

[2] National Ports Council. *Interim Report for Port Development*, HMSO, 1964, 2 Vols.

[3] Cf. also Chapter IX for the modernization of labour relations in the docks.

[4] Industrial Reorganization Corporation, Cmd. 2889, HMSO, 1966.

[5] Committee of Inquiry into the Aircraft Industry, Cmd. 2853, HMSO, 1966.

for military purposes were, in themselves, a sufficient motive for this, to which must be added the fact that the major clients for civil aircraft—the BOAC and BEA—are both publicly-owned corporations. To secure this, the Committee, in a majority view, recommended that the Government should acquire over half the equity capital of the British Aircraft Corporation and of the airframe elements of Hawker Siddeley. The Government's reactions to these recommendations should be seen against the background of the Labour Party's view that 'the aircraft industry was absorbing a disproportionate share of the country's resources'.[1] The view of the Plowden Committee that collaboration should be extended with Continental aircraft manufacturers was endorsed by the Government.[2] The partnership between the State and the private firms will be achieved by merging the BAC and Hawker Siddeley with a minority Government equity holding.

In a report by the Shipbuilding Inquiry Committee (the Geddes Committee) in March 1966[3] a recommendation for a far-reaching concentration of firms into larger units was made. Noting that there are sixty-two shipyards in the United Kingdom and nearly as many separate firms, the Committee considered that a rationalization of production could be achieved by concentrating the big firms in groups of four or five yards leaving some smaller, but geographically dispersed yards, to more specialized work. The Government should provide financial and other incentives to bring this concentration about. Discussions are now proceeding between the Government and the industry—as for the aircraft industry—on ways of implementing the report. Action along the lines of the Geddes Committee recommendations should be seen in a different light, it seems, from the decision by the Government, in January 1966, to go into partnership with private investors to keep the Fairfield shipyard on the Clyde in operation.

The decision to set up the Industrial Reorganization Corporation implies a new approach to the use of Government finance to help private industries in so far as the intention is not, as in the past, to help lame-duck industries to survive, or to reorganize, but rather to assist firms with a future to undertake the needed reorganization implied by technical progress and foreign competition. The Corporation was set up in May 1966 with a capital of £150m. It will be

[1] The Aviation Minister (Mr F. Mulley) in the House of Commons debate on February 1. *Hansard*, Col. 891. It will be recalled that, in 1964, as an emergency demand measure, the Government had cancelled work on the TSR-2 supersonic fighter.

[2] It will be recalled that the Government's initial intention to withdraw from the joint Anglo-French supersonic airliner scheme (the Concorde) was not carried out.

[3] Shipbuilding Inquiry Committee, 1965–6, Report, Cmd. 2937, HMSO, 1966.

able to provide capital for important new projects in the private sector, to facilitate new groupings and to make loans, or to take up equity holdings for these purposes. It is noteworthy that there are no Government representatives on the board of the Corporation, no doubt as an earnest of the Government's intention to let it run on commercial lines and not to represent 'nationalization by the back-door'.[1] The intention behind the setting-up of the Corporation is to favour concentration rather than diversification of industry which is considered to lead too frequently to unproductive units.

The Economic Development Committees: The 'Little Neddies'[2]

The increased activity of these committees since October 1964—they had got off to a slow start during the first two years of NEDC's existence as was noted in Chapter V—is one of the characteristics of Labour planning. By an irony of fate, it is the 'Little Neddies' which seem to have taken first place since 1964, rather than NEDC that has not yet found its place in the new planning arrangements, as was noted earlier in this chapter.[3]

Their contribution to the working out of the National Plan has already been described. What is original about the Labour experiment is the attempt to make them the instruments for the active prosecution of plans in particular industries. As the plan says, 'In many industries specific opportunities for greater efficiency and faster growth can be exploited on a basis of mutual agreement by those concerned. It is the function of the Economic Development Committees to identify these opportunities and to prescribe the measures that can be taken—within or outside their industries—in order to make the most of them.'[4] It is too soon to say whether these hopes will bear fruit, but the importance given to these committees in the British plan deserves to be stressed.

The present agenda of the committees includes methods of achieving greater efficiency, the possibility of substituting home manufacture

[1] Mr H. R. F. Catherwood to the Scottish Branch of the Confederation of British Industry, *Financial Times*, February 1, 1966.

[2] Diminutive of the name 'Neddy' (i.e. donkey) given to the big brother of these committees (NEDC). In August 1964, there were nine of them in operation; a year later there were fourteen and twenty by the beginning of 1966. By then two-thirds of firms in the private sector were covered by them.

[3] The following is the list of the twenty Economic Development Committees at work in 1966: Machine Tool; Chemical; Electronics; Chocolate and Sugar Confectioning; Paper and Board; Mechanical Engineering; Wool Textile; Electrical Engineering; Distributive Trades; Building; Civil Engineering; Movement of Exports; Food Processing; Rubber; Post Office; Hotels and Catering; Newspapers, Printing and Publishing; Clothing; Hosiery; Agriculture.

[4] *The National Plan*, p. 45.

for imports, greater standardization of production, and means of stimulating exports. In some cases the committees are studying questions of structural reform and rationalization of production. They have the advantage of outside help through the professional associations and by recruiting management experts. Programmes of work which require the co-operation of two or more committees exist in certain branches, as for example between electronics and machine tools, or between the manufacturers of equipment and their principal customers. There is a special committee to speed up the transport of export goods to the ports and abroad. This agenda thus prolongs the one drawn up for the committees before October 1964 and which was noted in the previous chapter.

In general, priority is given to the study of plans which will help improve the commercial balance. An example of this is the stepping up of national productive capacity so as to reduce the need for foreign manufactures; for example in the chemical industry it may be possible to save some £30m.[1]

Since the summer of 1965 the EDC for the Mechanical Engineering Industry has prepared a study that shows the United Kingdom to be too frequently an importer of modern, sophisticated types of equipment whilst exporting more traditional types. A study of imports of industrial electrical equipment has been carried out by the Electrical Engineering EDC. Action is being taken by firms and the Government to implement the recommendations of a report by the Civil Engineering EDC designed to raise productivity in road construction. An agreement between the Electricity Board and the cable-making firms to standardize purchases also results from the work of the EDC's.

The committees deal with a particular sector but the one for the movement of exports and, to some extent, the one for the distributive trades deal with more general issues. One nationalized industry only—the Post Office—is included. For the time being, there is no committee for the energy sector (coal, oil and electricity) or transport where the public sector is predominant.

When, eventually, the Government begins to prepare a new five-year Plan, it may be expected that the EDC's will play a more active role than was possible when the first draft of the Plan was being drawn up. As a general principle, it seems that, so far, the

[1] The pamphlet published in September 1965 by the National Economic Development Office on the competitiveness of the British economy gives some interesting information on all these problems. One point of special interest is that, although prices are often a decisive factor in the level of imports of manufactured goods, technical progress in the widest sense can be equally important. Cf. *An Inquiry into Competitiveness*, NEDO, September 1965.

committees have all been kept very active and have met regularly. A problem for the future will be to maintain this original enthusiasm and to persuade businessmen and trade unionists to go on devoting so much time to this absorbing task.

Productivity has become the leitmotif of declarations on economic policy in recent years. In addition to the work of individual EDC's in this field a Government-sponsored National Productivity Conference was held in October 1966. Its recommendations were hardly revolutionary and have yet to be followed by acts. But they indicate a trend of thinking. Among the recommendations of the Conference were: more exchanges of information between firms on productivity; more activity by the British Productivity Council; a joint reappraisal by both sides of industry of working methods; Ministry of Labour co-operation with the NEDC to devise schemes for rapid redeployment of labour; further study of wage bargaining schemes at plant level. Many business leaders urged the Government to take quick action to support the level of productive investment in industry during the 'squeeze'.

3. THE ECONOMIC SITUATION SINCE OCTOBER 1964

The balance of payments crisis which began in 1964 has not yet been successfully weathered. After October 1964 a large volume of foreign indebtedness was incurred to support the pound and to avoid a new 'stop' to growth. Despite this, harsh deflationary measures became inevitable in 1966.

This section will first study the sterling crisis in 1964–6, and then offer some provisional conclusions about possible consequences of recent stabilization policy.

The 1964–6 Crisis

A statement by the Labour Government,[1] issued a few days after the formation of the new Cabinet, announced the size of the balance of payments deficit almost certainly to be expected for 1964 as a whole. Estimated at about £800 million, this was the largest deficit since the end of the period of reconstruction after the Second World War. The Government stated further that the deficit could not be made good satisfactorily by any return to the much discussed 'stop-go' policy.[2] The corrective measures must therefore act directly upon the balance of payments. Unfortunately this innovation in stabilization policy did not succeed in reducing the external deficit fast enough and it became necessary to take other emergency measures of tradi-

[1] 'The Economic Situation.' A Statement by Her Majesty's Government.
[2] Op. cit., paragraph 7.

tional type under the threat of speculative movements which, otherwise, could have forced devaluation of the pound.

In October 1964, a special temporary levy of 15 per cent was imposed on imports of manufactured goods—nearly one-third of all imports—from all countries including those of the Commonwealth. This measure was a major innovation in demand management. But the objections which were raised, and most vigorously by the countries in EFTA (the European Free Trade Association) of which Britain is the most active member, showed that this approach was not without its drawbacks too. In part as a result of this, it was announced in February 1965 that the levy would be reduced by one-third at the end of April. This reduction in the rate of the duty must have weakened its effects on imports. Moreover, its main impact must be expected to have been felt through a running-down of imports of goods subject to the levy. In May 1966, it was announced that the levy would finally be abolished in November 1966. This long advance warning seems to have brought about a temporary reduction in imports similar to the one that occurred early in 1965. Altogether, then, the temporary levy on imports will have only succeeded in gaining time for other measures to take effect.

In October 1964, also, a system of export bonuses was introduced in the form of a reduction in some of the indirect taxes which exported goods carry. On average the bonus worked out at about 1·5 per cent of the value of the exports. Although it was raised marginally at the end of 1966, it remains slight and has not had much effect on the competitiveness of British exports.

A balance of payments deficit, considered in relation to the supply and demand of goods and services, clearly forms an addition to national production, and from this point of view its effect is deflationary. The elimination of the deficit has the contrary effect: goods and services are withdrawn from internal use. The logic of a policy of taxing imports and subsidizing exports, if demand is not to be excessive, calls for a reduction of home consumption by an amount at least equivalent to the estimated improvement in the current balance. This requirement was understood by the Labour Government and explains why in November 1964 it was decided to increase the petrol tax, the total additional receipts having been calculated in relation to the estimated improvement in the external balance.[1]

[1] Paradoxically enough, these restrictive measures were accompanied in the autumn of 1964, by a body of social legislation due to come into force in the spring of 1965, the effect of which on total demand was expansionist: increase in national insurance payments, abolition of national health prescription charges. This additional expenditure was only partially compensated in 1965 by an increase in income tax and by raising national insurance contributions.

Shortly afterwards, however, other forms of restraint of the traditional kind used in the past to cope with periods of crisis were introduced.

On November 20, 1964, there began a strong selling pressure on the pound. In spite of the support of the Bank of England, on both the spot and forward markets, an increase in Bank rate became necessary in order to demonstrate the determination of the British authorities to tackle the balance of payments deficit, and on November 23 the rate was raised to 7 per cent as in the earlier crisis in July 1961. But, in unprecedented fashion, this action proved ineffective and on November 25 the situation called for a large-scale international salvage operation for sterling. The equivalent of $3,000m. was made available to the Bank of England by the principal foreign countries and this assistance, combined with firm assurances that the British Government had no intention to devalue, was sufficient to maintain the rate of exchange of the pound.

Nevertheless, the months which followed brought no real stability. The United Kingdom had therefore to continue drawing on the 'swap' credit of $3,000m., and as part of this credit fell due for repayment in May 1965, the Government decided to draw $1,400m. from the International Monetary Fund (this withdrawal was in addition to the $1,000m. which had been borrowed in November 1964). When at last, in August 1965, the pound ran into calmer weather, partly as a result of the much better export figures, Britain had incurred obligations to repay the IMF, between 1967 and 1970, the equivalent of £850m., to which must be added considerable bilateral debts, particularly to the USA. The announcement in September 1965, of the creation of a network of very large supporting credits between the Bank of England and a group of foreign banks strengthened the position of sterling on the exchange market. These credits could be used as required to defend the pound against new speculative attacks. They were renewed, in an expanded form, in June 1966. Meanwhile, the United Kingdom's official reserves were bolstered by transferring to them $885m. the proceeds of the sale of part of the country's second line reserves held in US stocks.

But in July 1966 the weakness of the pound reappeared and, this time, the Government acted quickly with a full blast of well-tried deflationary measures. The 5 per cent ceiling on increases in bank credits that was imposed in May 1965 for a year was prolonged in 1966, credits to exports alone being exempted. In June 1965, Bank rate had been reduced to 6 per cent, but hire purchase minimum deposits had been increased. In February 1966, hire purchase controls were tightened, and again in July. Also in July Bank rate was put back to 7 per cent. The 10 per cent 'regulator' was used. Already in June 1965 there had been reductions in the official investment programme, and this decision was quickly followed by a system of building controls (from which house building was exempted). In July 1966 further cuts were announced in all categories of public investment—central government, local authorities and the nationalized industries. These measures should, it seems, mark the end of the Plowden doctrine—described in Chapter II—according to which public investment is intangible for demand management purposes. It would seem preferable to prepare flexibility rather than to make sharp emergency cuts.

The stagnation of demand in 1966 began to affect private productive investment and the latter has been estimated to fall by at least 10 per cent in 1967. In an effort to cushion the effects of deflation on such investments the Government announced an increase of 5 per cent in all investment grants for a period of two years, to take effect on January 1, 1967.

These various stabilizing measures still left unsolved the fundamental problem of the structural imbalance of the balance of payments. The Government's statement on October 26, 1964, had drawn attention to the high level of public expenditure abroad; and in this connection the Franco-British plan for a supersonic aircraft, the 'Concorde' was explicitly mentioned. Although it was later decided to continue with this particular plan, British Government spokesmen have several times emphasized their wish to cut spending down abroad and more especially military expenditure. But it has so far proved impossible to secure any really substantial economies of this kind.

On the other hand there was in April 1965, an important revision in the rules governing private investment abroad, in the form of exchange control and company taxation, with a view to curbing the export of capital. More rigid criteria were announced for the issue of currency intended for the financing of private investment outside the sterling area. Exchange control regulations lay down that in future certain categories of capital receipts arriving from abroad for United Kingdom residents, which could hitherto be sold at a profit must be handed over to the Bank of England at the official rate. If foreign portfolio securities are liquidated by British residents, a quarter of the proceeds must in future be sent home instead of being re-invested abroad. Exchange control has also been tightened up with regard to tourist travel allowances and the purchase of houses outside the country.

On the side of the private capital balance, there must be added to these measures the expected repercussions from the new companies tax which comes into force in 1966. Contrary to what usually happens on the Continent, a distinction is made between personal income tax, and companies tax which, as a result of somewhat complicated calculations, tends to discourage British residents from direct and portfolio investments abroad. In May 1966 controls on direct investment in non-sterling countries were imposed and a system of voluntary restraint on investment in four developed sterling-area countries was announced. Such measures, and doubts about the pound over recent years, have reduced the cohesion of the sterling area, many of whose members have been quietly building up their own gold and foreign exchange reserves.

The Present Situation and Short-term Prospects

The development of the situation in Britain from the autumn of 1964 was difficult both to predict and to interpret, and this certainly complicated the task of the British authorities who also, understandably enough, tried to minimize for as long as possible the effect upon home demand of the decisions directed at re-establishing external equilibrium. In the long run, though, the cumulative effect of the steps taken one after another from October 1964 to July 1966 brought about a flattening-out in production similar to the last phase of 'stop' in July 1961. But unemployment remained at a record level until well into 1966.

Even if the balance of payments can be brought into equilibrium as planned by 1967, the £357m. due to be repaid to the IMF in that year will have to come out of the reserves. The second-line reserves in the form of US portfolio have now been reduced to one-third of their amount in 1964 by sales of stock and transfers to the official reserves and the remainder (some £180m. in 1966) would only cover half the IMF debt. Further debt repayments can hardly be envisaged other than the proceeds of a balance of payments surplus. The National Plan looked forward to a surplus of £250m. on basic account by 1970. Even on present policies, it may be wondered if it will be achieved and, if it is, it may not prove adequate to repay debt.

If internal demand continued to rise hardly at all, as at present, for the next two or three years then no doubt import demand would be sufficiently slack for a substantial balance of payments improvement to take place. But this would be a short-sighted policy—as the experience of the 1950s described earlier showed—and would conflict with the aim of more rapid growth. The Prime Minister himself has stated that, in his view, the country should not 'get panicked into premature reflation'.[1] In particular, this means that the Government is prepared to face the prospect of rising unemployment and, once the crisis is over, a figure of 2 per cent is thought to be an 'acceptable

[1] Speech reported in *The Times*, November 12, 1966.

limit'.[1] The reader will recall the long debates in the 1950s on this issue that were mentioned in Part I of this book. There now seems to be agreement by Labour and the Conservatives that 'overemployment' has been nefarious to the cause of growth. Hence the stress on redeployment of labour and opposition by the Government, whereever possible, to half-time and other work-sharing reactions to the threat of unemployment.

An evident danger which hangs over the British economy today is that the need for modernization in both the public and the private sector will be frustrated by a general lack of buoyancy in demand. The happiest solution would be a rapid expansion of exports since this would carry with it an improvement in the balance of payments and in domestic demand conditions. Unfortunately, the outcome here is doubtful. No recent improvement in the competitiveness of British exports compared with those of other countries gives grounds for hope that exports will increase at all fast without a new element appearing in the present situation such as a change in exchange rate policy.

At one time it was intended that the 1970 plan targets would be revised late in 1966 to 'roll them on' to 1971. But new targets for 1971 would have remained as hypothetical as those previously assigned to 1970. Too many uncertainties overcloud the future at present, among them being the path out of deflation that will prove practicable and the fate of the new round of talks designed to get Britain into the Common Market.

[1] Mr Gunter, Minister of Labour, in the House of Commons on October 24, 1966, reaffirming the Prime Minister's statement on this point in July. Mr Heath, the Conservative leader, has gone on record as saying, 'The Government should run the economy on the basis that the number of vacancies only equalled the number of men unemployed.' This amounts to much the same thing. Cf. *The Times*, October 16, 1966.

CHAPTER VII

IN SEARCH OF AN INCOMES POLICY

Rising prices and difficulties affecting the balance of payments have often forced the British authorities to curb economic expansion in order to re-establish equilibrium. This 'stop' policy became the target of fierce criticism which ultimately brought into being the National Economic Development Council. It was therefore inevitable that, when the Council was working out its programme of medium-term development, it should direct its attention to ways and means of achieving competitiveness of prices. Moreover, many advocates of planning—particularly on the Labour side—considered that it held out an opportunity for a fresh approach to the problem of demand management. It should be no surprise, therefore to discover that the planning experiment under way in the United Kingdom since 1961 has attached considerable importance to the search for a workable incomes policy.

It is true that this recognition of the problem of keeping a proper relationship between the growth of incomes and output is not new. Between 1947 and 1951 the first Labour Government had obtained, from both trade unions and employers' representatives, undertakings to restrict wage claims and shareholders' dividends, and this certainly played a role in the restimulation of production and development of exports which marked that period. But in September 1950—that is, before the Conservatives returned to power—union dissatisfaction at the inflationary trends resulting from the Korean war brought about a vote at the TUC Congress condemning the policy of wage restraint. Looking back today, one may feel that the first Labour experiment in an incomes policy lacked a firm institutional basis which might have enabled it to withstand the stress of the Korean war. The breakdown of wage restraint in that period should be seen against the background of the demise of the Labour Party's post-war efforts to plan the economy in general.

So when the Conservatives returned in 1951 nothing remained of the first attempt at an incomes policy. As the Conservative leaders were unenthusiastic about economic controls, all that was heard of incomes policy for the next ten years were periodic Government appeals for restraint to which little attention was paid, occasional efforts (as in 1956) to stop rising wages by opposing wage claims, and recurrent bouts of deflation (as have been described in Chapter II).

Since 1961, a new approach to incomes, costs and prices has been outlined. The 'pause' in wage increases decreed in July 1961 was only the beginning of an incomes policy which had at last the merit of being coherent and of considering the problem as a whole. The return to power of Labour since 1964 has not carried much further the debate on general principles that was worked out between July 1961 and October 1964. Since that period it has been pretty generally recognized by both employers and unions that a policy of balanced growth must include an incomes policy, that this policy must be defined to include all incomes (wages, profits, other unearned income), and that permanent machinery is needed for attaining the desired objective. It must be added that the lack of any really significant results of incomes policy has been a major shortcoming of British economic policy in recent years, and helped to make the shock tactics of the summer 1966 inevitable.

This chapter will first set out briefly the facts relevant for an incomes policy in Britain. This analysis will make it easier to understand the discussions which took place between 1961 and 1964. The last part of the chapter will deal with the action taken by the Labour Government since its return to power.

1. THE FACTS

Without wishing to make an analytical study of the *raison d'être* of an incomes policy,[1] we give here certain statistical data which throw light on the question in the British context and we set out the chief practical problems inseparable from any policy of this kind.

Statistics

The determination of which factors have had, or might have, an influence on costs of production and hence on prices depends logically on the respective weights of the components of total costs in the gross national product (Table I). This Table shows the shares of factor incomes, of the cost of imports and of indirect taxation. The cost of imports plays an important part in determining costs; but these fluctuations are mainly beyond the control of the national authorities. Changes in indirect taxation, on the other hand, result from deliberate acts of economic policy. So the heart of the problem of rising prices must be sought in 'incomes' which, with 73 per cent of the

[1] The best introduction to the question is in two publications by OECD: *The Problem of Price Increases* (1961), and *In Search of a Policy of Prices, Profits and other unearned Income* (1964).

TABLE I

ELEMENTS OF THE TOTAL COSTS OF THE GROSS NATIONAL PRODUCT IN UK

	Per cent
I Factor incomes	73
II Cost of imports	17
III Taxes on expenditure	10
Total	100

Source: National Income White Paper.

total, largely dominates the two others. These incomes may be subdivided under earned income, gross profits, and other unearned income. Earned income represents about 70 per cent of the total income payments and have inevitably a special weight in determining the level of costs. We certainly cannot neglect the part played by profits; but to arrive at a similar increase in total costs we should need a rise in profits several times greater relatively than for earned incomes.[1]

Since the war, the movement of the total of money incomes compared with those of GNP at constant prices shows that incomes have increased at a relatively regular pace, and faster than GNP at constant prices, and that the price index of GNP rose considerably (see graph). The same effect can be found in all the countries of Europe, and it is perhaps the universality of this phenomenon which sometimes leads to its being overlooked. Before 1939 nothing of the kind existed; the total of money incomes had its ups and downs, but these were not, as is the case today, very largely independent of the growth of GNP at constant prices, as has been the case since 1945.

The existence of this persistent upward trend[2] is the reason why means are being sought through an incomes policy to reduce it without at the same time hampering the growth of GNP. The ideal would be to keep the cost of the gross national product per person employed constant in time. For this reason, without being over-sanguine about the results, it is convenient to take as norm for the maximum permissible—or desirable—growth of incomes, the growth of total productivity in the medium run. Although this recipe for ensuring price stability—by equating 'increases in income as a whole' and 'total productivity'—has the merit of being simple, in practice it raises a number of difficult issues.

[1] We shall come back to the *process* of inflation that raises different problems.

[2] Many reasons may be advanced to explain this phenomenon. We shall note some of them in the following pages.

Production and incomes since 1950
(1950=100)

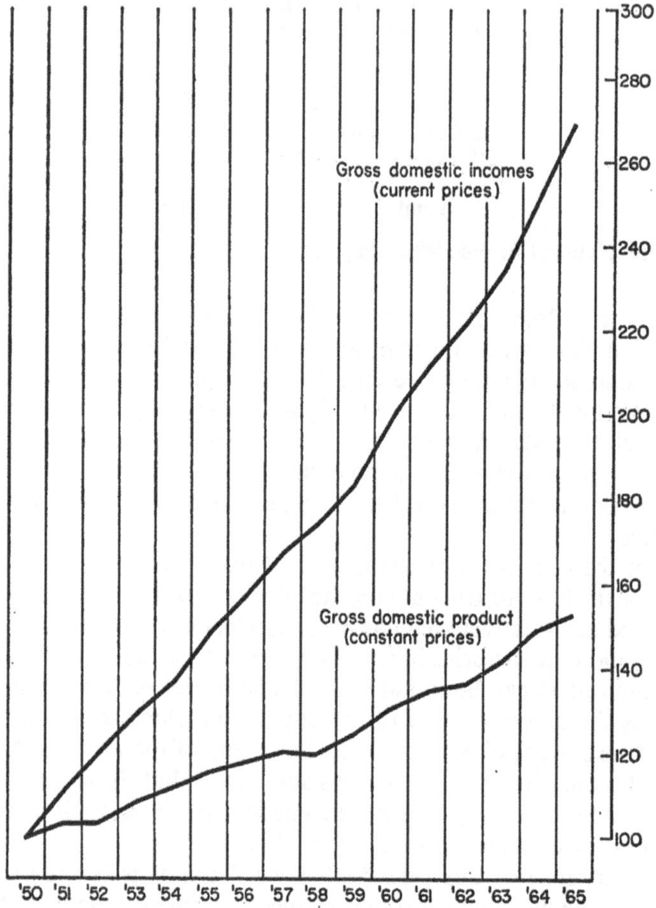

Source: Ministry of Labour Statistics and Incomes, Prices, Employment and Production

Practical Aspects

British incomes policy stems from the thought that the explanations of the phenomenon of inflation in a modern economy must be sought as much on the side of costs as on the side of demand. Therefore the measures suggested for stabilizing prices are an innovation as compared with the traditional ones which acted according to the principle that if prices rose there was excess demand and that eliminating the latter would cure the rise in prices.

Nevertheless demand factors cannot be ignored. British experience does show that the rate of growth of money incomes and of prices accelerates when the margin of productive capacity (capital and labour) becomes unduly narrow.[1] But, since 1945, wage increases have also frequently been noted during periods of economic stagnation and lowered industrial profits. Moreover, the movement of money wages is one way; though liable to rise, they never fall whatever the state of the labour market. It also happens fairly frequently that wage claims originate in the best paid industries, even if there is some unemployment in them, and then spread out. 'Cost inflation' is an aspect of the modern working of the labour market which must be taken into account by any economic policy dealing with costs and prices.

There is naturally no hard-and-fast point beyond which the pressure of demand also begins to have an effect. An active labour-market policy (cf. Chapter IX), for example, can certainly push back the limit of over-full employment. But, apart from the fact that such a policy is still in its infancy in Britain, it would be rash to identify 'faster growth' with an even lower level of employment than has pertained on average in the post-war period. Indeed, it is unlikely to prove possible to achieve reasonable stability of prices unless unemployment is rather higher than in the past. Since the summer of 1966, the Government has accepted this necessity despite trade union opposition.

Profits also play a part in rising prices but, as Table I shows, their share of the total costs of production is only a fraction compared with earned income (less than 17 per cent of the gross national product against nearly 70 per cent). The present structure of our economy, and especially the maintenance of full employment, have the effect that profit margins tend to be relatively stable over the years, so that rising costs—whether due to wages or other causes, including company taxation—tend to be passed on fairly quickly in selling prices. Also the abuse of monopoly, or quasi-monopoly, power allows some sectors of industry to raise their prices more than competitive conditions can justify. High, and rising, profits frequently make for wage and salary claims that neither market forces, nor considerations of equity, make it possible to oppose.

Whatever may be the practical importance of higher wages or profits, and their interaction, in the process of rising prices, it has been recognized for some years in Britain by both employers and unions that any discussion of an incomes policy must cover the whole field of different kinds of income, for reasons both of social justice

[1] NEDC recognized this when they wrote, 'A high level of demand and employment might also, on the basis of past experience, tend to be associated with pressure for higher money incomes.' (*Conditions Favourable to Faster Growth*, NEDC, April 1963, p. 50.)

and of economic necessity. In particular it has become very clear that the unions will never accept wage restraint unless profits are also restricted. No one can be in any doubt that such restraint will be extremely difficult to put into effect.

Except in the case of very vigorous intervention by the State, which neither employers nor unions would support, it is pretty generally admitted that an incomes policy must be based on a 'general will'[1] to make such a policy work. The concrete machinery for achieving the desired objective must lie within the framework of this general will. Nevertheless any such machinery will find itself up against formidable difficulties in practice.

For example, with regard to wages: how can an appropriate relationship be maintained between wages in different industries? How can a more efficient use of the labour force be encouraged? How can one equate the situation of workers whose productivity can be measured with that of workers where it cannot? How can one reconcile the interests of those whose productivity is rising rapidly and of those for whom it remains stagnant through no fault of their own?

Profits, from the point of view of economics, are in a different category from wages and cannot be subjected to quite the same treatment. Whereas the wage-earner's income is generally fixed by negotiation, profits are the outcome of the difference between a selling price and a cost figure; they are therefore closely bound up with prices. Further, although average profit margins remain stable over a long period, profits, unlike wages, do tend to fluctuate according to the economic situation and this makes it difficult to choose a base period from which to estimate their future growth. Also, to fix a profit norm for every firm, apart from the enormous practical difficulties, would cut right across the desire to secure a more efficient use of productive capacity. Nor is it very effective to use company taxation to 'mop up' profits judged to be excessive if, in the long run, direct taxes on industry tend to be counted as an element in the cost of production.

So it seems clear that, both for wages and for other forms of income and profits, the requirements of social justice and of economic growth by no means coincide, at any rate in the short run. Yet an incomes policy that stressed social justice at the expense of economic efficiency would court disaster. One that went all out for promoting efficiency would stand little chance of being accepted. Hence the complexity of the search for a viable compromise in Britain since 1961 to which we now turn.

[1] A favourite phrase of George Woodcock.

2. THE PERIOD 1961–4

July 1961 was a turning point, the importance of which has not always been realized, in the Conservative Government's prices and incomes policy. Till then the attitude had been one of 'exhortation in a vacuum'.[1] Numbers of speeches by Ministers had called for moderation in spiralling incomes, but without making any concrete proposals. Throughout the 1950s, the Conservative Government were probably embarrassed in opposing firm resistance to wage claims from the private sector by the fear that they might take on a political complexion, remembering the general strike in 1926.[2] But even in the public sector there was no trace of a coherent wages policy. Recourse to arbitration for the settlement of disputes usually resulted in unco-ordinated wage increases, since the tribunals lacked precise criteria. When in 1956 a White Paper on the conditions of full employment set out the problem of rising prices, there was no attempt at suggesting a remedy.[3] It is true that a committee of 'three wise men', set up in 1958, published four reports, but it had little influence in the private sector.[4]

After 1961 Government policy entered a new phase of activity. Let us look at this first, before considering the parallel development in the attitudes of employers and employed.

The Conservative Government

The policy adopted in 1961 laid down for the first time definite measures to be taken and attacked the problem on several fronts together. It was gradually translated into action and any analysis must start from the beginning—the 'pause' of July 1961. This decision was only a first stage, and the Government went on very quickly to a second novel step, the 'guiding light' for wage increases. At the same time they tackled the question of prices, costs and incomes from another angle by setting up a National Incomes Commission. This was followed by more direct action on prices through the strengthening of legislation dealing with restrictive practices. Finally, as was inevitable in the long run, the Chancellor of the Exchequer referred the question of an incomes policy to NEDC.

(a) *The 'Pause' of July 1961.* The 'pause' in the increase of earned income, announced in July 1961 and justified by the Chancellor,[5] was

[1] Cf. Hall, Sir Robert, 'Incomes Policy; the State of Play', *The Three Banks Review*, March 1964, p. 5.

[2] Cf. Maddison, A., op. cit., p. 159.

[3] *Economic Implications of Full Employment*, Cmd. 9725, 1956.

[4] Council on Prices, Productivity and Incomes.

[5] He said he considered a pause necessary until the progress of productivity made a fresh advance possible (cf. *Hansard*, July 25, 1961, p. 221).

accompanied by an undertaking to introduce in the next budget (April 1962) a capital gains tax—an indirect admission that profits were an element in an incomes policy. This admission also meant the abandonment of the thesis underlaying the work of the 'three wise men', that pressure of demand is the basic cause of inflation. The pause was criticized by the unions, although in fact it made little difference to the increase of wages in the private sector. As has been said, the bitterness felt by the unions at what seemed to them arbitrary unilateral action held up their decision to take part in NEDC. In the public sector the pause hit official salaries. Nevertheless in one nationalized industry, electricity, a wage increase was agreed that autumn which drew upon the management a public remonstrance from the Chancellor.

This incident provides food for thought about the laws governing nationalization. The nationalized industries have the legal status of 'public corporations', so that their management may be free from excessive Government interference. Nevertheless Ministerial responsibility, i.e. the responsibility of Parliament, remains in important decisions, and the Minister who nominates members of the Board of Directors can also issue directives. In practice, however, control has been fairly flexible and has concerned itself only with questions of investment and prices. Wage negotiations have been left to the management and unions, though the Government can exert discreet pressure, especially in industries which are in receipt of Government grant. Electricity in Britain was a prosperous industry and so could take an independent line in its wages policy. Even others which were much less prosperous observed the 'pause' far from completely—for example, British Railways where any strike threat always produced wage concessions.

The pause of July 1961, though approved by some people, like Sir Robert Hall, formerly economic adviser to the Conservative Government, for its salutary effect upon opinion,[1] nevertheless made the work of NEDC more difficult later on. If it had not been accompanied by other measures it would have been just one more palliative.

(b) *Working Out the 'Guiding Light' for Wage Increases.* During the second half of 1961 the authorities agreed to make the 'pause' more flexible. It was to come to an end on April 1, 1962, and to be followed by arrangements which would allow time for the working out of a permanent policy. The most unusual of the measures decided on was the fixing by the Government, for the first time, of an overall ceiling to the rate of annual wage increases. Calculated at 2·5 per cent, following the medium-term growth of total productivity, this rate was to serve as a 'guiding light' for future increases in earned incomes. A

[1] Cf. Sir Robert Hall, 'Incomes Policy: the State of Play', op. cit., p. 5.

White Paper published in February 1962[1] explained the proposal in detail. While confirming the end of the 'pause' and the substitution of a guiding rate of 2½ per cent, the Government urged that, in the immediate future, wages should not automatically go up with the cost of living, as had happened in the past. They felt that the shortage of manpower was not in itself sufficient to justify wage increases and that excessive weight should not be given to the pay rates for any particular job when wage claims were being examined. They promised to respect these principles in the public sector, including the nationalized industries. On the question of arbitration, the need to consider the economic situation as a whole was underlined. Last but not least, 'as a part of the incomes policy', the Government reaffirmed the statement made in the House of Commons in December 1961 that 'appropriate corrections would have to be taken if aggregate profits showed signs of increasing excessively as compared with wages and salaries'.[2]

(c) *The National Incomes Commission.*[3] The Government would have liked to support its policy by setting up a commission on which representatives of both employers and trade unions would have consented to sit. This hope having proved vain, in July 1962 when Mr Maudling replaced Mr Selwyn Lloyd as Chancellor of the Exchequer, the Prime Minister decided to create a National Incomes Commission composed of independent experts.

As for its competence,[4] the commission could have referred to it, either by the interested parties or by the authorities, all claims concerning remuneration or other conditions of work, except in the case of nationalized industries and those professions with arbitration machinery. The Government on their side could refer to it for retrospective examination any agreements already reached, except those awarded by arbitration. The commission sat as a tribunal, its deliberations were held in public, and it could hear evidence not only from the parties directly interested, but also from individuals or organizations of acknowledged competence on questions of pay.

The commission was to register the Government's undertaking that if a moderate growth of wages were accompanied by an unreasonable increase in aggregate profits these would be limited by fiscal or other means.[5]

The National Incomes Commission was abolished by the Labour Government in 1965 as part of the new incomes policy which will be

[1] *Incomes Policy: the Next Step*, Cmd. 1626, 1962.
[2] *Incomes Policy: the Next Step*, Cmd. 1926, 1962, paragraph 14.
[3] Immediately baptized 'Nicky' by analogy with 'Neddy' (NEDC).
[4] Cf. National Incomes Commission, Cmd. 1844, November 1962.
[5] Cf. op. cit., paragraphs 6 and 8.

discussed later in this chapter. The sum total of its activity seems rather slight. Nevertheless it served the useful purpose of bringing to the notice of the public one important aspect of the machinery of rising money wages in industry, namely the wage drift, and it is thanks to the commission that this question today naturally forms an essential part of any serious examination of wage movements.

TABLE II

GROWTH IN AVERAGE HOURLY WAGE EARNINGS AND 'WAGE DRIFT' (PERCENTAGE INCREASE COMPARED WITH PRECEDING YEAR)

	Average hourly wage earnings (1)	*Average hourly wage earnings excluding the effect of overtime* (2)	*Average hourly wage rates* (3)	*Wage drift (col. 2 minus col. 3)* (4)
October 1958	+ 3·1	+3·4	+3·7	−0·3
1959	+ 3·6	+2·9	+1·4	+1·5
1960	+ 8·1	+7·3	+5·5	+1·8
1961	+ 7·0	+6·9	+6·4	+0·5
1962	+ 4·1	+4·4	+4·2	+0·2
1963	+ 4·1	+3·6	+2·3	+1·3
1964	+ 8·2	+8·1	+5·7	+2·4
1965	+10·1	+9·5	+7·2	+2·3
April 1966	+ 9·8	+9·7	+8·0	+1·7

Source: Statistics on Incomes, Prices, Employment and Production, Ministry of Labour.

What does 'wage drift' mean? As Table II shows, the recorded increase in hourly earnings can be broken down into a number of elements. One of them, the increase in hourly wage rates, has traditionally been the centre of attention, for it is the outcome of wage negotiations and collective agreements. But although it is the main element, its importance is very variable and is not sufficient to account for the movement of the average rate of hourly earnings (corrected to allow for overtime). Comparison between columns 2 and 3 in the Table is significant here; it shows that the difference between hourly pay rates and hourly earnings is often considerable. This difference, in column 4 of the Table, is called the 'wage drift'. For the raising of wage earnings there are then not one but two procedures. They are partly linked, but they always work quite distinctly, one in full view and the other by means which do not attract attention.[1]

If therefore wage increases were calculated only in the light of increases resulting from collective bargaining, there would be a marked under-estimate of the rise to be expected in hourly earnings. Now it is

[1] Op. cit., paragraph 9.

clearly this rise which counts, both as regards incomes received and impact on costs of production. The wage drift does not exist in every industry. It is particularly noticeable in engineering construction, the electrical industry and in shipyards where it can reach as much as 2 per cent per annum, or even more.[1]

(d) *Restrictive Practices*. The importance of a prices policy in fixing the level of profits was stressed in the first part of this chapter. Vigorous action was initiated in this direction by the Government in January 1964. The parliamentary debates were lively and aroused energetic opposition by a large minority, consisting mainly of Conservative MPs. In spite of this, the Bill reducing the scope of retail price maintenance became law in the summer of 1964 and operative in July 1965. As regards legislation on monopolies, the case for it was presented by the authorities in a White Paper which the Conservative Party undertook to translate into a Bill if they were returned to power in the 1964 General Election.

Immediate public interest was concentrated on legislation directed against retail price maintenance.[2] This practice should be considered to be against the public interest except in particular cases capable of justification before a tribunal. To appreciate the full force of this statement one should remember that more than a third of consumer goods sold in Britain were subject at that time to agreements of this nature.

The law as finally passed in July 1964 largely followed the original plan, though opposition in Parliament forced the Government unwillingly to make concessions. Certain circumstances are accepted as justifying restrictive practices; imposed prices are not to be declared illegal for manufacturers who can justify them before a special tribunal. In spite of this loophole, a gap in British legislation has begun to be filled and the Conservative Party has shown that it is prepared to deal with prices and profits, as well as earned incomes. Since 1964 the sector where price maintenance was most marked, in durable consumer goods, has been freeing its prices more and more. Many manufacturers who have applied for temporary exemption from the Act have done so as a delaying tactic only. The first contested case is not scheduled to be heard until the beginning of 1967. Meanwhile the spearhead of the breakthrough as regards retail price maintenance has come from the modern retail outlets such as supermarkets and discount houses.

(e) *NEDC and the Incomes Policy*. When NEDC wrote in its second

[1] The 'wage drift' thus seems unjust as between groups of wage-earners if those who benefit from it can keep it dark.

[2] That is to say the obligation imposed by a manufacturer on the retailer not to sell his products below a minimum price.

report that 'there will thus be need for policies to ensure that money incomes (wages, salaries, profits) as a whole rise substantially less rapidly than in the past',[1] they were not just indulging in rhetoric but nor were they as yet committing both sides of industry. Subsequently, and owing to the vigorous way in which the economy responded to the expansionist measures contained in the Budget of April 1963, the Chancellor of the Exchequer tried to obtain from the representatives of both employers and unions an unequivocal commitment on the question of prices and wages.

In April 1963, after the Government had fixed a new 'guiding light' for the increase in incomes of 3½ per cent per annum, which was consistent with NEDC's growth target for the period 1961–6, discussion became active. Three meetings held in May, June and July were devoted chiefly to prices and incomes, and in July NEDO was instructed to prepare for the autumn meeting a document dealing with increases in prices and incomes within the framework of a programme of growth.

Discussions began again at the council in October and dragged on until January 1964 when the Office produced a study on possible methods of intervention. These were seen to include, besides action on earned incomes, the setting up of a prices commission rather like the National Incomes Commission, and the use of taxation to absorb some of the profits if they increased more rapidly than productivity.[2]

The employers on NEDC announced to the trade unionists that they would accept these measures if the trade unionists undertook to restrain wage claims. This offer was the high point in the attempt to work out an incomes policy before the change of Government. Caught on the wrong foot by the employers' proposal, the union representatives remained on the defensive,[3] and no further progress on this issue proved possible. It is true that, early in 1964, the prospect of imminent General Elections had begun seriously to hamper the work of the NEDC on this, as on other questions.

In sum, even if the concrete results of this period seem rather limited, at least it was no longer possible to discuss a British incomes policy in the same terms as a few years earlier. A threshold had been

[1] *Conditions Favourable to Faster Growth*, NEDC, April 1963, p. 51. The difficult task of securing trade union agreement to the drafting of this passage no doubt accounts for a slight delay in the publication of the document.

[2] An article on the working of a profits policy, written by a former collaborator with NEDO, sets out ideas which, even if they do not reflect the official attitude of the council, throw light on the thought which inspired its work. Cf. Scott, M. F.-G., 'Notes on Profits Policy', *Bankers' Magazine*, February 1964.

[3] George Woodcock is said to have remarked that it was too bold, too inopportune, too sudden. Cf. *Financial Times*, January 9, 1964.

crossed, and a retreat was unthinkable. This conclusion is reinforced by an examination of the respective attitudes of employers and trade unions towards an incomes policy, though it is clear that there were still serious difficulties to be surmounted after 1964, that unfortunately still remained two years later.

The Employers' Point of View

As we have seen, from 1961 to 1964, the employers' representatives on NEDC were nominated individually, in contrast to those of the unions. The question therefore arose as to whom they represented. They were certainly influential members of the FBI, the BEC or the NABM,[1] but these bodies had given them no mandate to represent them, still less to commit themselves in their name. Even if they had been plenipotentiaries, it is by no means certain that they could have carried the bulk of their followers as far as they themselves were prepared to go, for the provincial industrialist pretty certainly saw still the questions facing NEDC in a different light from those employers who sat on the council. As happens in the Trade Union Movement, the employers have to consider the average opinion of their organizations. The relevance of these considerations came out particularly strongly at the end of 1963 and beginning of 1964 during the marathon debate undertaken by NEDC on incomes policy. The debate also furnished a striking example of the dialectical process released by participation of both sides of industry in a body like NEDC and which clearly distinguishes NEDC from the traditional forms of Government 'consultation' with the private sector.

We have said that the proposals put forward at the beginning of 1964 by the employers' representatives on NEDC had found the trade union representatives somewhat unprepared. In fact they caught many employers unaware too. In January 1964 the Press reported a number of discussions between the employers' members of NEDC and the employers' organizations. Finally, in order to reach agreement among themselves, the FBI, the BEC and the NABM, in conjunction with the Association of Chambers of Commerce, set up a working party to study the application of a profits policy.

The results were published by the grand council of the FBI under the significant title 'The search for a national incomes policy'.[2] The temporary setback to NEDC as regards the debate on incomes policy was known by then and the FBI, by publishing its own study, was attempting, it seems, both to justify the action of the employers on NEDC and to demonstrate that they had been genuinely trying to find

[1] Cf. Chapter I.

[2] *The Search for a National Incomes Policy*, FBI, March 1964.

a solution. All the same, the document shows that there was not yet unanimity among the various associations.

The authors of the report make three complementary proposals for bringing profits within an incomes policy: a variable tax on profits; a monitoring of prices; a procedure for dealing with complaints about prices. With regard to the variable tax on profits, the idea was that on a three years' average the rate of growth of profits (distributed as well as undistributed) and of total earned income should keep in step. To achieve this the tax would vary up and down and this would resolve the difficulty of different rates of profits increase between one firm and another. With regard to prices, a list of key products would be drawn up and laid before a special commission which would be kept up to date with modifications. As to complaints, the same commission could be approached by any individual or organization, though the initiative would usually lie with consumer's association (on which the unions would be represented) or with the Board of Trade.

The FBI document examined with great impartiality the arguments for and against each method, but drew no conclusions. The introduction merely noted that the members of the working party could not reach agreement and recorded their disappointment at such a negative outcome. The president of the FBI,[1] on the other hand, made it clear that he was by no means resigned to the position, and that he thought further progress possible with the help of the Economic Development Committees just then being set up in each branch of industry. According to one representative of the employers on NEDC and a former president of the BEC, the setback of early 1964 was only temporary; after the General Election in October 1964 fresh discussions would take place at NEDC and between the BEC and the Government.[2] This proved to be the case as we shall see in a moment. The trade union representatives did not challenge this view.

The Trade Unions

If the employers' associations concentrated on defining their attitude towards profits in the context of an incomes policy, the trade unions were mainly interested in wages.

At their congress in 1962, the TUC recognized in a document about the National Incomes Commission that it was possible for incomes to increase without a rise in costs or prices.[3] But there was no unanimity about the working of an incomes policy covering wages.

In this respect the TUC were in the same quandary as faced the employers' representatives. Even if the members of the council of the

[1] Mr Peter Runge, quoted in the *Financial Times*, March 18, 1964.
[2] Sir John Hunter, quoted in the *Financial Times*, March 18, 1964.
[3] TUC, '*Economic Devolopment and Planning*', September 1963, p. 12.

TUC had been in agreement—which they were not—it was by no means certain that the TUC could make undertakings committing the unions as a whole. The precedent of 1950 showed that there was a mass of trade unionists sufficiently sure of themselves to reject if necessary a policy of moderation preached by their leaders. Moreover, the constitution of the TUC did not allow its interference in wage negotiations being engaged in by affiliated unions. This does not mean that a TUC declaration in favour of restraint in wage claims would be without influence on negotiations. But such influence would hardly be likely to be lasting in the absence of permanent machinery for constructing and applying an incomes policy.

The differences in opinion seem to have been due less to fundamental principles than to different tactical ideas, especially in view of a possible General Election, as was the case in 1963 and 1964.

The congress of the TUC in September 1963, for example, performed the feat of voting both for and against union participation in the working out of an incomes policy. Mr Ted Hill and Mr Frank Cousins, both members of the general council of the TUC and delegates on NEDC,[1] supported a resolution condemning any form of wage restraint.[2] The congress also demanded that the general council should withstand any incomes policy which did not include fiscal control of profits and capital appreciation, and price control.[3] But next month at the Labour Party conference Mr Hill, supported by Mr Cousins, agreed that the Government could be justified in asking unions not to support wage increases greater than economic growth would permit, though he added that he could never accept that the Government should block wages without blocking other forms of income.[4]

The unions, like the employers' associations and no doubt with similar reservations, continued to seek acceptable solutions to the problem of applying an incomes policy to wages. In this work the unions tend, quite naturally, to be more pragmatic than some theoreticians of the Labour Party.[5] It is probably George Woodcock who has laid the greatest stress upon the fundamental importance of the right frame of mind and a sense of responsibility among all concerned.[6] His attitude is much like that of many of the employers and his argument is not without force. He rejected, for example, as impracticable the idea that the TUC should place on the Chancellor of the Exchequer's desk in a little parcel the list of all the wage increases in every sector over a given period.[7] Since then, events have moved fast.

[1] Mr Cousins was later Minister of Technology until the summer of 1966.
[2] Resolution No. 58. [3] Resolution No. 10.
[4] Quoted by *The Times*, October 3, 1963. [5] Cf. the last part of this chapter.
[6] TUC Congress, September 1962, p. 370. [7] Ibid.

This remark does not alter the fact that a just and well balanced growth in incomes demands exact knowledge of all increases in income which have actually come about. In this connection many union leaders have given thought to the chaotic manner in which unions have set about getting wage increases. Improvements can no doubt be obtained in this way by workers in industries characterized by high productivity or a shortage of manpower. But the fate of many others whose working conditions are different is often overlooked and a situation where the most powerful unions push ahead with wage claims regardless of the fate of other groups of workers can, it seems, be as unjust as a tendency for profits generally to outrun wages. Many trade unionists are conscious of this problem.[1] There is thus a possible contradiction between the ideas of certain trade unionists who want no more than a general supervision of wage movements and the idea of others who are concerned about the inequalities in pay between one group of workers and another.

However that may be, it seems certain that the present complexities of wage negotiations put a premium on one union being able to outbid another and, at the level of individual firms, takes the effective control of fixing wage rates out of the hands of permanent union officials and generally leaves it to the shop stewards and shop-floor negotiation. In this connection the TUC document on economic planning already quoted had the courage to recognize that unions must ask themselves whether the structure of collective agreements and the methods of negotiation are entirely satisfactory, and whether tactics at the level of the firm cannot be better integrated into an overall strategy.[2] Some spokesmen of the Labour Party, before the General Election in October 1964, suggested going even further in this direction.

3. THE LABOUR GOVERNMENT

The following analysis is essentially devoted to the incomes policy adopted by the Labour Government since its return to power. This policy is sufficiently close to the ideas put forward by the Party before 1964 for these to be worth a moment's study.

Labour's Attitude Before 1964

The thesis that an expansionist economic policy calls for control of increases in incomes has been not only accepted but strongly pressed

[1] For example, Mr Ray Gunter—at present Minister of Labour—in the House of Commons on April 21, 1964, said: 'It is a repudiation of all the Trade Union Movement believes in for any trade union leader in a prosperous industry simply to turn round and say he is going to get his own pound of flesh regardless of his responsibility to other workers, particularly in the service industries.'

[2] Cf. TUC *Economic Development and Planning*, September 1963, p. 15.

by Labour since 1945, and this seems logical for a party whose post-war economic policy owed its success, among other things, to union sympathy. Before the General Election of 1959 (which kept the Conservatives in power) Hugh Gaitskell, then Leader of the Labour Party, looked forward, in the event of a Labour victory, to a climate which would allow the unions, in their own interest, to agree to co-operate so that wages and productivity increased together.[1]

The Party included in the final resolution of its annual conference in October 1963 a clause underlining the necessity of 'an incomes policy covering salaries, wages, dividends, profits and social security benefits'.[2] Harold Wilson, the present Leader and Prime Minister, took up this idea again at the beginning of 1964. According to him a Labour Government in contrast to a Conservative Government, 'will have the right to make this appeal [for wage restraint]. Because we shall be ensuring that those now making really big money the easy way are paying their full share.'[3] Mr Wilson returned to this theme in his speech to the TUC congress in September 1964 just before the last General Election.[4] Nobody could therefore be in any doubt about the Labour Party's intentions, least of all the unions. Their response, seen in perspective, appears rather half-hearted.

But it is Dr Balogh, an Oxford economist with an international reputation and at present personal economic adviser to the Prime Minister, who set out most completely the outline of an incomes policy for Labour. In his view, it is impossible to ensure the stability of the economy at the same time as its faster growth unless means are found to reconcile the claims of the TUC with the rate of expansion of productivity.[5] This problem is not peculiar to the United Kingdom; the question of an incomes policy is universal outside the Soviet orbit.[6] Taxation is the appropriate instrument for use as regards profits. As to wages, Dr Balogh recognized that it is essential to pre-

[1] Speech to the annual Labour Party conference, quoted in the *Financial Times*, October 2, 1958.

[2] Reproduced by *The Times*, October 3, 1963.

[3] Article which appeared in the journal of the National Union of General and Municipal Workers, quoted in the *Financial Times*, March 2, 1964.

[4] 'We have the right to ask for an incomes policy because we are prepared to contribute the three necessary conditions. First an assurance of rising production and rising incomes, so that the sacrifice, the restraint, for which we ask is matched by an assurance that it will result in increased production and increased rewards. Second, an assurance of equity and social justice in that our policies will be directed to the benefit of the nation as a whole and not to the advantage of sectional interests. Third, an assurance that what we ask for in wages and salaries will apply equally to profits and dividends and rents.' Quoted in *The Times*, September 8, 1964.

[5] Cf. Balogh, T., *Planning for Progress*, Fabian Society, 1963, p. 5.

[6] Cf. op. cit., p. 17.

serve the unions' freedom of negotiation; but he proposed the setting up of an arbitration tribunal, on which the unions would be represented and which would consider all wage agreements. This tribunal would have power to suspend any agreement judged to be incompatible with price stability or the healthy state of the balance of payments. Dr Balogh looked forward to the possibility of a system of wage fixing such as is used in Sweden, where negotiations take place at a high level between representatives of the employers and the unions, each of whom can speak for highly centralized organizations. Clearly the British tradition of very decentralized discussions puts an attempt of this kind out of the question at present, and the policy followed by the Labour Government since 1964 falls definitely short of such proposals though the influence of certain of the ideas expressed by Dr Balogh can be discerned in it.

Since October 1964

By the spring of 1965, less than six months after coming into power, the Labour Government had taken the essential steps towards a prices and incomes policy.[1] Even if the task were made easier by the long discussions which had taken place under the aegis of the NEDC (old style), between 1962 and 1964, the achievement is nonetheless considerable. The very fact that it is a medium-term policy makes it impossible to expect that it could reveal already everything that will ultimately come out of it. We shall return to an evaluation of the results achieved so far at the end of this chapter. Meanwhile, let us look at the Government's point of view before considering the various phases in the development of their policy.

(a) *The Labour Point of View*. In conformity with his election platform, the Prime Minister in assuming office lost no time in announcing his Government's intention to open 'without delay' discussions with representatives of employers and workers so that an incomes policy applicable to all types of income and linked with the development of productivity might become reality.[2]

A few days later Mr George Brown, Secretary of State for the new Department of Economic Affairs,[3] informed the House of Commons that, having been given the task of working out such a policy by the Prime Minister, he proposed to deal with the question within the framework of an overall medium-term economic plan and to include

[1] It is worth noting the title 'prices and incomes', for it clearly shows the Labour Party's intention to take action on both these components of real domestic purchasing power.

[2] 'The Economic Situation'. A Statement by HM Government, October 26, 1964.

[3] Cf. Chapter VI.

not only wages but incomes arising from profits and dividends. However, because 'profits differ in character from earned incomes, since they arise as a residual rather than a main element in costs' it would be appropriate to deal with them both by watching price movements and ultimately by taxation. Therefore, and as 'we shall never get agreement to an incomes policy which covers only one part of the field'[1] a price review body would be set up. Rigid control of incomes or prices was to be avoided. The success of the new policy would depend on the willingness of the interested parties to co-operate.

It should be noted that the first two budgets presented by the Labour Government after October 1964 contained measures aimed at making it easier for the unions to accept their policy. In November 1964 social security benefits and pensions were raised and, in April 1965, the tax on capital gains introduced by the Conservatives in 1962 was increased and its scope widened.

(b) *Setting the Stage.* The Government counted on three stages for the realization of their programme: the signature of a declaration of intent jointly by representatives of the State, the employers and the unions; an agreement between the same three parties on the machinery required for the carrying out of the new policy; the setting of norms to serve as terms of reference.

From the start the Government tried to move fast owing to the critical situation of the balance of payments. Although Mr Brown's statement, that he expected to reach the third and last stage of his programme by the spring of 1965, seemed to many observers to be somewhat ambitious, the Minister nevertheless succeeded in sticking to his time schedule.

In December 1964 a tripartite statement of intent was signed 'on productivity, prices and incomes'.[2] The value of this short text, consisting of twelve points, lies essentially in the fact that it is the first time that employers and unions have taken up a common position on this question. Even during the early post-war years when firms had voluntarily kept down their dividends and unions had restrained their claims, there had never been any joint declaration.

After referring to the serious situation of the balance of payments, the document defines the intentions of the three signatories. The Government reaffirm their desire to encourage economic growth and social justice within the framework of a medium-term plan, to create bodies with the duty of keeping a watch on the movements of prices and of incomes of all kinds, to use fiscal policy if need be to correct any rise in profits judged to be excessive. The employers and unions

[1] *Hansard*, November 4, 1964, pp. 221, 224.

[2] Joint statement of Intent on Productivity, Prices and Incomes, HMSO, December 16, 1964.

recognize the validity of three aims: an efficient and competitive industry, a growth of incomes within the limits of increasing productivity, the stability of the general price level. As a result the signatories undertake, in the name of those whom they represent, not to interfere with measures aimed at improving productivity and to co-operate with the Government in the setting up of the machinery necessary for putting a prices and incomes policy into practice.

The second stage of the programme was reached in February 1965 with the publication of a White Paper entitled 'Machinery of Prices and Incomes Policy'.[1] It was stated at the head of this document that it was issued by the Government in agreement with the employers' associations and the TUC. The text proposed that the supervision of the movements of prices and incomes as a whole should be entrusted to NEDC. But a special body would be set up to inquire, at the request of the authorities, into particular cases of prices or wages which did not conform to the established norms. This body would take the name of National Board for Prices and Incomes. The unions therefore agreed to co-operate with the Board, whereas they had always refused to recognize the validity of the National Incomes Commission—to which reference has been made earlier and which was dissolved early in 1965 in accordance with the promise made by the Labour Party before the election.

The Government refers cases to the new Board that has no statutory power to impose its findings. Initially divided into two sectors—for prices and incomes—in practice it has found these two aspects of each case too closely linked to separate them. Its chairman is a former Conservative MP and businessman,[2] who sits with a deputy chairman and three full-time and five part-time members including businessmen and trade unionists. The Board has a full-time secretariat of about 100 people at its disposal. The elements of the inquiries come from hearings, written submissions from the interested parties and from the Government, and from research by the secretariat. On the question of prices, the Board may be asked to report on those of nationalized industries as well as the private sector. Attention will not be restricted to cases of raised prices, but may also be devoted to those where a lowering of prices had not taken place when it was apparently possible. As for incomes, the Board may have cases referred to it while wage negotiations are still going on. Besides increases in pay rates and salaries, it must take account of the repercussions on costs of changes in hours, holidays and other working conditions. Here also, cases submitted by the Government may come from both the nationalized industries and the private sector.

[1] *Machinery of Prices and Incomes Policy*, Cmd. 2577, HMSO, 1965.
[2] Mr Aubrey Jones.

In April 1965 a new White Paper set out the norms which should serve as a basis for the work of the National Board for Prices and Incomes.[1] The key figure was the estimated average growth of production per person employed of 3–3½ per cent taken from the economic plan (1965–70). With the 'freeze' in the summer of 1966 the figure became zero for six months and a new one has yet to be fixed. The document does mention a certain number of exceptions to the general rule. This is the case with wage agreements which include as a *quid pro quo* undertakings aimed at increasing productivity more rapidly than in the past, higher wages offered as an inducement to recruitment in an industry judged to be of national importance, adjustments made necessary by a disparity of earnings in one industry by comparison with other similar jobs, low wages in unfavourably placed trades.

With regard to prices, the White Paper states that increases can be accepted only in certain conditions, for example where productivity in a branch cannot be improved for reasons over which those concerned have no control, and where increases in cost price caused by higher prices of materials or the financing of investment cannot be entirely absorbed by greater productivity. On the other hand there should be a drop in prices in branches enjoying a high rate of growth of productivity; this condition implies that wages in these same branches will rise less rapidly than productivity. Lower prices for materials should equally be reflected in the selling price.

(c) *Early Stages of Practical Application.* The sometimes rather laborious discussions which led up to the new policy involved a fairly small number of people on the employers' side and on that of the TUC. One of the concerns of the Government after the publication of the norms to be used in the carrying out of their policy was therefore to secure a wider approval from the unions. At a meeting of union leaders called for this purpose at the end of April 1965, Mr Brown succeeded in getting his policy approved by 6·6 million votes against 1·8 million; the powerful Transport and General Workers' Union, with 1·4 million votes, was the only large union to vote against.

In an eloquent speech, Mr Brown stressed that the new policy was concerned with every category of price and income, and that an increase in real purchasing power of 3·5 per cent a year was very much better than the 2·5 per cent achieved over the last fifteen years. To seek increases an aggregate earnings greater than the growth of national productivity must necessarily lead to higher prices which would weaken our competitive position, lead to a deficit in the balance of payments, reduce the real value of the higher wages, remove some of their purchasing power from pensions and others with

[1] *Prices and Incomes Policy*, Cmd. 2659, 1965.

fixed incomes, and penalize all whose negotiating position was weak.[1]

The Government found in George Woodcock a convinced, though realistic, supporter of the new policy which he had helped to develop. Without it, in his view, the authorities might just as well abandon the aim of full employment or put a stop to all wage increases. Nevertheless Mr Woodcock did not hide his opinion that nothing spectacular could be expected from it in the near future. In particular he felt that 'there is not the remotest chance that incomes and wages will be kept down to 3½ per cent in this year [1965]'.[2] Events since then have proved him to have been all too right, not only as regards 1965 but 1966 as well, unfortunately. Hence the moves undertaken by the Government to put more teeth into its prices and incomes policy.

A few days later Mr Brown sent to the National Board for Prices and Incomes the first files on price increases. They were concerned with detergents, bread and road transport. A fortnight afterwards a wage increase agreement in the printing industry which had just been concluded was also placed before the Board. From then on, references have followed at a steady, and rapid, pace and, by the closing months of 1966, the Board had published some twenty reports dealing with a wide variety of problems—price increases, wage and salary claims—in all sectors of national life—manufacturing industry, services, Government employment, the nationalized industries. The level of analysis and judgment in each report has remained consistently high and it is particularly noteworthy that the Board has insisted, in practically every case it has had to deal with, on the possibility of increasing productivity and on the almost universal harm done by restrictive practices. The stress upon productivity and competitiveness seems to be what is needed by the economy today and distinguishes the Board's work from that of its predecessor, the National Incomes Commission. This approach bears the personal imprint of the Chairman of the Board who has gone on record as saying that Britain suffers more from restrictive practices than any other industrialized country.[3]

The work of the Board up to the summer of 1966 reveals that the problems of implementing a policy for prices and incomes, which were noted at the beginning of this chapter, have suggested a number of general conclusions that will continue to influence policy-making in the new phase that opened in July 1966 with the 'prices and incomes freeze'. So, before discussing the 'freeze', it is necessary to look briefly at the record of the Board's work between April 1965 and

[1] Speech to TUC leaders, April 30, 1965.

[2] Quoted in *The Times*, May 1, 1965.

[3] Mr Aubrey Jones, Sidney Ball Lecture, quoted by the *Financial Times*, December 2, 1965.

August 1966. A first conclusion that has to be faced is that the voluntary experiment, with the Board as one element, failed. Otherwise the 'freeze' would not have been required. But this failure was due basically to continued excessive demand pressures on the labour market and too complacent lip-service paid by trade unionists and employers to the general principles for a prices and incomes policy they had previously agreed to. The Board itself has emerged with its reputation enhanced as a competent and responsible body. But, too often, the practical results of its recommendations have depended upon Ministerial bullying of the interested parties, a policy whose effectiveness is bound to wear off in time. The best hope for the future of the Board thus lies not mainly in giving its recommendations mandatory power, or in increasing the scope of its action—although steps in these directions may be needed—but basically in providing ways and means of giving institutional expression to the 'general will' of all interested parties to co-operate in making a prices and incomes policy work. This is the great task for 1967, the success or failure of which will very largely decide the fate of the National Board for Prices and Incomes.

A second conclusion from the work of the Board concerns prices. 'The main convention we have found . . . is that of automatically translating increases in wages into increases in prices regardless of the trend in output per man and regardless therefore of the ability to absorb them.' This view has led the Board, in addition to recommending short-run price restraint, to point out ways in which higher costs could be absorbed through increased efficiency, notably 'more critical methods of control in determining the investment of capital resources, the need to adapt manning practices to current technology and to the fact of higher employment, . . . the need to adapt the earnings structure so as to reflect high employment and thus help overcome resistance to change'.[1] The present system of setting incomes in industry is also criticized by the Board. In particular, the major argument justifying increases and which consists of comparisons with other sectors and jobs means that 'pay increases designed to improve productivity cease to be exceptional and become inflationary'. For that reason, since September 1966, the Board has begun a new series of studies of a number of 'productivity agreements' with a view to deciding what practical lessons can be learnt from them for incomes policy. This idea is in line with the renewal of favour for 'plant-level' wage bargaining. Clearly, this approach leaves open the questions of social justice and of treatment of sectors whose productivity cannot be increased that we mentioned earlier in this

[1] General Report of the National Board for Prices and Incomes, August 1966, HMSO, Cmd. 3087, Par. 80.

chapter. These issues are now squarely on the agenda of the new prices and incomes policy in 1967.

In the autumn of 1965 the experiment leaned towards the exercise of greater governmental authority. The Government intimated that Parliament would be asked to pass legislation introducing an 'early warning' system which would make it compulsory to inform the authorities of plans to increase prices or wages. This threat to reinforce the statutory character of the incomes policy stimulated the TUC to set up its own system of early warning in case of wage increases. As approved by the annual congress of the TUC by 5·3 million votes to 3·3 million, the general council must in future be informed by every affiliated union of its intention to ask for a pay rise. The council gives its opinion on each case and until it has done so the union in question is supposed to refrain from entering into negotiations with the employers. Such a decision contains the germ of a radical change in the traditional role of the TUC. We shall come back to this.[1] The TUC set up a special sub-committee to vet claims pending that unions are expected to submit to it before laying them before the employers.

In November 1965, the Department of Economic Affairs published a list of over eighty goods and services that would constitute an 'early warning' system.[2] Changes it was proposed to make in the prices of these goods and services had to be notified to the appropriate Government department at least four weeks before being put into effect, notification being accompanied by precise data justifying the increase. The Government—through the DEA—would decide whether or not to refer the case to the National Board for Prices and Incomes. In such instances, producers were expected to postpone the price rise until the Board had made its report. A similar system applied to wage and salary claims that must also be notified in advance, and irrespective of the TUC's own voluntary vetting procedure just noted.[3]

But this 'early warning' system still lacked legislative sanction and enforcement provisions. During 1966, before and after the spring general elections, there was considerable discussion of the nature of such legislation between the DEA and the representatives of both sides of industry. A draft Bill published in February 1966 lapsed following the elections in March. A new draft was put to Parliament in July 1966, which was profoundly modified by the announcement, on

[1] See Chapter IX.

[2] *Prices and Incomes Policy: An 'Early Warning' System*, HMSO, 1965, Cmnd. 2808.

[3] Unions and staff associations outside the TUC inform the Ministry of Labour directly without going through the intermediary of the TUC.

July 20, of a 'standstill' for six months on increases in prices and wages.[1]

In his statement to the House of Commons, the Prime Minister said: 'The Government are now calling for a six-months' standstill on wages, salaries and other types of incomes, followed by a further six months of severe restraint, and for a similar standstill on prices.' A new Part IV was added to the Prices and Incomes Bill to give effect to this policy.[2] As voted in August, the Bill established the National Board for Prices and Incomes on a permanent basis and gave it statutory powers to call witnesses. The Board could also have matters referred to it for permanent review. This seems to imply that the previous practice of appointing arbitrators in special cases, that had been heavily criticized, will cease. The early warning system became statutory and would take effect for 12-monthly periods after affirmative resolutions by both Houses. It would require 30 days prior notice of price increases and wage and income settlements and increases in company dividends. Except for dividends, a standstill period of three months can be imposed if the Government decides to refer cases to the National Board for Prices and Incomes. Fines can be imposed on those breaking 'standstill' orders.

But the debates on the Prices and Incomes Bill were dominated by Part IV. In August, when the Bill became law, the Government retained the right to bring Part IV into operation by Order in Council. The danger of too many cases of non-respect of the 'freeze' caused this to be done in October 1966. Part IV will lapse automatically on August 11, 1967. It gives the Government powers to issue orders that specific prices or charges shall not be increased and to reverse increases that have been introduced. Incomes can receive the same treatment and employers have been granted legal immunity from actions for breach of contract. Several such orders were issued at the end of 1966 regarding laundry charges, an electrical company's salary increases and the newspaper industry's agreements.

The CBI announced the decision of its members to co-operate in the standstill and the Trades Union Congress in September 1966 voted by a narrow margin its approval of the General Council's 'reluctant acquiescence'. In November, a White Paper—Prices and Incomes Standstill: Period of Severe Restraint—set out the views of the Government but not, it seems, those of the CBI or the TUC, on how to move after January 1, 1967, through the next six months of 'severe restraint' to the permanent arrangements it is hoped to set up to give the prices and incomes policy the firm foundation it had singularly lacked from 1965 to the July 1966 'standstill'.

[1] Publication of the Prices and Incomes Bill provoked the resignation of Mr Cousins who returned to his post as General Secretary of the TGWU.

[2] Prices and Incomes Standstill, Cmd. 3073, HMSO, July 1966.

CHAPTER VIII

REGIONAL RESTRUCTURING

As we have noted in Chapter IV, the years 1960–2 saw in Britain much heart-searching about regional development. This stirring of ideas from many different quarters led to severe criticism of the policy followed till then, including the 1960 Act, and finally inspired some constructive proposals. Both the Conservative Government between 1962 and 1964 and the Labour Government since then took new measures in this field and, at the present time, amid the new bustle of activity in regional affairs, it calls for some imagination to recall the atmosphere of the 1950s that was described in Chapter IV of this book. The title for the present chapter—'Regional Restructuring'—has been chosen for that reason to mark the difference in dimension of regional policy today compared with its predecessors.

The main lines of present policy may be summarized as follows. The sporadic piecemeal approach, based on the appearance of local pockets of unemployment—and which formed the core of the 1960 Act—has been abandoned in favour of a broad attack on the structural problems of large regions. Various incentives to renewal and development have been strengthened and expanded. New administrative structures have been put into place for implementing this approach. Finally, regional issues are now being viewed against the background of the aims of the plan for the economy as a whole and this explains why both the prosperous and the problem areas fall within the scope of regional policy.

In regional matters, where changes occur relatively slowly and where, in any case, there has been since 1962 less a break in policy than an intensification and broadening of the initial efforts and intentions, it is not useful to divide too rigidly the period considered here into two phases, corresponding to the periods of office of the Conservative and Labour Governments. Thus the following paragraphs will deal with in turn: 1, the new measures of the Conservatives; 2, the Labour Government's regional policy; 3, the new concept of the regions worked out since 1962.

1. THE NEW GENERAL MEASURES OF THE CONSERVATIVES

In 1962, even if they had wanted to, the Conservatives could not have claimed that the regional policy of the preceding years had been an unqualified success. The unusually hard winter of 1962–3 added its unfortunate effects on production to the stagnation already brought about by the restrictive measures of July 1961. There resulted an increase in unemployment which, as the graph shows, fell particularly heavily on the old depressed areas. The figures are sufficient by themselves to challenge, if not to condemn, the policy hitherto followed.

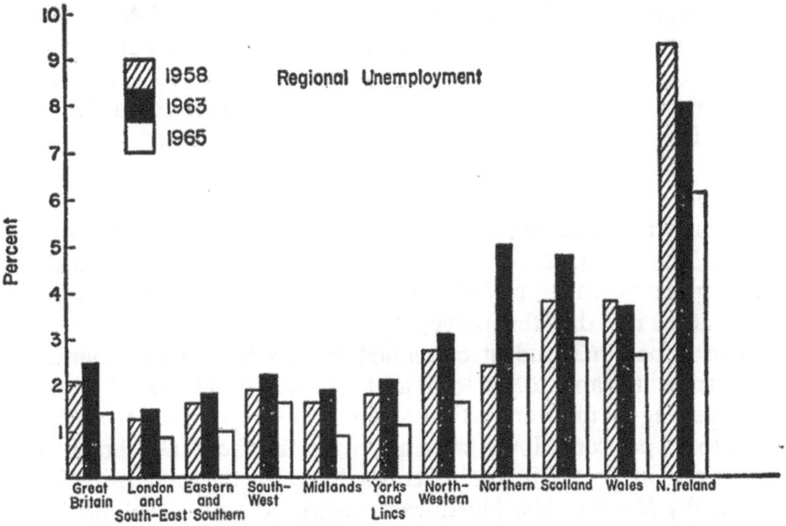

Source: Monthly Digest of Statistics

They called for action which the Government took in 1963, both on the financial side, increasing the aid already agreed to be essential, and on the administrative, introducing reforms of somewhat modest scope.

Financial Measures

The authorities had any number of different financial measures suggested from all sides to complete or replace the 1960 Act. The Government of Northern Ireland, for example, had suggested to the Hall committee[1] an unemployment grant applicable to the whole of productive industry. The North-East Development Council[2] wanted to see certain forms of fiscal discrimination. The Federation of British Industries,[3] realizing the importance of improving communications both within the development areas and between them and the South and the Continent, called for more expenditure on transport (railways, air services, ports). Many people agreed that public investment in social services in the depressed areas should be increased

[1, 2, 3] See Chapter IV.

(housing, schools, institutions for technical training and research). The fight against industrial concentration could be made more effective for example by the speeding up of administrative decentralization (had not the *Economist* proposed that the administrative capital should be moved to the North?[1]), and the introduction of a payroll tax.

Although the Conservative Government did not take up any of these suggestions, they introduced into the budget of April 1963 a certain number of financial stimulants intended to encourage firms more vigorously than hitherto to settle in depressed areas. These stimulants were in addition to those already offered in the 1960 Act.[2] They included two specially important measures.

One of these allowed the Board of Trade to give grants, at the rate of 25 per cent for the cost of building and 10 per cent for equipment, to firms which established themselves or expanded in development areas. The other, known as 'free depreciation', allowed firms in development areas to pay off their expenses on new plant and machinery at the rate they themselves chose.[3]

The same 1963 budget contained certain further arrangements: Government grants to the local authorities in development areas for the cleaning up and renovation of slum sites were raised from 50 per cent to 85 per cent; loans were approved for the establishment of a paper mill at Fort William in Scotland and for the modernization of Lackenby Dock in the North-east; restricted loans totalling £10m. were offered to underdeveloped countries for the purchase of heavy equipment from the depressed areas; another £10m. was set aside for doubling the capacity of the Government training and retraining centres, more than half of which was for Scotland and Northern England.

These stimulants seem to have been effective. The number of requests for help sent to the Board of Trade increased considerably; 435 plans were passed as suitable for aid in 1963–4; they were expected to produce 37,000 extra jobs, of which 16,000 were in Central Scotland and 12,000 in the North-East.

Administrative Measures

The Conservative Government remained somewhat tentative at both central and local levels.

[1] *The Economist*, December 8, 1962 ('North to Elizabetha').

[2] The methods of assistance in all its forms are summed up in a pamphlet by the Board of Trade, *Room to Expand*, 1964.

[3] For further details about these two kinds of stimulant, see the pamphlet *What standard grants and free depreciation can mean to you*, Board of Trade, 1964.

(a) *At central level.* At the beginning of 1963, however, there was a spectacular appointment—of Lord Hailsham as Minister with special responsibility for the North-east. But his main task was to preach patience in this region, where unemployment had reached 7·1 per cent by January 1963, until a comprehensive study of its problems was completed.

Another move was the change of title of the President of the Board of Trade, who became, in October 1963, the Secretary of State for Industry, Trade and Regional Development, and included among his functions the development of the North-east. The post was given to an outstandingly dynamic Conservative who had worked so energetically in Brussels during the negotiations for the entry of Great Britain into the Common Market, Mr Heath (now the leader of the Conservative Party). At the same time there was created at the Board of Trade a directorate for Regional Development, and an interministerial group was formed with four chief tasks: to decide on the general shape of regional plans to be drawn up; to supervise the execution of these plans; to prepare directives for any general policy having repercussions on regional development; to examine problems of research and statistics related to this development (a domain still relatively unexplored in England). At the same time some administrative decentralization was decided on and more extensive powers were given to the Ministries' regional officers.[1]

Some people would have liked to go further and looked forward to the creation of a Ministry of Planning on the lines of the Ministry of Town and Country Planning set up by the Labour Government in 1947. The idea foundered through the fear of seeing a vast organization come into being, controlling such different services as transport, agriculture, location of industry and housing, an organization moreover with ill-defined powers in relation to other Ministries and without effective authority—which had happened in 1947. There remained, then, the problem of co-ordination between the departments mainly concerned: Treasury, Trade, Housing, Transport and Labour.

(b) *At local level.* Although the need for some modernization of the administrative framework had long been recognized, reforms so far introduced have done little to shake up the existing structure. This consists of some 2,000 local authorities of different kinds, whose function when they were created were much more restricted than they are today. Also the local authorities are of unequal size and some are manifestly too small to accomplish the duties incumbent upon them today. Forty-four of the eighty-two county boroughs outside Greater London each contain less than 100,000 population.

The growing disparity between structure and functions led to

[1] See the final section of this chapter.

proposals for a fundamental change in the system. A suggestion was put forward by the committee under the chairmanship of Sir Geoffrey Crowther in 1963.[1] It proposed the setting up of Regional Development Agencies nominated by the Minister after consultation with the local authorities and endowed with considerable legal powers. The Regional Development Agency here envisaged would be an institution of an entirely new type. The best comparison would be with the corporations of the New Towns.[2] The Agency would, it seems, have had even wider powers, for, on top of administrative functions, such as the examination of regional plans and the giving or refusal of grants, it would have important prerogatives with regard to the right to buy and possess land.

This proposal, which aroused no hostility in the Labour ranks, also fitted in with the wishes of the employers. As was shown in Chapter IV, the FBI, in their pamphlet *The Regional Problem: a study of the Areas of High Unemployment* (May 1963), had come out in favour of autonomous regional organizations. The Liberal Party, which had wanted new regional bodies to be created, preferred Regional Councils elected entirely on a representative basis. Today, as we shall see in a moment, the Economic Planning Councils set up by the Labour Government go some way to satisfying these criteria.

The Conservative Government accepted none of these ideas and expressly rejected the conclusions of the Crowther Report. Sir Keith Joseph, Minister of Housing and Local Government, declared that he disagreed with the Crowther Committee, not only because he felt that the reforms proposed would destroy local government, but also because he disliked the idea of an agency.[3]

With regard to land, the Conservatives made no change either in the functions of local authorities, and although in the autumn of 1963 the Government seemed to have an ambitious plan to deal with land speculation,[4] not unlike the Labour idea of a Land Commission —a public body whose function was the acquisition of land—the plan did not come to anything before the elections in the autumn of that year.

[1] This Committee was set up to advise the Minister of Transport about the work of another Committee under Professor Buchanan (Traffic in Towns, HMSO, 1963). The Buchanan Report makes instructive reading. It reveals the enormous traffic problems in towns as a result of the growth in the number of cars, and does not hesitate to propose rigorous action to reduce traffic.

[2] Cf. The Crowther Report,

[3] Quoted by Chester, T. E., in 'The Challenge of Regional Planning', *District Bank Review*, June 1964, p. 16.

[4] 'Government Plan for Land Acquisition', *The Times*, November 20, 1963; 'The Conservatives' Dilemma over Land', *Financial Times*, July 17, 1964; 'Functions of Land Commission', *The Times*, July 27, 1964.

There was, though, one sector in which reforms did come about, in the administration of Greater London. Since the end of the nineteenth century a system had existed whereby a powerful and strongly centralized County Council dominated relatively weak metropolitan boroughs. This organization was hardly suitable any more, now that the limits of the London agglomeration stretched beyond the LCC area. In 1960, 5 million inhabitants lived outside the area and, in eighty years, the population within the LCC area had fallen by a quarter, while there were five times as many people in outer London. A Royal Commission was therefore nominated in 1957 to examine the question. Its report, issued in 1960,[1] was completed by a Government White Paper.[2] The Royal Commission proposed that larger basic units of local government should be created, called London boroughs, and these would be capped by a Greater London Council, directly elected.

The solution finally adopted is of the same type,[3] but the area chosen as the 'Greater London Area' has been reduced in size and population—a reduction which has been criticized. It covers some 600 square miles and includes 8 million inhabitants. On the other hand the London boroughs which were formed to the number of thirty-two are larger than those envisaged by the Royal Commission. They may nevertheless still seem too small, in view of the scope of the functions which they must undertake and which are much more varied than those which fell to the earlier eighty-five authorities. These functions include, *inter alia*, health, social services, housing and planning. We may note in passing one historical anomaly which the new Act retains: the City of London keeps its place apart and its independent statute.

The boroughs are administered by councils elected every three years. The same is true of the Greater London Council (GLC), which has more restricted powers than an ordinary County Council, though the Act gives it, transitionally, responsibility for the London education service. These changes are still too recent for us to judge the practical difficulties of carrying them out, especially those arising from decentralization in favour of the boroughs.

It seemed worth while to study these facts because London is the only example of a really positive local reform. For the rest of the country the authorities came out in favour, not of a reform of local

[1] *Local Government in Greater London*, 1960, Cmd. 1164.

[2] *London Government: Government Proposals for Reorganization*, November 1, 1961, Cmd. 1562.

[3] Act of July 31, 1963. The problems of local administration in London are reviewed in a pamphlet issued by the Conservative Political Centre: *Greater London Government*, March 1964.

government as a whole, but of a strengthening of regional action by the Central Government.[1]

We have already seen something of this strengthening when we noted the extended powers given to regional officers of various Ministries; it reflects a great change in regional policy by the authorities. The Labour Government carried this process further.

Meanwhile, from 1962 onwards, a new element in the situation was provided by the work of the National Economic Development Council. As a result, although the 1960 Act remained in force, the view of the regions and the policy followed by the Government departments were much modified.[2]

In its report, 'Conditions favourable to faster growth', the National Economic Development Council devoted a special chapter to regional problems.

The theme of the report was that regional phenomena are coming more and more to be considered, no longer in isolation, but as forming part of the economic life of the nation as a whole. For this reason the report concludes that aid in itself cannot guarantee success unless, at the same time, the national rate of economic growth increases faster. 'A high pressure of demand in the country as a whole would undoubtedly bring with it an improvement in the regional problem. . . . It will create a desire and need to expand.'[3] Further, the notion of 'areas of high unemployment', needed widening. According to the NEDC 'the less prosperous regions meant areas as wide as 'Northern England, Scotland, Wales and Northern Ireland'.[4] If the 1960 definition, though narrow, represented an interesting innovation, 'it is arguable that better results might be secured for the slowly expanding regions as a whole by identifying their natural growth points and seeking to attract industry to them. Within the bigger areas a wider choice of location than at present would be available to incoming firms'.[5]

This new philosophy brought about in Britain an attitude hitherto unknown in the study of regional problems, which was beginning to take place on the scale of large geographical regions: North-East, Scotland, South-East, South-West, North-West. The Conservative Government began a systematic inquiry into the first three of these regions, a theme to which we return in the concluding section of this

[1] Cf. Joseph, Sir Keith, quoted by Chester, T. E., art. cit., p. 11.

[2] This view was expressed forcibly by Mr Heath in October 1963, then Secretary of State for Industry, Trade and Regional Development, when he said: 'The concept of looking at the structure of a region as a whole is a new one. . . . The regional approach will mean looking at the problems of a region of all kinds as a whole so as to set it growing again.' Quoted in E. G. West's 'Regional Planning—Fact and Fallacy'. *Lloyds Bank Review*, April 1966, p. 34.

[3] Op. cit., p. 27. [4] Op. cit., p. 14. [5] Op. cit., pp. 25 and 26.

chapter. Meanwhile, we must take up the sequel to the renewal of ideas just noted from where the Labour Government began in 1964.

2. THE LABOUR GOVERNMENT'S REGIONAL POLICY

The Labour Party has traditionally been interested in regional problems, and local government affairs have often been the scene where future leaders of the party made their political début. As we have seen, both when in office after the war and during the years in opposition the party has sponsored ambitious plans for regional development. What has happened to this programme since Labour came to power in the autumn of 1964?

The policy of the Labour Government falls conveniently under three main heads: the setting up of new planning bodies at regional level; the introduction of additional measures of assistance to regional development and against urban concentration; planning of land administration.

Setting up of Planning Bodies at Regional Level

In its first months in office the Labour Government clearly stated that regional development is only one aspect of national development, that is of the National Plan that was to be drawn up, but it must be carried out with the collaboration of representative local elements.

Since regional development is regarded as a function of national expansion, it was to be expected that it would be controlled by the Department of Economic Affairs under Mr Brown. This Department has therefore been entrusted with regional planning and a regional directorate has been organized within it, absorbing the earlier directorate of regional development at the Board of Trade. However, the Board of Trade just as the Ministry of Housing and Local Government and the Ministry of Education, to mention only a few, retain executive responsibility for many aspects of policy.

The new administrative arrangements for implementing regional policy consist of a two-tier structure under the DEA—the Economic Planning Councils and the Economic Planning Boards. The outline of this scheme was laid before Parliament by Mr George Brown in December 1964.

There are eleven economic planning regions in the United Kingdom (see map). Scotland, N. Ireland and Wales each constitute, for historical and economic reasons, a region and there are eight in England. Each region has its Planning Council and its Planning Board. In February 1965, the Councils for Scotland, Wales and the North, North-West and West Midlands were established. Two months later followed those for Yorkshire and Humberside, the East Midlands and the South-West. There remained the South-East area where the Government did not decide until August what structure to adopt, after studying the White Paper—South-East England—prepared by its predecessor. The decision was to set up one region to be called East Anglia and another for the South-East proper. In each region, an administrative 'capital' has been designated which, in the case of East Anglia, rather paradoxically, is London.

Economic Planning Regions

The Economic Planning Councils are advisory in character and composed of a chairman and some twenty-five members, serving part-time, and who are appointed by the Government. About one-third come from local government, one-third from industry, commerce and the trade unions and the remainder from the universities and other activities that contribute to regional life. The chairmen are also appointed by the Government.[1]

[1] In Scotland and Wales, the respective Secretaries of State. In Northern Ireland, the Minister of Commerce.

The terms of reference of the Councils as announced in February 1965 are:

'to assist in the formulation of a regional plan having regard to the best use of the region's resources;
to advise on the steps necessary for implementing the regional plan on the basis of information and assessments provided by the Economic Planning Board;
to advise on the regional implications of national economic policies.'[1]

Unlike the part-time members of the Councils who act in an advisory capacity, the Economic Planning Boards are staffed by senior civil servants drawn from the interested Government departments and are chaired by an Under-Secretary from the DEA.[2] The task of the Boards is 'to provide machinery for co-ordinating regional planning work in the regions of the Government Departments'.[3] Both the Councils and the Boards meet in the 'regional capital'; and it is intended that, eventually, the members of the Board, and their staffs, should be housed in the same building.

Since they were set up, these two new bodies have been very active. The chairmen of the Councils keep in regular contact with the Secretary of State for Economic Affairs and with Government departments generally. The nature of their appointment, and the fact that they do not meet in public session, mean that they are brought closer to Government policy-making than the elected local authorities. Indeed, they have been described as 'essentially regional advisory bodies to Central Government'.[4] But the same authors note that some Councils are conscious of their delicate position *vis-à-vis* the elected local councils with whom they are now setting up liaison machinery, particularly those that are planning authorities under the Town and Country Planning Acts. As many elected councils are small, and there are many of them in a single economic planning region, liaison is not easy but is facilitated where local councils themselves—as in the North[5] and South-West,[6] for example —have taken the initiative of creating voluntary co-operation in

[1] Cf. Regional Economic Planning Machinery. *Board of Trade Journal*, June 17, 1966, p. 1,343.

[2] In Wales and Scotland, the Welsh and Scottish offices.

[3] Op. cit.

[4] T. E. Chester and I. R. Gough: Regionalism in the balance. *District Bank Review*, March 1966, p. 13. This article is an invaluable source for data on regional issues.

[5] The South-east Lancashire and North-east Cheshire Transportation Study which covers sixty-two local authorities.

[6] The Joint Committee for the Economy of the South-West.

particular fields (industrial development, tourism, airports, the arts, etc.).

The scope of the work of the Councils is vast, as their mandate quoted earlier indicates. The North-West Councils for example, has set up five committees to deal with: regional strategy, transport, industry, housing, and environment and arts.

The Economic Planning Boards did not innovate entirely in the field of decentralization of Central Government departments. Precedents may be found in the Scottish and North-Eastern Development Groups. Some Government departments, such as the Board of Trade and Ministry of Labour had regional offices already. New Ministries, like Technology and Land Use, have been quick to set them up. The authors of the study already quoted[1] note that, for the time being, active participation by the Central Government departments in the Economic Planning Boards still tends to be uneven and the responsibilities of the fifteen to twenty officials on each Board varies greatly from real executive power to simple liaison. But it is to be expected that an innovation in established administrative practices of the dimensions of the present regional policy will take time for adaptation to them fully to be achieved. Indeed, as was noted in Chapter VI, the proper functioning of co-ordinated regional boards depends, in part, on satisfactory solutions being found to the co-ordination of policy at the Central Government level between the DEA and the other departments.

A delicate problem that remains as regards the new machinery of councils and boards is that of their relations with local government bodies and, more still, of the real place of the latter in regional planning. The Government, understandably, has been at pains to stress the advisory status of the councils and the co-ordination functions of the boards. But, if the councils are to be no more than that, it may be that the present enthusiasm they have evoked will soon diminish; if, on the other hand, they clearly do begin to have an influence on Government policy, then difficulties in their relations with elected local councils are bound to arise. This would be the case, notably, if Government expenditure—as would be logical—was allocated not only according to departments but also by regions. A potential strength of the existing local councils is that they are better equipped to act as agents for regional *physical* planning, as opposed to *economic* planning, which will always remain an important element in regional policy.[2]

The next move in this matter may be expected after the publica-

[1] T. E. Chester and I. R. Gough, op. cit.

[2] Cf. on this point D. Rigby Childs: 'A new approach to Regional Planning', *The Listener*, May 1965.

tion of the report of the Royal Commissions (one for England and one for Scotland) on local government that were set up in May 1966. The mandate of the Commission for England is: 'To consider the structure of local government in England, outside Greater London, in relation to its existing functions and to make recommendations for authorities and boundaries, and for functions and their discussion, having regard to the size and character of one as in which these can be most effectively exercised and the need to sustain a viable system of local democracy.'

Other recent pointers suggest that an overhaul of local government may now be undertaken. The latter is characterized in Britain by the co-existence of two systems—the all-purpose county borough and the two-tier county/county district—that live in uneasy harmony. The spread of conurbations, and the need for wider scope for some services, would suggest that big all-purpose local government units are the most appropriate solution. But a basic principle of local government is that small units provide a guarantee of active local democracy.[1] In this connection, a solution that began to enjoy the favour of many observers, and of the Ministry of Local Government too it seems, is that of the 'city-region'. The latter would be defined as a city and its hinterland and would form a new local government unit replacing the existing counties and county boroughs.[2]

Measures to assist Regional Development and against Urban Concentration

The creation of the new bodies just described to work out regional development plans left intact the system of incentives to encourage development in backward areas and the definition of those areas (the development districts). The Labour Government has taken action to increase the effectiveness of Government incentives as well as tightening the 'disincentives' to expand in the congested areas.

(*a*) *Increased Incentives.* Advance factory building—a technique used for some years by the Board of Trade—has been speeded up. New investment incentives are now being provided. An Industrial Development Bill sets the stage—among other measures—for a reform of the existing development districts.

[1] The present Minister of Local Government (Mr Crossman) expressed the problem as follows, when speaking of the need for an authoritative analysis of 'the relation of size and function in local government under modern conditions, where many services are regional in character [and of] the way to resolve the conflict between local democracy, which is inherently small, and efficiency, which is sometimes large'. Quoted by Sir William Hart, 'The Conurbations and Regions', *Political Quarterly*, April–June 1966, p. 134.

[2] See *The Regional City*, ed. by R. Senior, Longmans, 1966, and the article by Sir William Hart, op. cit.

By the end of 1966, the Board of Trade had announced four new programmes for building advance factories to be completed during 1967. The first two programmes were for fifty-five factories, covering an area of nearly 900,000 square feet, of which thirty-two are situated in coalmining areas. The third, announced in May 1966, for eighteen factories (380,000 square feet), is also directed chiefly at providing alternative employment for coal miners. In November 1966, a further twenty-one factories (475,000 square feet), mainly in Wales, the North-West and Scotland, were planned.

The existing Board of Trade industrial estates are being expanded and new areas constructed (notably in Lanarkshire and South Tees-side). Private industrial schemes are being helped by the Board of Trade, particularly the Ford Motor Company at Swansea, Firestone Tyre and Rubber Company at Wrexham and ICI at Ardeer in Ayr-shire.

All in all, by 1966, there were 260,000 people working in factories owned by the Board of Trade, comprising 57 million square feet, an area that will rise to 60 million square feet when the current programme is complete.

Total financial assistance by the Board of Trade to private industrial schemes in development districts reached £42m. in the fiscal year 1965–6, compared with an annual rate of £30·2m. during the period 1960–4. When it became necessary, in July 1965, to cut back public expenditure on social infrastructure, schemes in the development districts were exempted.

When the Government issued—in January 1966—its White Paper on 'Investment Incentives' attention was directed, in the first instance, to the effects of the new scheme on private investment in general. It may be that, in future, the implications of this White Paper for regional policy will be seen to have been more important still. Henceforth, manufacturing and extractive industries will receive from the Exchequer investment grants for plant and machinery at double the national rate, 40 per cent instead of 20 per cent.[1] A significant change compared with previous practice is that these grants will be paid irrespective of the extra employment generated by the investment.

In the eighteen months after October 1964, the new Government extended considerably the area covered by the development districts, adding some 440,000 extra population. This step was a stop-gap measure only and, in the summer of 1966, new 'development areas' were announced. The investment grants just described apply to firms in these areas.

The new development areas are shown on the map. It will be seen

[1] 45 per cent instead of 25 per cent up to December 31, 1968.

that they cover considerably larger areas than the old development districts.[1]

Thus the criticisms directed against the concept of these districts[2] have now led to a radical change in approach. Not only are the development areas much larger, but they have been fixed once and for all and are not based upon narrowly defined high-unemployment criteria.

The Industrial Development Bill that was voted in 1966 is designed to give legislative force to these proposals. The Bill adds construction and search for oil and natural gas in the North Sea to the activities qualifying for the special rate of investment grants. Industries in development areas that do not qualify for the double rate of investment grants will continue to receive initial investment allowances for tax purposes at an increased rate of 30 per cent. The definition of the new development areas is confirmed with the provision that the Board of Trade will be able to include, where justified, certain overspill areas within their scope. The present arrangements for providing advance factories, grants and loans to firms giving employment are to continue as are building grants at 25 per cent. The grant can be raised to 35 per cent in special cases or, for advance factories for rent, a rent-free period may be offered. Where the employment effects of industrial projects are insufficient to qualify for such grants the Board of Trade is empowered, nevertheless, to propose a lower rate.

A feature of the new Bill that has attracted attention is the

[1] They are defined as follows:

(1) The whole of Scotland, except the Edinburgh, Leith and Portobello employment exchange areas.

(2) The Northern Development Area consisting of the Ministry of Labour Northern Region, plus the Furness peninsula (i.e. the Barrow group and Ulverston employment exchange area and Grange-over-Sands sub-office area).

(3) The Merseyside Development Area consisting of the existing development districts with the addition of St Helens, Runcorn, Ellesmere Port, Neston and Hoylake employment exhange areas. Skelmersdale new town, which draws its population mainly from Merseyside, will also qualify for the benefits available within the development area.

(4) The Welsh Development Area consisting of the whole of Wales and Monmouthshire, with the exception of the following employment exchange areas:

a. South-East Wales—the Cardiff and Newport groups, Chepstow, Abergavenny and Cwmbran and the Monmouth sub-office area; and

b. North Wales—the Chotton group and Rhyl, Colwyn Bay and Llandudno.

(5) The South-Western Development Area consisting of the employment exchange areas in Cornwall (excluding Devonport, Saltash and Gunnislake but including Launceston and Bude), and the North Devonshire employment exchange areas of Bideford, Barnstaple and Ilfracombe.

[2] See Chapter IV.

provision which allows the Board of Trade to offer financial assistance to undertakings in development areas by subscribing for shares or stock or by making a loan with an option to convert into equity.

The investment grants are expected to cost £250m. a year in the development areas. The existing cost of other forms of assistance is higher by £35m. to £40m. due to the effect of the enlarged development areas. These sums are large and the Exchequer will soon have to face some hard problems of choice now that the previous target for the overall growth of public expenditure is to be cut back.

(b) *The Congested Areas.* An early measure introduced by the Labour Government was a strict control over office building in an area roughly 40 miles from Charing Cross in London, and in the built-up area in and around Birmingham (see map). In August 1965, the Industrial Development Certificates were extended to new industrial buildings of 1,000 square feet (instead of 5,000 square feet as previously) in the Midlands and South-East England and, in 1966, to all buildings to be used for scientific research by private firms. Since July 1966, IDC's are granted more stringently still, except in development areas.

Clearly, the Board of Trade now has at its disposal a very powerful instrument for directing building for manufacturing or other purposes away from the congested areas. Flexibility in the use of these new powers under the IDC's will be necessary, however, as the areas of the Midlands and South-East England do not constitute, as a whole, congested regions. There are many rural areas included, as well as some new towns.[1]

It is still too early to see the full effects of these measures to stimulate investment in less-prosperous areas and to direct new development away from the congested areas. But it may be noted that the North and West received a much larger share of factory building in 1965 than in the period 1960–4 and the South and East much less. Fifty per cent of new factory approvals, compared with 39 per cent, went to Scotland, Wales, the North and North-West. Also in 1965, the three congested areas of London and the South-East, Eastern and Midlands received 30 per cent compared with 40 per cent from 1960 to 1964.

(c) *The Land Commission.* The struggle against land speculation and, to this end, the creation of an official body capable of acquiring land destined for development have long been one of the major themes in Labour's programme.

A White Paper, published in September 1965,[2] set out the pro-

[1] See, on this point, B. J. Loasby: 'Location of Industry—Thirty years of "planning"': *District Bank Review*, December 1965.

[2] *The Land Commission*, Cmd. 2771, 1965.

posals being put forward by the Government in this field. Before the elections in March 1966, a Bill giving legislative force to the ideas in the White Paper received a Second Reading but then lapsed. It was brought forward again later the same year and was approved by Parliament in the autumn and began work before the end of 1966.

The legislation was described by the Minister of Land and National Resources[1] as being 'founded on the proposition that the value attached to land by the right to develop it was a value which had been substantially accrued by the community'.[2] It followed that the community was justified in appropriating a share of such increased value. Furthermore, as owners were not always willing to make land available for desirable development projects, the latter could be frustrated by an insufficient supply of land which the community should be armed with compulsory powers to correct.

The original proposal for a Land Commission, put forward in the Labour Party's election manifesto in 1964, suggested that the scope of the legislation would cover all land on which building or rebuilding was to take place; such land being acquired at below market prices. The Land Commission Bill is more limited, but it nevertheless gives the Commission the same powers of compulsory purchase as a Minister, except that an order would have to be authorized at ministerial level.

Compulsory purchase would presumably be an exception. In the normal case the Commission would acquire land by purchase on the market. From the enactment of the Bill all sales of land in private transactions or to public bodies, including the Commission, would attract a levy of 40 per cent of development values. The rate chosen is a low one so that owners are not deterred from selling their land. It is to be increased subsequently with the same object in view. The levy will be paid by the purchaser who—in theory—will be able to recuperate the cost in the price he pays.

The Land Commission would be able to manage land thus acquired before disposing of it either by sale or lease. It is intended that prices fixed by the Commission shall be related to the purpose to which the land is to be put. There is even provision for disposal at discretionary prices below normal values.

The Commission will consist of a Chairman and at most eight members, nominated jointly by the Minister of Land and Natural Resources and the Secretary of State for Scotland. It will work within the framework of regional development plans and in collaboration

[1] A new Ministry created by the Labour Government.

[2] Mr Willey reported in *The Times*, February 1, 1966.

with the local authorities whose existing powers of acquisition of land remain in force.

3. THE NEW REGIONS: SOME CASE STUDIES

A new regional policy has been emerging rapidly in recent years as we have seen under the impetus, first of the Conservatives and then of the Labour Party. But action by the State, from the top downwards, should not lead to neglect of the numerous local initiatives that, over the years, have been instrumental in bringing regional development issues to the notice of national opinion and, hence, of Governments. The two examples that come immediately to mind in this connection are Scotland and the North-East. The circumstances of the London area are so different from these two regions that it seems appropriate to note also the work in progress in the South-East as an illustration of what was said earlier regarding the fresh concept of regional policy which attempts to see the problems of all regions in the light of the development of the economy as a whole.

Scotland

A pioneering report in Scottish development dates from 1952 and it was the first to launch the idea of a co-ordinated approach to the problems of the area seen as a whole.[1] The early 1960s saw increased interest in Scottish matters. In 1961, the Toothill Committee published a Report on the Scottish Economy under the auspices of the Scottish Council, a voluntary association with wide membership including local authorities, trade associations, chambers of commerce and co-operatives. Following the publication of the NEDC's programme for 1961–6 a White Paper was published in 1963 which outlined proposals for action in Central Scotland.[2] In 1966, the Labour Government carried a step further the process of defining a development policy for Scotland by publishing a plan for the years 1965–70.[3]

Before examining the contents of these plans and the results achieved to date, it will be appropriate to recall briefly what are the major development issues for Scotland.

With a population of 5·2 million for an area of 20 million acres, one-third of the United Kingdom, Scotland's overall population density is the lowest of all the planning regions, 0·17 persons per

[1] Scottish Council (Development and Industry), Report of a Committee on Local Development in Scotland, Edinburgh 1952.

[2] *Central Scotland—a programme for development and growth*, HMSO, Cmd. 2188, 1963.

[3] *The Scottish Economy, 1965–70: a plan for expansion*, HMSO, Cmd. 2864, 1966.

acre compared with a national average of 0·59 persons. But there are wide differences in population density as between Central Scotland, where 1·8 million persons live in conurbations along the Glasgow-Edinburgh belt, and the sparsely populated Highlands and Western islands.

In the period 1953–63, the average unemployment rate in Scotland was 3·4 per cent, the highest in the country except for Northern Ireland and double the national average. Employment grew hardly at all in those years, by less than 1 per cent, compared with 9 per cent in the United Kingdom as a whole and only one-fifth of the area's workers were in industries with expanding employment and 18 per cent in contracting ones. As a result, migration southwards accounted for nearly 30,000 persons a year. In 1965, before they were abolished, development districts in Scotland accounted for 68 per cent of insured workers.

It was therefore to be expected that plans for Scotland would place special emphasis on the employment prospects in the region. The present plan 1965–70 sets itself the aim of raising the number of jobs by 50 to 60 thousand. As many industries in decline will continue to reduce their employment levels, this will call for the creation of some 130,000 jobs by 1970. This target necessitates an acceleration of training and retraining schemes and an expansion of educational facilities generally.

Development of employment will be concentrated mainly in Central Scotland where four-fifths of the Scottish population live. This is in line with the views of previous studies of the Scottish economy. Major expansions are foreseen in North Ayrshire—where a new town is to be built—Lanarkshire and the Falkirk-Grangemouth region. The four existing new towns in Central Scotland are to be expanded further to accommodate the growth of industry and the number of workers. Manufacturing industry is considered to be the key to development but the service industries, that employ half the labour force, will also have to expand.

The 1966 Plan innovates, compared with the 1963 White Paper, in that it covers the whole of Scotland and not just the central area. In the Borders area, the development of the Galashiels district is expected to accommodate an extra 25,000 people. Advance factories are being prepared with this end in view. In the South-West agriculture—particularly dairy farming—is to be the mainstay of development policy. In the Highlands, the Forestry Commission will raise its current tree-planting programme to 20,000 a year. The whole of Scotland, except for Edinburgh, Leith and Portobello, is now a development area and benefits from the various incentives being made available by the Board of Trade.

The 1963 programme placed considerable emphasis upon the role of public expenditure in the development of the Scottish economy through improvements in housing, urban renovation and roads. The present plan carries this programme further. In 1966, public investment in Scotland should reach £360m. compared with £312m. on average over the previous five years. By 1970, the figure is planned to reach £390m. Housing is the largest single item. The nationalized industries will invest large sums. Roads, education and health and welfare services will absorb the remainder.

The growth projections for Scotland up to 1970, compared with the average for the United Kingdom, are summarized in the following table:

TABLE I

GROWTH PROJECTIONS 1964–70 (ANNUAL PERCENTAGE RATES)

	Production		*Employment*		*Output per head*	
	UK	*Scotland*	*UK*	*Scotland*	*UK*	*Scotland*
All Industries	4·5	4·8	0·4	0·4	4·1	4·4
Manufacturing	4·4	4·6	0·5	0·6	3·9	4·0
Construction	4·6	5·8	0·9	1·6	3·7	4·1
Gas, electricity and water	8·4	8·4	1·7	1·8	6·5	6·5
Mining and Quarrying	—	−0·5	−5·1	−6·8	5·4	6·7

Source: The Scottish Economy, 1965–70.

The sustained efforts in recent years to stimulate the growth of the Scottish economy have begun to yield results. Industrial production in Scotland, in 1965, was 19 per cent higher than in 1960, whereas, in the United Kingdom, the rise was 16 per cent. Unemployment in Scotland in mid-1966 was 2·7 per cent, lower than for some years and nearer the national average (see graph). With such massive increases in public expenditure as those now taking place, in addition to the inducements being offered to private industry, it would indeed be surprising if the Scottish economy did not progress rapidly. In so far as Scotland contains the largest pool of unused labour in the country, the stress being given to Scottish development is in line with the thinking expressed in the now defunct National Plan. Meanwhile, the big question is whether Scotland, like other development areas, can come through the present 'squeeze' without too much harm.

The Northern Region

This region, comprising the whole of the North of England, became a single planning unit in 1965 when the system of regional councils already described came into existence. Previously, the problems of the region had been dealt with under two heads, the North-East and the North-West. The former took shape as a planning unit under the

Conservative Government when Lord Hailsham received a special mission for the North-East. The North-East Development Council—a private body—was set up in 1961 and it remains today the prime mover for development issues.[1] The problems of the North-East were thus studied, and solutions found for some of them, earlier than in the North-West.[2] For the time being, no comprehensive programme for the whole of the northern region, analogous to the Scottish plan, has been published. In any event, such a programme will have to lean heavily on the work done for the North-East and, in the following paragraphs, we shall therefore concentrate attention on that part of the northern region.

The North-East comprises the counties of Northumberland, Durham and the North Riding of Yorkshire. But the growth centre of the area that has been recognized is bounded by the Tyne, the Tees and the North Sea and stretching westwards a little beyond the Great North Road (A1), covering the eastern half of County Durham. The two urban agglomerations of Tyneside and Tees-side and the Darlington-Aycliffe area are specially singled out as centres for expansion.

The industrial structure is particularly unfavourable. In the early 1960s, coal-mining—the chief industry losing manpower today—employed 16 per cent of male labour, or four times the national average, and shipbuilding 7 per cent. In total, nearly half the region's male workers were employed in a handful of industries—coal, steel, shipbuilding, marine, electrical and general engineering, chemicals. Long years of depression and neglect of infrastructure had left in inheritance poor and obsolete communications and much sub-standard housing. Early in 1963, at the peak of winter unemployment, there were 7·4 per cent out of work and it was estimated that some 12,000 workers left the region each year.

The 1963 policy consisted essentially in focusing increased public expenditure on the core of the North-East just defined, expenditure being due to rise from £55m. in 1962–3 to £90m. in 1964–5. Investment in roads, railways, ports and airports was stepped up. A housing target of 25,000 new houses was fixed compared with the existing rate of 18,000. Town improvement generally, and the expansion of social services and educational facilities were decided. Industrial training centres were opened. With the help of the North-East Development Centre, the Board of Trade took the lead in co-ordinating the activities of Government departments in the North-East. At one time it was expected that the GPO might be decentralized to

[1] Cf. Chapter IV.

[2] *The North-East: a Programme for regional development and growth*, HMSO, Cmd. 2206, 1963.

the North-East, but Scotland was finally chosen. The greater part of the offices of the Ministry of Pensions and National Insurance is now in Newcastle. At the administrative level, the ten regional offices of Government departments concerned with the North-East were grouped symbolically, in the same building, Welbar House in Newcastle. Thus the North-East represented already the embryo of the present regional planning set-up of Economic Planning Councils and Boards.

The Labour Government has placed practically the whole of the northern region—and all of the North-East—in the development areas where the new assistance to industry that was described earlier will apply. Policy with regard to infrastructure and industrial training—inaugurated by the 1963 White Paper—is being continued in its main lines, but intensified. The implementation of the Geddes report on the shipbuilding industry[1] and the nationalization of the ports are both measures that could bring benefit to the traditional industries of the North-East, The Board of Trade continues to make vigorous use of IDC's in favour of the region that received 11 per cent of certificates issued in 1965 for 5·7 per cent of the insured population. By 1966, in three years, thirty-one advance factories had been completed or were in course of construction. If the prospect of big resources of natural gas from the North Sea transpires, the North-East will become a favourable location for industries like chemicals.

In 1966, there were signs that this intense activity was bearing fruit. Unemployment had fallen to 2·5 per cent, or 30,000, and the North-East Development Council calculates that there are at present 38,000 new jobs in the pipeline up to 1970. In many skills, shortages of labour exist and employers find difficulty in recruiting extra manpower despite the expansion of training facilities. In 1965–6, five-sixths of IDC's concerned firms already established in the region compared with less than three-quarters in the previous year. In sum, more even than in Scotland, the new regional policies of the 1960s have begun to pay dividends in the North-East.

The South-East

The National Plan characterizes the South-East as a 'congested area'.[2] This is taken to mean that there is pressure on space around the London conurbation and that such pressure is steadily increasing due to internal migration from other areas and to immigration from abroad. Despite the resulting above-average rate of increase of the labour force, there is heavy 'demand for labour, low unemployment, rapid growth of employment, high activity rates'.[3] These characteristics call for a different approach through regional

[1] See Chapter VI. [2] Op. cit., p. 89. [3] *The National Plan*, p. 89.

development policy from the ones just described in Scotland and the North.

Two official documents had been issued in 1964 by the Conservative Government to set guidelines for policy in the South-East.[1] The general tenor of these studies was that, whilst the further growth of population was inevitable, in future Government policy should not encourage it. Meanwhile, the most urgent task was to bring about the more harmonious development of a region whose past growth had been left too much to chance.

Plan for the Development of the London Area

The Labour Government has not yet taken up position officially on growth prospects in the South-East so the South-East Study and the 1964 White Paper remain the basic documents. The new Economic Planning Council is, at present, working on this.

The 1964 study concluded that the South-East, which was defined as the region lying to the south-east of a line running from the Wash to Dorset, with 18 million inhabitants would grow by 3½ million by 1981, of which 1 million would be in Greater London. Seven-tenths of this increase will come from the natural surplus of births over deaths and the rest from outside the area.

The 1964 White Paper envisages that this rise in population—

[1] *The South-East Study* (1961–81), Ministry of Housing and Local Government, HMSO, 1964, and *South-East England* (White Paper), HMSO, Cmd. 2308, 1964.

which it accepts—must be accommodated outside of the London area either through local authority development schemes or in new towns and expanded towns. This raises, of course, the question of finding land for such a massive building programme. The Conservative White Paper contented itself with advising local authorities to acquire sites well in advance. The newly created Land Commission, which was described earlier, will no doubt be very much concerned with the problems of the South-East. A related issue is where employment expansion will take place, in London (thus increasing transport problems), or on the periphery. The Conservative Government had not taken up position on this matter before the 1964 elections. The Labour Government seems to have opted in favour of fairly strict limitations on the creation of jobs in London. Control on office building within a radius of 40 miles of Charing Cross, new and stricter limits for the delivery of building licences, more active use of IDC's to favour the less prosperous regions, all these are pointers towards the present Government's policy.

The prospect of continued urbanization during the rest of the century—there are likely to be 20 million more people in Britain in the year 2000—raises the problem of the choice of areas that can accommodate such an increase. The northern areas, as we have seen, are now likely to play a more important role in this respect and the Home Counties will also have to receive more population. The Government have also decided that new areas for urbanization should be studied. Three of these that have been chosen are Humberside, Severnside, Dundee.[1] A new Central Planning Unit, set up inside the DEA, began work in 1966 on the Humberside project. Large-scale development is envisaged including cities with populations of a quarter to one million, new docks and transport systems and industries.

As has been seen, the task of translating the general principles of the National Plan regarding the regions into concrete programmes for action is not yet complete. But already, thanks in part to earlier efforts, the results as regards the northern areas of the country are substantial. The Department of Economic Affairs is at present engaged in a review of population trends, the pattern of settlement and related factors up to the year 2000. This review will pin-point the areas suitable for large-scale development in the long term. It must be admitted that all regional studies are hampered by lack of statistical knowledge on such elementary facts as employment, skills, production and investment. These gaps are now being filled in and

[1] Humberside includes both banks of the river from Goole to the sea; Severnside both banks of the river from Gloucester to Bristol/Newport; the Dundee area extends from the north and south of the Firth of Tay to west of Perth.

in 1966 a new Abstract of Regional Statistics began publication.

But the really major issues for the task of regional restructuring that lies ahead are not ones that can be solved by better data, though the latter are needed to ensure that decisions are soundly based on facts. The last word on this may appropriately be left to two authors who have already done much to enrich our statistical knowledge of regional matters: 'The real issue of regional development is . . . nothing less than the problem of replanning the whole urban life of the country . . . [but] our political system with its relatively short-term horizons is not in fact well adapted to taking the kind of long-term decisions required for regional development. It is the lack of central machinery for taking long-term decisions rather than deficiencies of regional government or regional statistics that constitute the main obstacle to regional development at the present time.'[1] It is to be hoped that the changes in policy, and in machinery for implementing them, which have been described in this chapter will contribute to overcoming this obstacle.

[1] Mrs M. F. W. Hemming and Mrs H. M. Duffy: 'Regional Statistics', *District Bank Review*, March 1965.

CHAPTER IX

MODERNIZATION

In spite of obvious exaggerations, the English *mal du siècle* struck the imagination of thinking people quite apart from any political considerations, and the electors could not fail to observe, during the election campaigns in October 1964 and March 1966, that each of the three political parties made the modernization of the British economy one of their principal electoral platforms. In doing so, they were responding to the desire of public opinion because, just before the elections, a sample survey showed that 81 per cent of the electorate thought that there was either an 'urgent' or 'some' need to modernize Britain.[1]

The theme certainly requires definition, for it sometimes tends to mean no more than a rejection of the past and a preference for change for its own sake. The wished-for modernization goes beyond the narrow technical meaning of the word; it seems to imply first and foremost the re-thinking of methods of managing the economy in both the official and the private sector. Profound changes in the habits of mind and action of officials, businessmen and trade unionists are needed to bring about a new dynamism, a new flexibility and adaptability of the economy to the modern world. In October 1964, the electors confided the responsibility for this task to the Labour Party, who inherited the plans already started by their predecessors.

We can pick out three leading motifs in the movement for modernization in Britain today: the *élites*; labour-market policy; science and technology.

1. THE ELITES

It is now generally admitted that in any process of development the quality of men, institutions and methods of work is of capital importance. The traditional methods of administration have been strongly criticized, in both the official and the private sector, and held responsible for the unsatisfactory functioning of the British economy.[2]

[1] When asked what needed modernizing the replies were: the transport system, the trade unions, the nationalized industries, the civil service, business management. See R. McKenzie, 'Between Two Elections', *Encounter*, January 1966.

[2] A subject analysed in the first part of this book.

It could therefore be expected that both the second report of the National Economic Development Council, analysing the 'conditions favourable to faster growth', and Labour's National Plan should deal with the part played by Government, by employers and by union leaders, three themes which we will now consider.

The Public Sector

If English officialdom has been criticized—and has criticized itself—for a certain amateurishness and a tendency to isolation, it would be quite wrong today to describe the situation in black and white terms, for important changes have taken place in recent years in both the recruitment and the training of civil servants.

(a) *Recruitment.* Although the overall method of recruitment to the higher ranks of the Civil Service remains unchanged, there are now new possibilities for recruits from the world of business and from academic life to enter the public service.

In June 1964, the Minister of State at the Treasury authorized a widening of the rules of recruitment. In future nine senior civil servants, aged between 30 and 45, will be selected over and above the usual contingent of young men and women from the universities. The candidates must have held responsible positions in private business, the university or liberal professions. At the same time the rules applicable to officials leaving the service have been made more flexible, and an official who resigns under the age of 50, with his Minister's agreement, does not as a result sacrifice his rights to a proportionate pension. In 1962 the secretariat of NEDC recruited the larger part of its staff outside the Civil Service. In February 1964, when the Bank of England reorganized its economic service, it put it under the direction of a university economist. The field of action for the new Government was therefore already prepared.

The most important innovation of the Labour Government, the creation of a Department of Economic Affairs,[1] brought about a large recruitment of non-officials, especially men from the higher ranks of industry and the banks. Apart from these full-time members, the Ministry makes great use of occasional help, especially from the universities. A similar development will be found in other parts of the public service. Apart from Professor Balogh, economic adviser to the Prime Minister with a personal secretariat, the Chancellor of the Exchequer has two private advisers. The Ministries of Overseas Development, Technology and Transport have also recruited many people from outside the Civil Service. It has been estimated that there were some thirty professional working economists in Whitehall in October 1964 and over 100 eighteen months later, seventy of them

[1] Cf. Chapter VI.

full-time but of those only seventeen were established civil servants.[1] Another sign of changed times is that, in 1965, 24 per cent of new entrants to the administrative class had not been to Oxford or Cambridge compared with 16 per cent in 1964.[2]

The recent changes in the selection of senior officials in the public service were a bold move. The present experimental phase has perhaps swung the pendulum too far and there will probably have to be some adjustments. Those who set out to reform the British Civil Service are aiming especially at introducing elements from the private sector, inspired apparently by the system of ministerial cabinets to be found on the Continent. Now the latter, at any rate in France, are in fact mainly recruited from the Civil Service and not from the business world.[3]

However that may be, the most important outcome of these reforms is the opening up of the British administration to the outside world. Such efforts at co-operation between the official and private sectors are a characteristic very wide-spread in the development of modern industrial economies.

(b) *Training and Promotion.* Changes in the recruitment of officials inevitably bring in their train changes in the training of young entrants to the Civil Service.

Without going so far as to open a special school which, like the National School of Administration in France, would have taken care of both the recruitment and the training of future high officials, the British Government nevertheless organized a Centre for Administrative Studies in 1963.

Today all recruits into the administrative class must follow the course at the Centre. For three weeks they attend courses on the structure of the administration, then, after three years of normal work in a department, they return to the Centre for twenty weeks. The teaching deals mainly with political economy, micro- and macro-economic analysis, and statistics. Part of the time is devoted to the study of industry and modern administrative methods. The Centre does not classify its students nor is there an examination. Its function is to provide courses of lectures, seminars and study groups. The courses of study are undoubtedly an innovation in the training of high officials; but they remain a little narrow and could usefully include such subjects as the study of social phenomena.

One of the questions which have been discussed is the creation of a

[1] J. Rogaly in the *Financial Times*, January 27, 1966.

[2] Annual Report of the Civil Service Commissioners, 1965.

[3] See A. Dutheillet de Lamothe: 'Ministerial Cabinets in France', *Public Administration*, winter 1965.

Civil Service Staff College to which high ranking officials with several years' service could be seconded for a year.

In 1966, the Treasury proposed to a committee inquiring into Civil Service structure (the Fulton Committee) ways of opening up to officers in the professional and scientific classes access to senior posts responsible for policy formulation and managerial functions. The means of doing this would be to introduce a new grading structure that would merge the existing administrative and executive classes into a single general management group. The Treasury memorandum says that, in this way, 'more scientists and professionals who have the potential for top management might be attracted into the Civil Service if they knew that the higher posts in the general management field were open to them and that training courses would be provided to equip them for management and to bring out their aptitudes for it'.[1] It is likely that the report of the Fulton Committee will recommend a number of changes in Civil Service recruitment and training.

The Leaders of Private Industry

Old-fashioned institutions are perhaps a more serious danger to our Western countries, now entering a phase of accelerated change, than out-of-date technology, though the latter is often bound up with institutions. Indicative planning imposes heavy responsibilities on the private sector and inevitably calls for an 'agonizing reappraisal' of methods of thought. At present the changes are more marked at the top than lower down. The reader will notice a similarity between what is happening among the employers—which is discussed here—and among trade unionists—which will be examined later.

(a) *History*. Whereas the reform of the TUC appeared on the agenda of the General Council in 1962, the employers' organizations did not begin to modernize themselves until 1963. It was in March 1963 that the congress of the British Employers' Confederation raised the question of the structural unsuitability of their organizations to meet their tasks. One of the employers' representatives[2] on NEDC, and the then Minister of Labour who also sat on NEDC, strongly supported the idea that the employers' organizations should be merged. Among other arguments in favour of fusion, they pointed to the employers' participation in NEDC, the need to face a contribution by the employers to the implementation of an incomes policy, and the indispensable recasting of labour policy and working relationships—all tasks for which the employers were still unprepared.

In July 1963, the three principal employers' organizations decided to entrust two delegates with the task of preparing a report on the

[1] Quoted in *The Times*, June 30, 1966.

[2] Mr Hunter.

creation of a single unified body. Ready in April 1964, the report came out in favour of the plan and proposed the following organization:[1] application would be accepted from individual firms, professional associations and employers' federations, and—a new idea—the nationalized industries could join as associate members.[2] The same report stresses the need for a firm regional structure. It makes clear also that the organization would not replace the existing employers' federations in collective contracts and wage agreements.

As a result of this work, agreement in principle was reached in December 1964 between representatives of the three employers' organizations. In February 1965, the president, the two vice-presidents and the director-general of the new body were nominated, and the organization began to function in August 1965, under the name of Confederation of British Industries (CBI).

The fusion is too recent for any judgment to be passed on the results, especially as hard work will be necessary to bring the local organizations throughout the country up to date with their leaders at the centre. A dissident minority group, the Society of Independent Manufacturers, has already been formed among small and medium-sized firms which refuse to join the CBI, but its numerical importance is slight. At regional level negotiations are going on between representatives of the three former organizations with a view to fusion. There seem to be fewer difficulties in a modern industry like chemicals than in more traditional sectors like the clothing trade, which has some ten groups for dealing with wage negotiations or building and civil engineering which, though both employing many qualified workmen belonging to the same trade, negotiate their collective agreements independently.

(b) *Questions on the Agenda.* The principal questions awaiting the leaders of the unified employers' organization[3] seem likely to be: taking part in the plan; implementing the prices and incomes policy; and rethinking of the whole business of labour relations, including industrial training which will be referred to later.

The six employers' members of NEDC are sitting as delegates of the employers—which was not so before 1965. On the Economic Development Committees of the Plan, now increasing in number and the object of great activity at the Department of Economic Affairs, the employers' representatives are often the local chairmen of their

[1] Report on the Formation of a National Industrial Organization, by Sir Henry Benson and Sir Sam Brown, FBI, BEC, NABM, April 1964.

[2] By 1966, ten of them had done so.

[3] It is interesting to note that these are a definitely younger team than their predecessors, and that the first president, Sir Maurice Laing, was one of the most active of the employers' members on NEDC.

professional associations. As regards the prices and incomes policy, the most important thing at the moment is that the employers' members should serve as efficient 'transmission belts' between the leaders at the centre who have subscribed to the policy and the average businessman who is certainly less convinced of the need for it, and also less prepared psychologically to take part. The prices and incomes policy will inevitably affect relations with the trade unions. It is to be hoped that the stress on increased productivity among the criteria on which the policy is based in practice will lead to a modernization of the traditional working contracts and methods of payment.[1] At the same time there will have to be some rethinking about the relations between employers and employees as a whole.

All these tasks are bound to change the character of the work of the professional associations and will demand an increase in the number of qualified personnel they employ. This transformation, similar to the one the leaders of the trade unions must be prepared to face, must lead to a recasting of the finances of many associations who at present receive very small subscriptions from their members.[2]

A fitting final comment on the changes now taking place in the employers' organizations, and which illustrates the need for new attitudes and methods on both sides of industry, was given by the present Minister of Labour—himself an ex-trade union leader—on the eve of the official setting up of the CBI. 'Strong, responsible and unified central organizations of employers and trade unions alike are needed, not only in their own interest but also in the interest of the nation as a whole.'[3]

The Trade Unions

The supporters of progress in British trade unionism managed to get the question of changes in union machinery debated at the TUC congress in 1962. It is true that the results so far lag behind what had been hoped, as regards both the reform of the General Council and the modernization of the whole structure. But a process was started which seems unlikely to stop.

(a) *The motion passed in 1962* suggested changes of three kinds, in

[1] An example of the results which can be obtained from patient and thorough discussions between employers and unions is furnished in the petroleum industry, where substantial increases both in wages and in productivity followed a complete reorgnization of job allocation and the system of pay. See Flanders, A., *The Fawley Productivity Agreement*, Faber, 1964.

[2] The Federation of Building Employers, for example, has only an annual income of £500,000, of which one-third goes to the central organization.

[3] Speech at the last Annual General Meeting of the BEC before it joined the FBI and the NABM in the Confederation of British Industries, March 17, 1965.

the structure and function of the General Council of the TUC, in the structure of the unions, and in methods of union action.

It is significant that it was proposed by one of the six TUC representatives on NEDC, who is also the youngest general secretary of a British union. It is the first motion of its kind since 1944, a time when, in the euphoria of the war's ending, an inquiry was launched into the problems of post-war adaptation which faced British trade unions. It was never followed up. The statement of 1962 seems likely to enjoy a better fate. Congress, it says, feels that the time has come to adapt British trade unionism to modern conditions. It 'instructs the General Council to examine and report . . . on the possibility of reorganizing the structure of both the TUC and the British Trade Union Movement with a view to making it better fitted to meet modern industrial conditions'.[1]

Among the speeches of those who supported the statement the remarks of the general secretary of the TUC, Mr George Woodcock, are worthy of special attention. In his view the proposed study's recommendations for future action must turn on the fact that trade unionism functions today in very different conditions from those of pre-war, especially in its relations with the State. The president of the Transport Salaried Staff Association,[2] with a return to power of the Labour Party in mind, warned his colleagues that a Labour Government would expect co-operation from the unions in laying down and carrying out an incomes policy, and also in changing the methods of wage negotiations, so that the less favourably placed categories of workers got a fair share as well as the members of the more powerful unions. The Government would also expect the unions to surrender some of their autonomy to the General Council of the TUC.

Another sign of the times, in September 1962, after a visit to Sweden by a group from the General Council, the TUC published a study on the aims of Swedish trade union action. The group found that the Landsorganisationen[3] is of the opinion that the improvement in the standard of living, the maintenance of full employment and price stability are indissolubly linked. It gives to their realization a higher priority than to other aims, such as maintaining the existing shape of the union movement, the autonomy of each union and keeping the worker in the same job, to which British trade unionism attaches much importance.[4]

It must be noted though that no plan for radical reform has

[1] Annual Report of the TUC, September 1962.
[2] And today Minister of Labour.
[3] The Swedish TUC.
[4] Cf. *Sweden. Its Unions and Industrial Relations*, TUC, 1962.

followed the debates in 1962. At the congress of 1963, the general secretary himself recognized that the process of revision of union structure must necessarily be slow. To conclude that the period since 1963 has been entirely sterile would however show a failure to realize the importance of the forces now active in the British trade union movement. The following paragraphs will show this.

(b) *The General Council.* The council considered collectively or as represented on a great number of bodies, and particularly NEDC, shoulders much greater responsibilities than it has powers. The question therefore arises whether it should not be in a position to commit, in its name, the Trade Union Movement and whether, with this in mind, its composition should not reflect more accurately that of the movement.

A TUC report in 1947 had proposed a pyramidal organization which would make the General Council the plenipotentiary of the unions. But two main reasons prevented the change, the unions' clinging to their autonomy and the refusal of the members of the General Council itself to take an initiative which they thought dangerous.

It would be wrong to assume from this that the council has regularly refused to commit itself with the Government so as to avoid trouble within the Trade Union Movement. For example, after the Labour victory at the General Election of 1945, it invited the unions, with quite a degree of success, to moderate their wage claims. Again in 1964, it agreed to sign, along with the employers, a declaration of intent on incomes and prices. Since the summer of 1965 the General Council has struck out in quite a new direction, as an informal review body for wage claims put forward by its member unions. If it were to continue further in this direction its function in the Trade Union Movement would inevitably be altered.[1] But it would at the moment be premature to draw such a conclusion.

On the other hand, the council has remained cagey in everything to do with union business and especially the structure of the unions, and some trade unionists think this will always be the case until it becomes more representative of the British Trade Union Movement.

At present its thirty-five members are elected on a trade basis, each group having the right to propose one, two or three candidates for election by the TUC as a whole. This system which was developed just after the First World War has remained the same although changes have come about in the composition of the active population, some branches dropping into the background, relatively or absolutely, while others came into being or expanded. Union representation therefore no longer corresponds to the membership of the various

[1] Cf. Chapter VII.

groups. Textiles, coalmining, railways and iron and steel are over-represented, whereas the electrical and engineering industries, transport other than the railways and 'white collar' unions are poorly represented, a situation which does not strengthen the moral prestige of the council.[1]

At the beginning of 1965 the need to find two representatives, one for the Civil Service Clerical Association (recently affiliated to the TUC) and the other for the electricians' union, gave the general secretary of the TUC the opportunity to suggest the creation of five new seats. This would have made it possible to correct obvious disparities by a general increase (it having been found impossible to withdraw seats from the over-represented unions). But at the 1965 congress the council contented itself with ratifying the creation of only two seats. The present system of election therefore remains unchanged, but it seems unlikely that the problem can be artificially postponed much longer.

(c) *Rationalization.* Since the inquiry opened by the TUC in 1962 the question of simplifying union structure has been kept on the agenda thanks to the general secretary's persistence. Having been forced to recognize that a radical reform could not be contemplated in present circumstances, he has restricted himself to encouraging fusions or the creation of federations between unions. His efforts have indeed been seconded by a number of trade unionists.

One special initiative of the TUC since 1962 has been to bring about exploratory meetings between unions in the same industry or trade to see whether fusions or amalgamations are possible.[2] Altogether, by 1965, 170 unions had begun discussions with a view to fusions or amalgamations, of which a majority seems likely to be successful;[3] in 1966, the movement appeared to be gathering momentum. But since the unions concerned are mostly small ones, this process of simplification, though it is necessary, can scarcely result in any very marked rationalization of union structure.

In parallel with this policy inspired by the TUC, some of the big unions have recently been showing a new dynamism as regards the rationalization of their structures. In April 1966, the three largest unions—Transport and General Workers, Amalgamated Engineering Union and General and Municipal Workers—set up a joint relations

[1] Mining (500,000 employees) and the railways (400,000) each have a right to three delegates, which is the same representation as for engineering (1,600,000 employees) and transport other than the railways (1,500,000). The 'non-manuals' are represented by a solitary member on the General Council.

[2] In 1964 a Bill encouraged fusions between unions by removing certain obstacles of a fiscal and financial nature.

[3] V. Feather, deputy general secretary of the TUC quoted by *The Times*, May 24, 1965.

committee to standardize benefits, reduce competition for members and limit demarcation disputes. It would be premature to speak of amalgamation between the three; but something like it appears to be the aim. The UGMW is decentralizing its internal organization into distinct trade groups, aligning itself with the TGWU. Five such groups are likely—engineering, nationalized industries, chemicals, clerical workers and miscellaneous. Thus a step towards industrial unionism under another form would have been accomplished.[1] Such a massive trade union group would, however, create other problems as it would dominate the TUC and the labour market generally in a great many occupations.

It is likely, therefore, that over the next few years, the structure of British trade unionism will undergo major transformation, the greatest since the appearance of the general unions in the closing decades of the nineteenth century.

(d) *Modernization.* Faced with the more complex problems of modern industry and caught up in a network of negotiations and discussions of an increasingly technical nature, the traditional union official often finds himself out of his depth, and even if he possesses the necessary training, is often overwhelmed by the multiplicity of his problems and the paucity of the means at his disposal. The result is loss of efficiency and recourse to the easy solution of reducing action essentially to regular claims for basic wage increases, while complex questions of capital importance to union members are neglected.

The rule books of many unions have not been revised for a generation. The Prime Minister told the AEU congress in 1966 that theirs 'belonged to an industrial museum'. Since then, the union's leaders are exploring ways of modernizing it.

More and more the unions are seeking to train their officials by attendance at conferences and courses and some officials with university qualifications are now being used.[2] Improving the technical competence of union officials will never really go very far without a reform in their pay structure. Here, too, some progress has been made. Raised subscriptions are becoming more frequent, and the concentration of unions which is beginning to take place will, on the one hand, allow economies in administrative personnel, and, on the other, will ease the fear that too many unions feel now of losing members to rival unions if they raise the cost of the union card too much.

[1] Industrial unionism is favoured by the past President of the CBI (Sir Maurice Laing) in evidence to the Royal Commission on Trade Unions and Employers' Associations, quoted in *The Times*, February 9, 1966.

[2] For example, in 1965, the National Union of General and Municipal Workers started a programme of training for young permanent union officials, some of whom will spend a year at Ruskin College, Oxford. Ultimately the number of full-time officials will be 50 per cent greater than now.

All these topics for thought and action will doubtless remain on the agenda of both employers' organizations and unions for years to come. But a powerful catalyst that will prevent either side of industry from seeking to smother the present pressure for reform is the Royal Commission on Trade Unions and Employers' Associations that had been mooted for some time and was finally set up in February 1965.[1] This Royal Commission is due to report towards the end of 1966.

If it lives up to the hopes it has raised its report can hardly fail to deal with a number of major issues that arise for labour market policy and employer-worker relations, and which are seen today to be bottlenecks impeding the modernization of the economy. Those issues are: the status of collective agreements; the right to strike; the closed shop; the right of appeal against dismissal; company law; joint consultative procedures.

2. AN ACTIVE LABOUR MARKET POLICY

By showing how basic to the success of a programme of faster growth was the improved use of available labour, NEDC gave the Ministry of Labour a somewhat unaccustomed star part. Since 1962 this Ministry—under successive Conservative and Labour Governments—concentrated mainly on recasting the system of technical training and on increasing the mobility of workers. In 1965, the Minister of Labour went much further than any of his predecessors by putting into effect structural reforms in labour relations in two sectors (docks and car manufacture) where these relations had for long been very unsatisfactory, though for different reasons.

Industrial Training

1962 was both the nadir of industrial training and the starting point of renewed interest in this important subject.

Although the demobilization of the forces in 1945 had led to the opening of a very extensive network of training centres administered by the State, only thirteen of them remained in 1962, attended by 3,300 people, mostly ex-soldiers or the physically handicapped. Essentially therefore, industrial training remained the business of each employer setting about things in his own way or occasionally following apprenticeship agreements with the unions. The training methods were nearly always 'on the job', the apprentice being attached to a qualified workman who taught him empirically the elements of his trade.

[1] The Royal Commission's terms of reference are: 'To consider relations between management and employees and the role of trade unions and employers' associations in promoting the interests of their members and in accelerating the social and economic advance of the nation with particular reference to the law affecting the activities of these bodies.'

The weaknesses of this system are obvious. It could in no way guarantee that a sufficient number of apprentices would be trained each year; retraining was scarcely provided for at all; the industrialist who spent time and money training his personnel was at the mercy of others who could attract away his labour once trained; a too empirical training tended to perpetuate outdated methods. However, neither the employers nor the unions—mainly interested in maintaining the closed shop where it existed or getting as near to it as possible—had any direct interest in changing the *status quo*; it was therefore essential that some urge to change should come from outside. This is what happened when Parliament passed a law which is now, and will be for many years, the basis of a new system of industrial training.

The proposals of the Government were published as a White Paper[1] at the end of 1962 and were incorporated into the Industrial Training Act 1964. The fundamental point is that industrial training becomes obligatory. The industrialist has the choice between training his personnel himself or contributing to a pool in each branch of industry, the money being used to finance the establishment and working of apprenticeship centres for each industry. The organization is based upon Industrial Training Boards, one for each branch of industry, topped by a Central Training Council which advises the Minister of Labour. Each Board is responsible for fixing the contributions for its branch, keeping an eye on standards of training, opening and managing a sufficient number of apprenticeship training centres. Firms which, after inspection, are deemed to be providing adequate training are entitled to receive grants from the Board, these being drawn from the contributions of others which do not train their own workers. In addition the Government contributes towards financing the Boards. The latter will recommend, after close analysis of each industry, standard conditions for the nature, length and content of training. Some form of further education must be combined with practical training, and will be provided by the local educational authorities. Clearly, the advent of the Boards will call for drastic changes in many 'craft' unions' approach to apprenticeship but, conversely, the Boards should be welcomed by the 'general' unions who have often found irksome the exclusiveness of the craft unions.

By the end of 1966, or early 1967, it is expected that there will be over twenty Boards and, eventually, some thirty are envisaged.[2]

[1] *Industrial Training: Government Proposals*, Cmd. 1892, December 1962.

[2] At mid-1966, Boards existed in the following branches: agriculture; ceramics, glass and mineral products; construction; electricity; engineering, furniture and timber; gas; horticulture and forestry; hotels and catering; iron and steel, man-made fibres; road transport; shipbuilding; textiles; water; wool. Others it is intended to set up are: chemicals; oil; plastics; rubber; civil aviation; fishing; clothing.

As had been foreseen, the employers' contributions are somewhat heavy. The engineering board's levy is equal to 2·5 per cent of the payroll of firms, a higher figure than in most industries. But money, though indispensable, cannot settle every problem, for example, the difficulty in persuading each industry to accept proper standards and in seeing that they are adhered to. Again, an expansion of industrial training as great as is now expected will run up against the lack of qualified teachers. This problem is already acute since it is proposed to raise the number of staff in centres administered by the State from 3,000 to 12,000.

More Government Training Centres are being provided. Six new ones were set up in 1965 and two in 1966, bringing the total to thirty-two with 6,000 places able to train 12,000 men a year. Eventually a total of thirty-eight centres, training 15,000 men a year, is aimed at. The stress being placed today upon re-deployment of labour as a substitute for 'stop-go' unemployment underscores the urgency of training in industry and, equally important, of re-training.

The Mobility of Labour

The efforts which we have described to achieve improved industrial training—and those noted in Chapter VIII to promote regional development—are not enough in themselves and efforts are needed to make changes of employment easier, especially as such changes often entail removal from the neighbourhood.

In many countries—but it is scarcely true of Britain—collective agreements include the measures necessary for the re-employment of redundant workers. In the United Kingdom only a few industries, mainly the nationalized ones, have shown any interest in this,[1] and it was not until 1961 that the authorities began to take up the question systematically.

Discussions organized by the Ministry of Labour between 1961 and 1963 had held out the hope that it might be possible to lay a Bill before Parliament in the autumn of 1963 to improve the mobility of labour. But very soon snags appeared. The Government favoured compulsory compensation to be paid by employers to workers laid off owing to the disappearance of their jobs, the sum being calculated according to seniority and pay. The employers, however, were opposed to a universal compulsory system which would have meant their losing once and for all in the negotiation of collective agreements the trump card of guaranteed compensation for loss of employ-

[1] In 1963, only 4½ million workers were covered against loss of employment, of whom 3 million were in the public sector; for many of them the protection was poor and included no money compensation.

ment. For their part, the unions would have liked to see unemployment benefit raised and fixed in relation to the last wage earned. Because of all these disagreements nothing was done before Labour came into power.

In April 1965, a Bill was laid before Parliament by the new Government. It follows the Conservatives in proposing a universal system of compensation for loss of employment. As *The Times* commented, in future the worker has a right to his job in the same way that the employer has a right to his business, and the workers' right grows stronger with time.[1] Moreover—and this may become more important in years to come—the special tribunals set up under the Industrial Training Act will interpret the legislation, so that perhaps in this way Britain will have arbitration tribunals like most Continental countries.

As for the details of the proposal, it applies to wage-earners between the ages of 18 and 65 (60 for women) who work at least 21 hours a week and have had a minimum of 2 years in the same employment. If a worker is laid off owing to personnel reduction, compensation is payable according to the following scale:

Age	*For each year of service*
18 to 21	½ week's wage
22 to 40	1 week's wage
41 to 65	1½ week's wage

A maximum of 20 years' service is fixed and earnings above £40 a week are not counted in calculating the compensation which cannot therefore exceed £1,200. The system is financed from a central fund which collects a compulsory levy from employers for each employee and pays an average 60 per cent rebate to employers who have to make payments. When the wage-related scales of unemployment pay were implemented at the end of 1966, the obstacles to worker mobility due to loss of income were considerably reduced.

The Act came into force in December 1965 and, in the first six months, 42,000 workers received redundancy payments, an average of £190 each. This was more than had been estimated, and, since then, a very substantial increase has occurred following the rise in unemployment. The Government aims at re-deployment of labour rather than short-time working. Here the redundancy payments and re-training facilities are the incentive and, for employers, the Selective Employment Tax the goad.

Labour Relations

The Ministry of Labour's action with regard to the docks and the car

[1] April 3, 1965.

industry seems to be inaugurating a much more vigorous policy than in the past.

From time to time in the past the labour situation in the docks has been the subject of official inquiries without any practical results. The facts of the case have never been set out so clearly as in the Devlin report[1] published in August 1965. While condemning the inefficiency in the docks and the bad relations between employers and labour, the members of the committee of inquiry attribute this state of affairs to three causes: an excessive number of employers, the traditional methods of signing on casual labour, and the lack of authority over the dockers shown by the principal union, the Transport and General Workers' Union.

The employers number more than 1,500, many being small firms which have not even got offices of their own and which work irregularly. The system of casual labour suits them very well, especially as it exempts the employer from any social responsibility towards his employees—who are continually changing in any case. The Devlin Report reckons that 75 per cent of dockers are casual labourers, and examines all the unfortunate consequences both for the worker (lack of security, mysterious systems of priority in securing jobs), and for the efficiency of the docks (excessive labour force, impossibility of introducing modern methods requiring specialist training).

The Transport and General Workers' Union also bears a heavy responsibility. The members of the committee were struck by the supine reaction of the union officials in the face of a situation which they nevertheless deplored. The failure of the attempts made in 1961 to do away with casual labour came in part from the inability of the Transport and General Workers' Union to convince its members of the need for reform. The report comments that this union too often lacked ideas of its own and when it wanted to carry out some policy did not have the conviction necessary to persuade its members. This explains why there has been for many years a powerful unofficial movement in the docks and why strikes are nearly always called without union approval. The Devlin Committee came out firmly in favour of decasualization and regular employment guaranteed by a much reduced number of employers.

Since taking note of the Devlin Report, the Minister of Labour has played the part of goad to force the interested parties to take action. It may therefore be hoped that at last something will be done to remedy this unhealthy situation. But, so far, progress has been difficult. The Joint National Modernization Committee for the docks,

[1] Committee of inquiry into the Port Transport industry, Cmd. 2734, August 1965.

set up following the Devlin Report, has made proposals and the Docks and Harbours Bill, published in the summer of 1966, provides for a licensing system for port employers, those refused a licence being compensated. Parallel with this reduction in the number of employers, local port authorities will be empowered to allocate dock labour to permanent employers. This scheme continued to attract criticism from both the employers and the workers. Now that the principle of dock nationalization has been adopted by the Government, a new element has been introduced into the situation.

In the motor industry the problems are quite different. We noted in Chapter I how the multiplicity of unions, and in some firms the absence of any determination to improve labour relations, had made motor manufacture the prey of many wild-cat strikes, often quite out of proportion to the seriousness of the real or trumped-up grievances causing the stoppage. It is thanks to the initiative taken by Mr Gunter, the Minister of Labour, that employers and unions agreed in October 1965 to the setting up of a joint labour council,[1] with the task of promoting good working relations and of studying the present situation in each motor company with this in view. An important innovation is that the chairman of the council is empowered to inquire into the problems of the industry and to call representatives of the employers and the unions to give evidence before the council. The British Press has baptized him 'the ombudsman of the motor industry'.[2] In 1966, the Council published several reports on labour troubles in the industry that laid special emphasis on the need for an overhaul of payments systems as a means of preventing disputes.

3. SCIENCE AND TECHNOLOGY

The electoral campaign of autumn 1964 included one theme unusual in British politics, that of science and its application to methods of production. Mr Wilson had said some months before becoming Prime Minister that if he had to define modern socialism in one word he would answer 'Science'.[3] The leaders of the other parties in their speeches showed themselves equally aware of the possibilities offered by science. It is not surprising therefore that the Labour Party on coming to power should seek to create a public image of a modern

[1] Joint Labour Council for the Motor Industry.

[2] By analogy with the Danish ombudsman which has already inspired the creation of a British 'parliamentary ombudsman'. The 'ombudsman' of the motor industry is one of the members of the Devlin Committee (Mr Scamp).

[3] Wilson, H., *The Relevance of British Socialism*, London, Weidenfeld and Nicolson, 1964.

government anxious to use scientific methods of administration and inquiry.[1]

This seems then the appropriate moment to look into what has been happening during the last few years in the fields of research and development,[2] science and teaching, and the introduction of scientific methods of management into business.

Research and Development

As in most big industrial countries—Germany is an exception—research and development (R and D) is in Britain largely financed by the State to the tune of about half the total. The return to be expected from the money spent thus depends to a great extent on Government decisions. The total expenditure on R and D reaches today 2·6 per cent of the gross national product, a figure below that of the USA (3·7 per cent), but higher than on the Continent. Expenditure is increasing rapidly. Between 1955–6 and 1961–2 expenditure on scientific and technological research rose from £300m. to £634m. and to £756m. in 1964–5. The Government's contribution to civil research rose from £130m. in 1961–2 to £204m. in 1964–5.[3]

The amount devoted to fundamental research is only 11 per cent of the total, but 90 per cent is spent by university laboratories. Elsewhere research is mainly in applied science. About 40 per cent of the total expenditure on R and D goes to defence, which absorbs 60 per cent of the official contribution. Hence the predominant share of industries associated with defence, such as the aeroplane industry in particular, and also electronics and electrical engineering. Some 20 per cent of all scientists and engineers in the country work on R and D.

The theories of the two main political parties in Britain differ on a number of points. The Conservatives prefer not to use direct State control except where no other initiative is forthcoming, whereas Labour is much readier to consider active participation by the

[1] Mr Crossman, now Minister of Housing and Local Government, said in 1964 that a future Labour Government 'may well be the first science-based government this country has ever known'. *Encounter*, July 1964.

[2] When a scientific discovery has resulted from research, the task of 'development' is to work out methods, materials and techniques which will enable the discovery to proceed to the stage of practical application or a prototype. We shall follow current practice and call it 'R and D'.

[3] In absolute value there is a great difference between the USA and European countries. American expenditure on R and D is about $94 per head of population per annum, while it is only about $34 in Britain and less than $24 in France. Cf. *The Effort at Research and Development in Western Europe, North America and the Soviet Union*. OECD, 1965. Estimates in this field tend to diverge—partly for reasons of definition. The reader should consult also *Country Report on the Organization of Scientific Research: the United Kingdom*, OECD, 1966.

authorities. While the Conservatives can justly pride themselves on having greatly increased expenditure on R and D. Labour feels that the effort is still not enough. And Labour has often criticized the disproportion which has been noted between the share of R and D expenditure going to certain industries like aeronautics and the share of some other industries which are very important for British exports, such as machine tools.

(a) *The Part Played by the State.* In spite of the line taken on the organization of science, the Conservative Party nevertheless created a Ministry of Science in 1959. However, this Ministry never seems to have found its true vocation and with a very small staff it has not had much scope for action[1] (in 1964 for some months it was combined with the Ministry of Education). Meanwhile, in 1963, the NEDC made certain suggestions as regards industry and, the same year, the report of a committee of inquiry into the organization of civil science[2]—the first on the organization of civil science since the Haldane Report in 1918—drew attention to certain institutional problems.

NEDC was specially concerned with reducing the time lag between the results of pure research and their application in practice.[3] The vertical committees of the National Plan for each branch of industry seemed the ideal instrument for achieving this aim. As was seen in Chapter VI, the Labour Government has given considerable stress to this issue in the work of the Economic Development Committees.

The Labour Government has kept the portfolio of 'Education and Science', but a newcomer, the Ministry of Technology,[4] shares the responsibility for science and R and D. The Department of Education and Science has two sections, one for education up to and including the secondary stage, and the other (under a Minister of State) for higher education and scientific matters. This association of higher education and science is in line with the proposals made by the Trend Committee. As for the Ministry of Technology, it is still somewhat difficult to distinguish its particular function from that of the Department of Economic Affairs set up by the Labour Government and in charge of the implementation of the medium-term plan.[5]

The present organization of civil science in Britain results from

[1] As the other Ministries retained responsibility for their own science programmes, the Ministry of Science was responsible for general scientific policy only, except in the field of defence.

[2] Committee of Inquiry into the Organization of Civil Science (Trend Committee), HMSO, Cmd. 2 71, 1963.

[3] *Second Report. Conditions favourable to faster growth.* NEDC 1963.

[4] From 1964 to 1966 the Minister was Mr Cousins, now again General Secretary of the powerful Transport and General Workers' Union.

[5] This is discussed in greater detail in Chapter VI.

the Science and Technology Act 1965, inspired by the report of the Trend Committee. Under this Act, the Department of Scientific and Industrial Research, that had been charged since its creation in 1916 with promoting scientific research and its applications to industry, was abolished. Two new research councils—the Science Research Council, that takes over the university grant awarding functions of the DSIR and responsibility for 'basic' science, and the Natural Environment Research Council, with tasks of broadly 'ecological' character—and a Ministry took its place. At first this Ministry of Technology controlled research stations run out of public funds and supervised the Atomic Energy Commission and the National Research Development Corporation. In 1966, the aircraft industry—with its very large research programme—as well as shipbuilding also passed to the Ministry of Technology.

At the advisory level, a Council for Scientific Policy attached to the Ministry for Education and Science, was set up in 1965. The same year, a Committee on Manpower Resources for Science and Technology was created to advise jointly the Ministries of Education and Science and of Technology. The latter Ministry also has, since 1964, an Advisory Council on Technology and, in 1966, the Government's Chief Scientific Adviser became chairman of a Central Advisory Committee on Science. In 1964–5, the Secretary of State for Education and Science was responsible for about 40 per cent of Government funds for civil research, the Ministry of Technology 31 per cent, the Ministry of Aviation 23 per cent and other departments 6 per cent.

(b) *Size and Allocation of Funds for R and D.* Size too small and allocation unsatisfactory—such were the chief criticisms levelled by the Labour Party at their predecessors. Various steps have been taken since Labour came to power to remedy these defects.

In his budget speech in April 1965, the Chancellor of the Exchequer announced the Government's intention to recast companies' taxation in such a way as to favour the reinvestment of profits in modernization. The details of this plan are complex and its repercussions, which are still vigorously debated in Britain, fall largely outside the question which interests us here. It is sufficient to say that the fundamental principle of the reform is to separate the taxation of individuals from that of corporate bodies by creating a special single tax on the profits of firms known as Corporation Tax.[1] As the rate of this new tax would be about 35 per cent to 40 per cent, that is, lower than the combined effect of income tax plus taxation on profits

[1] The plan is essentially like one of the ideas put forward some years ago by Professor Kaldor, at present adviser to the Chancellor of the Exchequer on fiscal matters.

(56·5 per cent), companies keeping a high percentage of their profits for reinvestment and, hopefully, for R and D instead of distributing them as dividends would benefit.[1]

The Labour critics had for long pilloried the unsatisfactory allocation of expenditure on R and D. A much-quoted example is the aeroplane industry which absorbs 38 per cent of expenditure on R and D though it provides only 4 per cent of British exports, whereas the engineering and electrical industries which get only 17 per cent of grants provide one-quarter of all exports. Therefore, in April 1965, work on the prototype military aeroplane TSR-2 was stopped so that skilled manpower could be released for more urgent civil jobs.

The Ministry of Technology is also responsible for implementing the policy of 'development contracts', and the National Research and Development Corporation (NRDC) which has already undertaken operations of this kind on a small scale[2] has been attached to the Ministry for the purpose. So far four industries have been selected because of the importance of science and research for their development—machine tools, electronics, computers and telecommunications. In 1966 'pre-production contracts' that offer a firm Government outlet for new products were awarded for the supply of advanced machine tools and the NRDC is to operate a £1m. scheme to enable producers of numerically controlled machine tools to offer 'trial period terms' to prospective buyers. A National Computer Centre has opened in Manchester. Contracts worth £10m. are forthcoming from the universities for British-made computers and another £5m. from private industry. The recommendations of a special committee (the Flowers Committee) in favour of public sector support for a British computer industry are behind these, and other, initiatives.[3] Another field of activity of the Ministry is in measures to correct the present shortage of engineers and insufficient attention paid by private industry to engineering design. This activity results from the findings of DSIR Committee on Engineering Design (the Feilden Committee) that reported in 1963. The Ministry has set up the first of a series of State-sponsored institutes in modern technology—the Institute of Advanced Machine Tool and Control Technology.

[1] Paradoxically, companies tax in the Common Market countries works the other way round, since it tends to unite the taxation of individuals and of corperate bodies and to favour the payment of dividends.

[2] Set up in 1949, the Corporation's main function has been to develop inventions derived from public expenditure on research. Examples are electronic computers, hovercraft, fuel cells and towed flexible barges. Its capital was increased in 1965 from £10m. to £25m.

[3] Professor Flowers is now Chairman of the Computer Board for Universities and Research Councils that will spend up to £30m. over the next few years.

The boost to spending of public money on science in recent years is certainly very welcome. But, as with other items of public expenditure, there are limits to what can be usefully absorbed in a short space of time and delicate problems of choice in the overall use of resources have to be solved. The first annual report of the Council for Scientific Policy, published in 1966, stresses these issues.[1] If the present rise in expenditure continued until 1984, the authors note, R and D expenditure would increase eightfold and the Research Councils would be spending £500m. annually—instead of £28m. at present—on the basis of the present annual growth of 13 per cent. One problem, in deciding how to allocate funds, arises because no one knows what types of pure research are likely to pay the best dividends in terms of practical application. Another is the persistent 'brain drain' to the United States of British scientists who are attracted not only by higher salaries but by vastly superior equipment for research. Finally, it is hardly likely that a small country like Britain can survive without active co-operation in R and D with Continental countries.

Science and Education

The adaptation of the structure of education, especially higher education, to fit new programmes and the rapidly increasing number of students arises in every country and has so far found a satisfactory solution in none. It is not surprising therefore that discussions about the future of education in England are conducted mainly in terms of investment needs and pay-offs, international competition and future manpower balances for scientists and technicians. Moreover, the discussions are complicated by the criticism, especially from the Labour ranks, that the educational system maintains class distinctions that should be abolished.

In 1964–5, 13·5 per cent of total public expenditure was being allotted to education, about 60 per cent of it on schools. The National Plan expects the percentage to rise to 14·5 per cent by 1969–70, about half the increase being for schools.[2] This is because the school population, following the higher birth rate since the mid-1950s, will rise by 695,000 in England and Wales between 1965–70 compared with 160,000 over the previous five years. As more pupils will stay on after fifteen, there will be an increase of some 109,000 in senior pupils. This will call, among other things, for 11,000 extra teachers a year compared with 5,000 in recent years. The school-building programme in Great Britain is estimated in the Plan to rise from £143m. in 1965–6 to £195m. in 1969–70.

Turning to higher education the Plan notes that there was an in-

[1] *Report on Science Policy*, Cmnd. 3007, HMSO, 1966.

[2] Op. cit., p. 192, et seq.

crease in students of 50 per cent between the years 1953 and 1964 but that there will be a further substantial increase to meet which current expenditure on further and higher education will rise by 50 per cent between 1964–5 and 1969–70 and capital expenditure wil ldouble.

The fundamental document which influences British policy today, and will continue to do so for many years to come, is the report of the Committee on Higher Education, known as the Robbins Committee.[1] It is therefore essential to study it before examining recent changes in official policy.

Set up by the Conservative Government, the Robbins Committee reported in 1963.[2] It came out strongly in favour of greatly increasing the pace at which additional places in higher education are provided. By 1973–4 there should be 390,000 places in higher education of which 218,000 should be in university institutions. This would mean an 80 per cent increase in the numbers of higher education places in ten years. An interim objective of 197,000 places was suggested for 1968. In order to meet an increase of this magnitude it was urgently necessary to provide budgetary credits for grants towards the construction of new buildings, in particular as the student population is likely to rise rapidly up to 1967–8 before slowing down somewhat.

This drive for university building should not, in the opinion of the Robbins Committee, be concentrated exclusively on existing universities, and the creation of six new universities was recommended. With regard to teaching staffs, the committee felt that higher salaries were necessary, together with other measures to attract young graduates. Noting that the demand for scientists and technologists was likely to increase more rapidly than for people with other qualifications, the committee suggested that the science departments in universities should receive special grants, and that certain existing technical colleges should be upgraded[3] so that their degrees might be on a level with those of universities.

The numerical conclusions of the Robbins Committee were accepted at once by the Conservative Government,[4] and since then the target of 390,000 places in higher education by 1973–4 has become common doctrine in the two chief political parties.

Since their return to power the Labour Government have renewed their predecessors' pledge on the increase in university places but 122,000 of the Robbins' target of 390,000 places in higher education

[1] Report of the Committee on Higher Education, Cmd. 2154, HMSO, 1963.

[2] A very large document, with five volumes of appendices, this report gives a thorough analysis of every aspect of higher education, and detailed comparisons with other countries. It is therefore impossible to provide any detailed summary of it here.

[3] As Colleges of Advanced Technology (CAT's).

[4] Government's Statement on the Robbins Report, Cmd. 2165, HMSO, 1963.

by 1973–4 will be in colleges of education that train teachers. This move will double the numbers of teachers in such colleges. The Robbins report had called for 50,000 places by 1973–4 in technical colleges and other, non-university, institutions of further education. In 1966, the Government proposed to create 'multi-level polytechnics' which would complement universities and the colleges of education and would help to ensure over 70,000 places by 1969–70 compared with the lower Robbins Committee's target of 50,000 four years later.[1]

The present Government has departed from the Robbins proposals, however, in that the separation between the universities proper and other establishments for further education (colleges of education, technical colleges and the new 'polytechnics') is being maintained, if not reinforced, whereas the Robbins report looked forward to an upgrading of certain CATs to put them on a par with the universities. In future, all degree work being done in technical colleges will be concentrated in some thirty of the new 'multi-level polytechnics' and withdrawn from the others.

The Government has decided not to build more new universities as it appears to be less expensive to increase the number of places by extending universities already in existence or under construction. According to the Ministry of Education, even allowing for this change, the average size of English universities will not be greater than 5,000 students (a figure already much exceeded in the USA). One possible snag may, however, appear in a few years' time, now that the decision has been taken not to open any more universities. If the increase in the number of students should continue beyond 1973, say for another ten years, a bottleneck would occur owing to the impossibility of the existing universities absorbing any more students. The recommendation of the Franks Committee as regards the future of Oxford may be noted. A rise of one-third in the student population over the next 15–20 years is postulated.[2]

With regard to secondary education at the end of 1965, the Minister of Education appointed a commission (the Newsom commission) to examine ways of carrying out the Government's intention to integrate the 227 public schools with the State system of education. One objective will be to reduce the present 'socially divisive influence' of these schools.[3] The policy of the Minister is to achieve a generalization of the comprehensive school for secondary education. This will

[1] *A plan for Polytechnics and other Colleges*, Cmd. 3006, HMSO, 1966.

[2] *Report of a Commission of Inquiry*, 2 vols., Oxford University Press, 1966. This committee was set up as a direct response to the remarks concerning Oxford in the Robbins Report.

[3] Mr Crossland, reported in the *Financial Times*, December 23, 1965.

apply not only to State schools but to the direct-grant schools also and would presumably imply the disappearance of the traditional grammar schools to make way for very large institutions taking in less selected children. For the moment therefore, unless the quality of comprehensive schools is raised and the gap between State and public schools narrowed, the prospect exists of an aggravation of the disparity between the quality of teaching offered to the ablest pupils in fee-paying schools and in the schools within the State system.

Management Training

The training of the higher ranks in industry is a subject which has only recently attracted the attention of the authorities. NEDC can take credit for having been first to place the question on the agenda. This marks the disappearance of the myth of the business chief whose success depends exclusively on innate qualities which cannot possibly be transmitted by organized teaching. In reality there is a body of intellectual disciplines which have become indispensable for the managerial class and which are very much the province of education.[1] Once this point of view was accepted it became obvious that, generally speaking, neither the universities nor business firms could offer sufficient training facilities.

Therefore in 1963 NEDC charged one of its members with the preparation of a report on management training in the private sector. This document recommended the setting up of Business Schools in Britain.[2] According to the Franks report, these institutions should not follow the model of universities. They would provide teaching of two kinds, for the young university graduate and for executives with several years of professional experience. Representatives from the private sector would be closely associated with their management, and this being so, private industry should provide most of the necessary money.

In May 1964, the Conservative Government gave the plan financial support and a committee of businessmen—the Foundation for Management Education—began to collect contributions in the private sector amounting to £5m. The Government and the Fund have contributed equal amounts to set up three new business schools, two are already at work in London and Manchester; the third will be in Oxford.[3] In 1966, a new advisory body on management studies was set up. The Board of Trade is sponsoring a scheme

[1] For example, the modern techniques of communication, analysis and decision.

[2] Lord Franks, *British Business Schools*, British Institute of Management, November 1963, and *British Business Schools—the Cost*, FBI, May 1964.

[3] London Graduate School of Business Studies and the Manchester Business School. The third, the Oxford Centre for Management Studies.

for sending fifty top executives in British industry to the Harvard Business School. Under private initiative, the College of Production and Industrial Administration at Cranfield is introducing in Britain the techniques of the Harvard Business School.

Meanwhile NEDC has continued its work and published in 1965 the results of the first inquiry into the present state of management recruitment and training,[1] which makes it possible to get some idea of the size of the problem. For manufacturing industry alone an annual recruitment of some 20,000 higher executives is necessary simply to keep up present numbers. At the present time only about half the managers have a degree or diploma and only a quarter of them are scientists. It is true that the percentage of recruits with university degrees is going up fairly fast, but it is rather striking that many firms of whom inquiries were made complained that the young graduates were over-specialized and lacking in general culture. With regard to training after recruitment, although most large firms have organized training courses, these are rare in small and medium-sized business. The latter are discouraged by the cost of an organization suited to training their executives and also by the lack of interest shown by many professional associations. They maintain that it is impossible for them to face the prolonged absence of their management staff and often prefer part-time arrangements. Asked about the teaching offered by the universities and specialized institutes, most of them complain that too many subjects are taught and that it is difficult to compare the various programmes. The age group whose training needs are still largely unsatisfied is that between 28 and 35. This means that the business schools will cater for a different public from the traditional university one.

On the whole it seems possible to conclude on an optimistic note with regard to the increasingly wide-spread introduction of training in modern methods of business management. The new business schools can meet the needs of only a part of those capable of benefiting from their teaching, but their example may perhaps move the universities to develop their courses in business management and to co-ordinate their teaching programmes better.

[1] *Management Recruitment and Development*, NEDC, 1965.

CONCLUSION

It was the conviction that, since the early 1960s, there have been unmistakable signs in the United Kingdom of a change of 'climate' in attitudes towards economic questions that led us to make that change the *leitmotif* of this book. We have tried to show how, after a period during the 1950s of growing dissatisfaction and self-questioning about the future, there followed another dominated by the desire to break with a number of traditional habits of thought and action and the determination to carry out changes, radical if necessary but agreed to be essential. Further, it seemed to us that this new 'climate' had found its most notable expression in a system of indicative planning whose ramifications spread right through the economy. This opinion is justified, in our view, not because planning could ever be an 'open sesame' to the solution of all difficult and complex problems, but because in Britain it acted as a catalyst. Planning has provided positive support, and constructive outlets, for initiatives that, otherwise, would have remained disorganized and incapable of making themselves heard. This will appear, looking back in future years, to have been its principal merit, and a very considerable one it is.

Yet it must be admitted that the planning 'honeymoon' between 1961 and 1966 was carried on in a spirit of optimism which, though fundamentally justified, was nonetheless premature. The feeling of relief at having finally broken with a rather disappointing past was certainly at the base of this optimism, but the efforts required to achieve the objectives fixed in the plan were seriously under-estimated. From this point of view it is symptomatic that the first document dealing with the plan (1961–4) set out the targets to be reached and was only then followed by a statement of the conditions necessary for success. The serious sterling crisis which began in 1964 came as a timely warning that, although the will to act is the first requisite in transforming a situation, the acts themselves must follow or the penalty will be failure and fresh disappointments. The wish to reach the growth target too quickly brought about exaggerated pressures of demand, excessive increases in costs and prices, and a need for imports out of proportion to the likely rise in exports.

Not only was the truth of the adage 'more haste, less speed' lost sight of during the brief euphory of the years 1962–4, but the underlying long-term trend in the growth of output was too lightly ignored. It is now clear that the 4 per cent annual growth target for GNP fixed by the first plan exceeded, and still exceeds, what can reasonably be expected despite the continued rise over recent years in productivity.

The decision, taken after October 1964, to scrap the first plan and to draft another could have provided an opportunity to bring the aims of policy closer to the harsh realities of the United Kingdom's position. Unfortunately, this opportunity was not grasped and the second plan's growth target remained as unrealistic as that of the first.

The drawn-out payments crisis which began in 1964 and, at the end of 1966, was still latent, has proved to be costly. Heavy foreign debts have been incurred that will burden the balance of payments for many years. Confidence in sterling—a prime objective of policy from 1964 onwards—has been severely, and perhaps irrevocably, shaken. The hope that it would prove possible to weather the storm without sacrificing the growth prospects of the domestic economy has proved to be an illusion. The bout of 'stop-go' imposed in the summer of 1966 was all the more severe for having been postponed.

It was to be expected that this unhappy situation would lead to a swing of opinion in some circles against the 'new look' in economic policy that is discernible after 1961. A reassessment of economic policy, including a frank recognition of the causes of the disappointments of the 1960s that have followed those of the 1950s, is now urgent. But to incriminate the whole renewal of ideas and methods that can best be described by the convenient short-hand of 'indicative planning' would be a council of despair and, worse still, another error of diagnosis coming on top of so many earlier ones.

The basic change implied by the adoption of 'indicative planning' may be summed up by saying that the old preoccupation with 'full employment' gave way to a new concern with 'growth'. Nothing in recent events invalidates the soundness of this—if the experience of other countries is considered—sadly belated conversion. But the difficulties of the task, and the very considerable leeway that had to be made good in Britain, were seriously under-estimated.

'Full employment' can be seen as basically a question of annual juggling with the balance between overall demand and supply. 'Growth' is quite another matter although, and this is clearly one major lesson of recent years, short-term demand management should be viewed as an integral part of indicative planning and not as its antithesis. Attempts to use an expansion of overall demand as a painless short-cut to a solution of the twin obstacles of low productivity and a loss of international competitiveness have been both costly and self-defeating.

For the time being there are no medium-term targets. Those in the second plan drafted by Labour in 1965 are irrelevant and it is not easy to see what useful purpose would be served by 'rolling on' the targets for 1970 in the National Plan to, say, 1972. The present painfully obvious gap between aims and realities would remain as wide as ever. The task of drafting a new medium-term plan is not urgent until the way out of present difficulties can be seen more clearly. More pressing is the need to strengthen the links between medium-term planning in the public sector—broadly defined—and the annual budgetary process and to decide how to apportion the permissible volume of public expenditure between rival claimants.

The new consultation procedures—through the NEDC, the Economic Development Committees or the Regional Planning Councils—made a sharp break with previous practice and, aided by the changes under way in the structure and attitudes of the Civil Service, they are unlikely to be given up by any government in future. The gain to the economy from these institutional changes seems to us to be established beyond doubt. That more has not been achieved in this way has been due, in no small measure, to the upsetting influence of demand mis-management. This overall judgment concerning the value of the planning machinery does not exclude the need for a reconsideration of the appropriate spheres of action of the Treasury, the Department of Economic Affairs and the NEDC.

Prices and incomes policy is another example of the 'new look' in economic policy-making that has developed out of the experiment with indicative planning and which would have little hope of surviving without it. Here again, the errors made in setting the macro-economic targets of the medium-term plan have placed a severe strain on a new policy approach when the latter was still in a formative stage. But it is heartening to note that the events of 1966, culminating in the price, wage and dividend 'freeze', did not wreck the whole experiment which has thus shown more resilience than many sceptics were inclined to credit it with. The next testing time for prices and incomes policy will come when the present restrictive measures can be loosened a little. Indeed, the main danger of the shock tactics resorted to in 1966 is that they will breed the impression that, at some future date, the flood gates will be flung open again. In that case, the pressures now being bottled up may prove irresistible. If, on the contrary, the present period of savage restraint can be put to good account to achieve agreement on permanent mechanisms for price and income surveillance in the framework of modernized negotiating procedures, good may emerge from unavoidable evil.

The painful gestation of incomes policy illustrates a more general problem for Britain. Since the war, our society has found itself freed —and happily freed—from the terrible disciplines of mass unemployment and the spectre of business bankruptcy. But it has not yet been able to substitute for these harsh auto-mechanisms of the market a workable form of self-discipline that would allow the country to achieve the twin goals of growth and social justice to which it aspires.

We know too little about the secrets of the springs in any human society that cause phases of dynamic progress and rejuvenation to give way to periods of stagnation and frustration. Social scientists concerned with development in the backward areas of the world are coming increasingly to see their problems in terms of 'modernization'. The merit of this approach is to broaden the debate about growth and to generalize it so as to encompass the already developed economies as well. We have noted, in the chapters of this book, a number of measures initiated in Britain during the 1960s that point in the right direction. Among them are improved labour market policies, the reappraisal of their methods by trade unions and business associations, expanded facilities for education and systematic training, changes in the structure of industry—both public and private, regional re-activation and the improvement in research and development activities. But these are only the beginning of the changes that are called for. Present policies will have to be pursued actively and extended to other fields.

The Government, aided by the *élites* in the private sector that are ready and willing to accept their responsibilities, can do much to help in the process of modernization. But change by consent may not be sufficient. Modernizing out-dated structures is bound to upset many time-hallowed ways of acting. The pressure of the market, if adequate safeguards against injustice and hardship are provided, remains without rival as a means of bringing about required adjustments. Unfortunately, British policy towards restrictive practices remains timid and recent events have served to increase the protection from foreign competition enjoyed by domestic producers.

In the present economic situation, which is scarcely favourable to expansion, a major problem is to keep up the momentum of private productive investment. It has not proved possible to secure the stabilization of these investments at their 1966 level. Yet a drop of any size would gravely prejudice the future. The Economic Development Committees have a part to play here, quite apart from selective measures of encouragement. Eventually, however, the fact must be faced that investment cannot stay buoyant for long unless demand conditions—either on the domestic market or for exports—are favourable. There is, unfortunately, little in the international price competitiveness of the British economy that suggests a likely acceleration in the growth of exports. If this proves to be the case, the question of the exchange rate for sterling will have to be considered objectively and without sentimentality. But devaluation would provide only temporary relief to the balance of payments if it were not accompanied by more moderate pressure of demand as a permanent state of affairs, at least until present efforts to modernize economic structures and to achieve a workable policy for prices and incomes have borne fruit.

Finally, we believe that participation in an area of development which is sufficiently large and dynamic—such as would be found in the European Common Market—would bring to the British economy both the stimulant and the discipline which are needed for the attainment of its aims. But such a plunge into Europe will call for difficult decisions and the dimming of some illusions that die hard in Britain when economic policy is discussed.

INDEX

For Product Safety Concerns and Information please contact our EU representative GPSR@taylorandfrancis.com Taylor & Francis Verlag GmbH, Kaufingerstraße 24, 80331 München, Germany